School Bullying and Mental Health

Risks, Intervention and Prevention

Edited by Helen Cowie
and Carrie-Anne Myers

Routledge
Taylor & Francis Group
LONDON AND NEW YORK

First published 2018 by Routledge

2 Park Square, Milton Park, Abingdon, Oxfordshire OX14 4RN
52 Vanderbilt Avenue, New York, NY 10017

Routledge is an imprint of the Taylor & Francis Group, an informa business

First issued in paperback 2018

British Library Cataloguing-in-Publication Data
A catalogue record for this book is available from the British Library

Library of Congress Cataloging-in-Publication Data
A catalog record for this book has been requested

ISBN: 978-1-138-67412-7 (hbk)
ISBN: 978-0-367-19018-7 (pbk)

Typeset in Bembo
by Apex CoVantage, LLC

Contents

List of figures xii
List of images xiii
List of tables xiv
Series editor's foreword xv
List of contributors xvii
Permissions xxiv

THEME 1
The nature of bullying 1

1 **What we know about school bullying** 3
HELEN COWIE AND CARRIE-ANNE MYERS

2 **Theoretical perspectives on the continuities of bullying over time** 12
MAILI PÖRHÖLÄ

THEME 2
The interface between bullying and crime 25

3 **Boundaries of bullying: when does bullying behaviour become criminal?** 27
CARRIE-ANNE MYERS

4 **Homophobic, biphobic and transphobic bullying in schools** 35
IAN RIVERS

5 **Contested and complex terrain: sexual violence in UK schools** 46
KERRY LEE

6 **Exploring the nature and extent of hate crime in schools and interventions to combat it** 58
RASHID AZIZ

7 **Bullying of religious minorities and asylum seekers** 67
ANA AZNAR, HARRIET R. TENENBAUM AND MARTIN D. RUCK

THEME 3
Bullying: its impact on emotional health and well-being 79

8 **The bullied child in the vulnerable adult: therapeutic work with adults bullied in childhood** 81
MARIA LUCA

9 **Addressing the mental health and emotional needs of children who bully** 90
HELEN COWIE AND PAT COLLIETY

10 **The moderating role of father acceptance in the relationship between victimisation and depressive symptoms** 101
THEODOROS GIOVAZOLIAS AND MARIA MALIKIOSI-LOIZOS

THEME 4
The social and cultural contexts which challenge or promote school bullying 113

11 **Bullying and social media** 115
HOLLY POWELL-JONES

12 **Fostering resilience in vulnerable children** 130
CARMEL CEFAI

13 **Bullying and resilience within a neoliberal framework: implications for mental health and well-being** 144
WENDY SIMS-SCHOUTEN AND SIMON EDWARDS

14 **School culture as a determinant of bullying: exploring the participant roles** 154
RUBINA HANIF AND SADAF ZAHEER

'*School Bullying and Mental Health: Risks, Intervention and Prevention* is a unique book that covers a broad variety of relevant and cutting-edge topics spanning from theory to practice. The book discusses the tipping point at which bullying becomes a crime and considers bullying involving sexual violence and bullying targeting minorities. As well as the school setting, bullying in university and workplace settings is covered in this book, giving the reader an overview of bullying across the life-span. The consequences of bullying are considered while accounting for therapeutic work and interventions within specific social and cultural contexts. A must-read for anyone with an interest in this increasingly recognised world-wide problem.'

–**Professor Muthanna Samara**, *Department of Psychology, Kingston University London, UK*

'This is a very important book for anyone who is concerned with the nature of bullying, its consequences for the mental health and well-being of young people, and the measures that can be taken to ameliorate and prevent this ubiquitous but often hidden problem. The editors, Helen Cowie and Carrie-Anne Myers, are distinguished authorities in this complex area and bring to bear their extensive knowledge in the creation of a scholarly and very well constructed book. In dividing the volume into five distinct themes, elaborated by a wide array of international expert writers, they provide the reader with an invaluable resource that illuminates the multifarious nature of bullying in ways that are always informative, engaging, and thought-provoking. The writing is clear and accessible, but never at the expense of complexity.

School Bullying and Mental Health: Risks, Intervention and Prevention offers many important insights, none more important than the fact that bullying in schools has immediate, extensive, and, in some cases, lifelong negative consequences for its victims that can be prevented through timely, informed and carefully targeted intervention. This book deserves a very wide readership among school leaders, teachers, educational psychologists, and school governors, as well as policy makers. Academics in education, and their Masters and Doctoral students studying bullying and mental health, will also find this book an indispensable source.'

–**Paul Cooper, CPsychol, FBPsS**, *Emeritus Professor, Brunel University London, UK*

'Bullying was for long spared full censure, the rigours of the criminal law and the criminological gaze, as if it were a fleeting and marginal form of misbehaviour that should be treated with an indulgence akin to benefit of clergy. But a changing understanding of childhood, greater publicity and an enhanced appreciation of who and what it is to be a victim have begun to translate it into a complex and consequential social problem. It is apparent that it is not simply confined to the playground; that it may take multiple forms and that its impact is often far from ephemeral. It is not always easy to make sense of everything that has been learned, and Helen Cowie and Carrie-Anne Myers are greatly to be thanked for having mustered educationalists, sociologists, criminologists, and psychologists from across the globe to produce such a timely and comprehensive review of the state of expert, legal, practical, and policy-relevant knowledge of the field.'

–**Paul Rock**, *Emeritus Professor, London School of Economics, UK*

'Helen Cowie and Carrie-Anne Myers realize that such an important issue as bullying needs to be viewed from different angles, based on current scientific data and appropriate methods in the field of research, intervention, and prevention. They gathered scientific researchers as well as practitioners in bullying prevention and treatment from various countries: UK, USA, Greece, Malta, Sweden, Spain, Pakistan, Australia, Ireland, and Finland. All of them share with us their impressive knowledge and practical experiences for dealing with bullying. Therefore, the book will be of great value for a range of practitioners (teachers, psychologists, etc.), but also for university teachers and students, interested parents of both bullies and victims, and all those victimized people who are searching for the right answers.'

–**Renata Miljević-Riđički**, *Professor in the Faculty of Teacher Education, University of Zagreb, Croatia*

School Bullying and Mental Health

Bullying amongst young people is a serious and pervasive problem, and recent rapid advances in electronic communication technologies have provided even more tools for bullies to exploit. *School Bullying and Mental Health* collates current research evidence and theoretical perspectives about school bullying in one comprehensive volume, identifying the nature and extent of bullying and cyberbullying at school, as well as its impact on children and young people's emotional health and well-being.

There are many negative consequences of bullying, and children and young people who have been victimised often suffer long-term psychological problems, such as increased levels of anxiety, depressive symptoms, social isolation, loneliness and suicidal ideation. Perpetrators of bullying also have a heightened risk of experiencing problems such as anxiety and depression, as well as eating disorders and antisocial behaviour. Founded on rigorous academic research, this important book tackles the negative consequences of bullying, and bullying culture itself, by examining the social and cultural contexts that perpetuate such behaviour from childhood through adolescence and potentially into adulthood.

Containing contributions from an international team of authors, this book explores current interventions to prevent and reduce school bullying and to alleviate its negative effects on the mental health of children and young people. In-depth discussion of the profound implications of this research for researchers, practitioners and policymakers makes this book essential reading for those interested in bullying culture and the mental health and well-being of children and adolescents.

Helen Cowie is Emeritus Professor in the Faculty of Health and Medical Sciences at the University of Surrey, UK, and a Fellow of the British Psychological Society. She has authored and co-authored a number of influential books on mental health and youth, emotional development, bullying, cyberbullying and peer support, including *From Birth to Sixteen* (Routledge 2012) and *Bullying Among University Students* (Routledge 2016), which she co-edited with Carrie-Anne Myers.

Carrie-Anne Myers is a senior lecturer in Criminology and Sociology at City, University of London, UK, where she researches and publishes in a number of key fields: school violence and bullying, victims, victimology and criminal justice policy, and gendered criminology. She co-edited *Bullying Among University Students* with Helen Cowie (Routledge 2016).

The Mental Health and Well-being of Children and Adolescents

Series Editor: Garry Hornby
University of Plymouth

Mental health disorders in children and young people are increasing, with one in four under-16s experiencing mental health difficulties which will disrupt relationships, education and work. In addition to this, one in ten under-16s suffers from a diagnosed disorder. Access to up-to-date research and appropriate interventions minimises the mental health challenges these children and adolescents face and reduces their potentially lifelong impact.

It has been internationally recognised that the scale of mental health research is low in relation to the burden of the disorder. This research-focussed series will consist of titles that consider key issues affecting young people's mental health and well-being, exploring preventative measures, promoting positive behaviour, and sharing research to develop effective and efficient treatment.

Aimed primarily at researchers and postgraduate students, this series will also be of interest to practitioners in the mental health field, such as psychologists, and some in the field of education, such as counsellors, who would like to implement research-based findings in their clinical practice.

Please visit www.routledge.com/The-Mental-Health-and-Well-being-of-Children-and-Adolescents/book-series/MHWCA.

Books in the series include:

School Bullying and Mental Health
Risks, Intervention and Prevention
Edited by Helen Cowie and Carrie-Anne Myers

To Spiros and Constance

THEME 5
Effective interventions and policies to counteract school bullying 167

15 **Paper tiger or effective guidelines: the use of policies and procedures to address school bullying** 169
MARILYN CAMPBELL

16 **Reducing school bullying: a whole-school approach** 180
JAMES O'HIGGINS NORMAN AND KEITH SULLIVAN

17 **Convivencia: a strategy that prevents school bullying and promotes emotional health and well-being** 192
JOSÉ MARÍA AVILÉS MARTÍNEZ, TRANSLATED FROM SPANISH BY SARAH GRIFFIN-MASON

18 **The impact of Social and Emotional Training (SET) on school bullying in Palestine and Sweden** 202
BIRGITTA KIMBER

THEME 6
Commentaries and epilogue 211

19 **Continuities into the university** 213
SHERI BAUMAN

20 **Continuities into the workplace: what can we learn from research into workplace bullying?** 217
IAIN COYNE

21 **The perspective of the Special Educational Needs Co-ordinator (SENCO)** 223
ANNA BARKER

22 **Epilogue: implications and considerations for future research in the field of young people's mental health** 226
HELEN COWIE AND CARRIE-ANNE MYERS

Index 231

Figures

4.1 Five stage model of bullying perpetration (PAPER) 41
9.1 The interrelationship between factors leading to bullying, the impact on bullies and approaches to changing bullying behaviour 96
10.1 Graphical representation of the simple moderation effect of paternal acceptance in the relationship between victimisation and depressive symptoms scores 107
18.1 Bullying scores over five years of SET 205

Images

12.1 RESCUR Teachers' Guide 133
12.2 Theme 3 poster 135
12.3 Sherlock and Zelda, the two curriculum mascots 137
12.4 Puppets of Sherlock and Zelda 137
12.5 The Parents' Guide 139

Tables

5.1 Exclusions due to sexual misconduct in England and Wales, 2011–14 50
6.1 Hate crime by type 2014/15 59
11.1 Examples of criminal legislation in England and Wales relevant to discussion of cyberbullying in schools 123
14.1 Simple linear regression showing the effect of school culture on bullying 161
14.2 Stepwise regression showing the effect of subscales of school culture on bullying and participants roles 162
16.1 Seven core elements in a checklist for schools 181
18.1 Reliability (Cronbach's alpha) and re-test correlation for the bullying scale 205
18.2 Regression coefficient and effect size for SET/No-SET by group 205

Series editor's foreword

This book is the first in a series addressing the mental health and well-being of children and adolescents. It presents international perspectives of the latest research, theory and practice on bullying, with contributions from countries spanning the world.

Among the wide range of important topics addressed are the relationship of bullying to hate crime and sexual violence, as well as its impact on asylum seekers, religious groups and the LGBT community. The roles of counsellors, mental health specialists, families, bystanders and peers in bullying are discussed. Also, the influence on bullying and mental health of school ethos and social media, plus cultural and economic aspects, such as neo-liberalism, is addressed.

The book emphasises the pervasiveness of cyberbullying and the potential continuation of bullying roles from school into college or university as well as the workplace. It also focusses on strategies for promoting emotional health and well-being in schools, including programmes of Social and Emotional Training.

Bullying is set within the context of the wide range of mental health issues affecting children and youth that are encountered in schools (Atkinson & Hornby, 2002). Several chapters focus on the necessity for promoting mental health and well-being in schools (Hornby & Atkinson, 2003). Others focus on developing whole-school anti-bullying policies and ecological approaches to intervention for bullying, which are now widely supported in the bullying literature (Hornby, 2016).

The editors are to be commended for bringing together an outstanding group of contributors who are involved in bullying research in a wide range of countries. The book provides a scholarly, up-to-date and comprehensive coverage of issues relevant to bullying, as well as their relation to children's and young people's mental health and well-being, which means that it makes a major contribution to this field.

Professor Garry Hornby
University of Plymouth

References

Atkinson, M., & Hornby, G. (2002). *Mental health handbook for schools*. London: Routledge Falmer.

Hornby, G. (2016). Bullying: An ecological approach to intervention in schools. *Preventing School Failure*, *60*(3), 222–230.

Hornby, G., & Atkinson, M. (2003). A framework for promoting mental health in schools. *Pastoral Care in Education*, *21*(2), 3–9.

Contributors

José María Avilés Martínez is Professor in the Psychology Department at the University of Valladolid, Spain. He is an expert on convivencia in schools, in the prevention of bullying and of cyberbullying, and on the risks involved in social interaction on the Internet. He has investigated peer support and its impact on the prevention and reduction of bullying. He has been honorary professor in la Universidad Nacional Mayor de San Marcos de Lima, Perú since 2012. He has published extensively in national and international journals and has written many books and manuals, including, 'INSEBULL, instrumentos para la evaluación del bullying' (2007, CEPE, España), 'Manual contra el bullying' (2012, Ediciones Libro Amigo, Perú), 'Bullying, guía para educadores' (2013, Mercado de Letras – SP, Brasil), 'Proyecto Antibullying, prevención del bullying y el cyberbullying en la comunidad educativa' (2015, CEPE, España).

Rashid Aziz is Senior Lecturer in Applied Criminology at the School of Law, Criminal Justice and Computing, Canterbury Christ Church University, UK. His main research interests are in the areas of informal social control and British Asian Muslim communities, forced marriage and bullying among university and high school students. He has recently been awarded his PhD; his thesis explored British Asian Muslims and decisions taken with regard to leisure and marriage. He is also a member of the Canterbury Centre for Policing Research.

Ana Aznar is Lecturer in Psychology at the University of Winchester. She is a developmental psychologist and was previously a Postdoctoral Research Fellow at the University of Surrey. She has two main areas of research. Firstly, she is interested in how parents and children talk about emotions and the relationship with children's understanding of emotions. Much of this work has examined gender differences in parent-child emotion talk. Her second area of research focusses on children's reasoning about social issues, such as peer rejection and children's rights.

Anna Barker is Assistant Head Teacher for Inclusion at St Mary's Church of England Primary School in Hackney, London, and works as part of the Senior Leadership Team. Qualified as a teacher for ten years, she has taught in Key Stage 1 and 2 and had a range of school roles including head of year and reading coordinator. Her previous career was in health promotion and education and she is a trained counsellor who specialised in working in sexual health clinics and drug education.

Sheri Bauman is Professor of Counselling at the University of Arizona, USA. Prior to earning her doctorate in 1999, she had been a teacher and counsellor in primary and secondary schools. Her research interests revolve around peer mistreatment (bullying and cyberbullying), with a focus on teacher responses to peer victimisation. She is currently studying the impact of police personnel on actual and perceived safety and climate in secondary schools in the US. She is the author (or co-author) of six books and numerous articles in peer-reviewed journals, and is a frequent presenter at local, national and international conferences.

Marilyn Campbell is a professor at the Queensland University of Technology, Australia. She is a registered teacher and a registered psychologist. Previous to this she supervised school counsellors and has worked in infants, primary and secondary schools as a teacher, teacher-librarian and school counsellor. Her main clinical and research interests are the prevention and intervention of anxiety disorders in young people and the effects of bullying, especially cyberbullying in schools. She is the author of the Worrybusters series of books for anxious children.

Carmel Cefai is a fellow of the British Psychological Society and is the director of the Centre for Resilience and Socio-Emotional Health, and Associate Professor at the Department of Psychology, at the University of Malta. He is Joint Honorary Chair of the European Network for Social and Emotional Competence and joint founding editor of the *International Journal of Emotional Education*. His research interests are focussed on the promotion of resilience, well-being and mental health in children and young people and he has led various national and international research projects in these areas. Recent publications include *RESCUR Surfing the Waves, A Resilience Curriculum for Early Years and Primary Schools* (2015) published in seven languages and *Social and Emotional Education Primary School. Integrating Theory and Research into Practice* (Springer Publications USA, 2014).

Pat Colliety is Senior Teaching Fellow at the University of Surrey, UK, and has a professional background in children's nursing and health visiting. She has a particular interest in bullying and cyberbullying and has recently been collaborating with school nursing colleagues to explore what the role of the school nurse is in relation to bullies. She has also been involved in teaching ethics using theatre and performance simulation.

Helen Cowie is Emeritus Professor at the University of Surrey, UK, in the Faculty of Health and Medical Sciences and a Fellow of the British Psychological Society. She has numerous publications in refereed journals on the subject of mental health and youth, emotional development, bullying, cyberbullying and peer support. She has authored and co-authored a number of influential books, including *Managing School Violence* (with Dawn Jennifer, Sage Publications), *New Perspectives on Bullying* (with Dawn Jennifer, Open University Press), *From Birth to Sixteen* (Routledge) and *Bullying among University Students* (with Carrie-Anne Myers, Routledge). *Understanding Children's Development* (John Wiley), co-authored with Peter K. Smith and Mark Blades and now into its 6th Edition, remains one of the most popular undergraduate texts in the field.

Iain Coyne is Senior Lecturer in Organisational Psychology in the School of Business and Economics, Loughborough University, UK, a Registered Occupational Psychologist and an Associate Fellow of the British Psychological Society. He is focussed on understanding bullying/cyberbullying at work, publishing his research in peer reviewed journals, book chapters and presenting at national/international conferences for both academic and practitioner audience groups. He is co-editor (with Claire Monks) of *Bullying in Different Contexts* (Cambridge University Press, 2011). Previously, he was a task force member for the Chartered Management Institute project on workplace bullying (2005) and an elected member of the Management Committee for a European COST Action on Cyber-bullying (2008–12).

Simon Edwards was appointed Senior Lecturer in Youth Studies at the University of Portsmouth, UK, in 2014 following a career as a youth worker and secondary school teacher working with educationally and socially marginalised young people. He maintains his practitioner experience through voluntary youth and community work carried out in his home town of Lancing, West Sussex, UK, as a director and manager of Electric Storm Youth and through research projects developed in his academic role at Portsmouth University. These voluntary and research activities are underpinned by his interest in Freire's liberation education enabling him to carry out his conviction to present young peoples' voices on a range of issues related to communities and schools including school exclusion, crime, cyberbullying and bullying.

Theodoros Giovazolias is Associate Professor of Counselling Psychology at the Department of Psychology, University of Crete. His main research interests include the examination of bullying in children and adolescents, as well as its effects in adult psychosocial adjustment. More specifically, he tries to understand how both family and school factors are related to the occurrence of the phenomenon. Additionally, he has participated as educator and co-ordinator in various seminars and educational programmes (both on a national and European level) on school bullying. He has presented his work in national and international conferences and has published in peer-reviewed scientific journals. He is a Chartered Counselling Psychologist with the British Psychological Society (BPS) and Director of the University of Crete Student Counselling Centre. In 2015, he received the Annual Award of the European Association of Counselling Psychology for Outstanding Contribution to Counselling Psychology across Europe.

Sarah Griffin-Mason is a career translator who first trained with the InterPress Service in Montevideo, Uruguay in the 1990s. She is currently Chair of the Institute of Translation and Interpreting and also a Senior Lecturer in Translation Studies at the University of Portsmouth. Sarah also runs a small freelance translation and editing business dealing with direct clients in her fields of expertise see: www.griffin-mason.com.

Rubina Hanif is currently working as Tenured Associate Professor at the National Institute of Psychology, centre of excellence, Quaid-i-Azam University, Islamabad, Pakistan. She has worked as a post-doc fellow at Goldsmiths University, London, UK, and as a Fulbright scholar at the University of Houston, US. Her research interests are Educational Psychology, Developmental Psychology, and Interpersonal Relationships and Conflicts. Furthermore, she works in survey, experimental, qualitative and longitudinal research designs and targets cross cultural populations.

Birgitta Kimber is a school teacher, psychotherapist and post-doctoral researcher. She is the creator of the Social and Emotional Training (SET) programme that has been used in Sweden and Palestine. She is the author of several books and many articles in both Swedish and English, including stringent evaluations of the SET programme. Currently she works partly as a teacher of newly arrived immigrants in Sweden and is very involved in bettering their prospects in all regards. For details of her career, see www.birgittakimber.com.

Kerry Lee is a research fellow at City, University of London, UK, in Criminology where she researches and teaches in a number of key areas including Domestic and Sexual Violence, Gender, Victimology, Feminist Criminology and Criminal Justice.

Maria Luca is Senior Research Fellow at the School of Psychotherapy and Psychology, Regent's University London, UK, head of the Regent's Reflections Research Centre, manager of the PhD programme and Editor of the *Journal of Psychotherapy & Counselling Psychology Reflections.* Her previous administrative roles include Head of the School of Psychotherapy and Counselling Psychology at Regent's. She made a television appearance on Sky News (25/03/2016) on sexual bullying among young people. Included in her publications are: *Sexual Attraction in Therapy: Clinical Perspectives on Moving Beyond the Taboo – A Guide for Training and Practice* (London: Wiley, 2014); Trainee therapists' moralistic reactions and defensive handling of client sexual attraction in therapy, *Journal of Psychotherapy & Counselling Psychology Reflections*, 1(1): 27–3 (2016);

The role of the therapist in helping university students who have been bullied: a case study of sexual bullying, in Helen Cowie and Carrie-Anne Myers (eds.) *Bullying Among University Students* (London: Routledge, 2016); Containment of the sexualized and erotized transference, *Journal of Clinical Psychoanalysis*, Vol. 11 No. 4, Fall 2002, International Universities Press.

Maria Malikiosi-Loizos is Professor Emeritus at the University of Athens in Greece. She is a counselling psychologist. She has participated as educator, trainer and coordinator in various programmes concerning the applications of counselling in primary, secondary and higher education. She established the first peer counselling centre at the University of Athens in 1995 and also started the first post-graduate programme in counselling psychology and counselling in Greece in 2009. She is recipient of honorary awards for her contribution to Greek but also European counselling psychology. She is a humanistic psychologist who nurtures the principles of positive psychology in promoting human well-being.

Carrie-Anne Myers is a senior lecturer in Criminology and Sociology at City, University of London, UK, where she researches and teaches in a number of key areas including: Childhood, Youth and Adolescence, School Violence and Bullying, Victims, Victimology and Criminal Justice Policy, and Gender and Feminist Criminology. She has published in refereed journals, focussing on young people bullying, cyberbullying and violence, including *Pastoral Care in Education, Emotional and Behavioural Difficulties* and *The Journal of Cross-Cultural Psychology*. In 2016 she co-edited, with Helen Cowie, *Bullying Among University Students*, published by Routledge.

James O'Higgins Norman is Associate Professor in Sociology and Director of the National Anti-Bullying Research and Resource Centre at Dublin City University, Ireland. He has authored a number of books on aspects of equality and bullying in schools. He is best known for his research on homophobic bullying in schools in Ireland which has drawn international media attention and was referenced in parliamentary proceedings in Ireland and at the EU Commission. He is a co-editor of the *International Handbook on Education for Spirituality, Care and Wellbeing* (Springer, 2009) and his current research projects include gender and cyberbullying, parental Internet usage and knowledge of cyberbullying, and workplace bullying.

Maili Pörhölä is Adjunct Professor in the School of Humanities at the University of Eastern Finland. Her areas of research include bullying at school, in higher education and in the workplace, as well as aspects of peer relationships, peer community integration, and psychosocial well-being. She has worked on steering committees to provide advice on the development of anti-bullying policies and procedures for kindergartens in Finland, and been invited as a presenter at seminars and workshops aimed at preventing bullying at school and university levels. She has published a number of research articles in peer-reviewed journals as well as authoring several book chapters. Among other publications, she has co-edited with Terry A. Kinney the book *Anti and Pro-Social Communication: Theories, Methods, and Applications* (2009, Peter Lang Publishing Inc.) and co-authored with Terry A. Kinney the book *Bullying: Contexts, Consequences, and Control* (2010, Editorial Aresta).

Holly Powell-Jones is a former broadcast journalist who has been designing and delivering media law and ethics training for schools, businesses and charities since 2013. Her course, 'Online and Social Media Law and Ethics', has received substantial investment from the Police and Crime Commissioner's Office for Surrey and reaches approximately 50 secondary schools every year. She is also a visiting lecturer in Media Law and Ethics at Goldsmiths, University of London, UK, and currently is completing a PhD at the Centre for Law, Justice and Journalism at City, University of London. She also runs CityCyber Research.com and @OnlineMediaLaw.

Ian Rivers is Professor of Education for Social Change at the University of Strathclyde, Glasgow, Scotland. He is a developmental and health psychologist and was previously Professor of Human Development at Brunel University London. He is a fellow of the American Psychological Association, the British Psychological Society and the Academy of Social Sciences. He is the author of *Homophobic Bullying: Research and Theoretical Perspectives* (2011, Oxford University Press) which has now been translated in Italian (2015, Il Saggiatore). He is also co-author (with Sheri Bauman) of *Mental Health in the Digital Age* (2015, Palgrave). He is a past recipient of the British Psychological Society's Award for Promoting Equality of Opportunity in the United Kingdom.

Martin D. Ruck is Professor of Psychology and Urban Education at the Graduate Center of the City University of New York, USA. His research examines the overall process of cognitive socialization – at the intersection of race, ethnicity and class – in terms of children and adolescents' thinking about human rights, equity, and social justice. Much of his research has addressed how children and adolescents view their protection and participation rights across various settings. His work has appeared in many prestigious journals. He is co-editor with Stacey S. Horn and Lynn S. Liben of the 2-volume *Equity and Justice in Development Science* published by Elsevier in *Advances in Child Development and Behaviour* (2016). With Michele Peterson-Badali and Michael Freeman he is co-editor of *Handbook of Children's Rights: Global and Multidisciplinary Perspective*, published by Taylor & Francis in 2017.

Wendy Sims-Schouten is Senior Lecturer in the School of Education and Childhood Studies at the University of Portsmouth, UK, where she specialises in research on mental health and well-being in childhood and education. She has published in the areas of early years education, bullying, resilience and childhood obesity, and stigmas and labels. In addition, she has presented her work at several national and international conferences, invited lectures and research seminars and panel discussions. Current projects include research on mental health and well-being of young care leavers, mental health literacy of HE students, and issues around (cyber-)bullying, resilience and well-being.

Keith Sullivan's research and practical solution-finding has focussed on real-world and cyber bullying within education and the workplace. His concern has been to establish knowledge about its nature and through lived-experiences to create holistic, humane solutions that neutralise and address the damage it creates. His work has been published in hardcopy and e-books in English, Spanish, Chinese, Japanese and Estonian. Professor Sullivan has taught in universities in England, New Zealand, the South Pacific and Ireland. He held the Charter Fellowship in Human Rights at Wolfson College, Oxford, UK, and gained practical experiences for understanding and dealing with bullying through his work as a child care worker, a school counsellor and teacher in secondary schools in Canada, England, and New Zealand. He has presented his bullying work to many international audiences.

Harriet R. Tenenbaum is Reader in Psychology at the University of Surrey, UK. Her research examines social, cognitive, and emotional development to understand how children understand social issues and how these views are formed in social context with important others. Her work has appeared in journals such as *Child Development,* the *Journal of Educational Psychology*, and the *Journal of Experimental Child Psychology* and has been funded by the British Academy, Leverhulme Foundation, and the European Commission. She is a former editor and current associate editor at the *British Journal of Educational Psychology* and is also a current associate editor at the *British Journal of Developmental Psychology.*

Sadaf Zaheer was formerly a research scholar at Quaid-i-Azam University, Islamabad, Pakistan. Currently, she is working as a lecturer in psychology at Foundation University, Rawalpindi, Pakistan. She is also an article and content writer with years of experience in academic writing. Her areas of specialization include social, educational, organizational and positive psychology.

Permissions

Consent to use clinical material in this book has been given by the clients and other relevant parties. All identifying features of the clients have been removed.

Theme 1

The nature of bullying

In chapter 1, Cowie and Myers consider key aspects of the nature and incidence of bullying in schools and its impact on the mental health of children and young people. They explore the moral disengagement that characterises bystanders' apathy in the face of an episode of bullying. Bystanders who do nothing or who actively rejoice in the victim's humiliation and shame demonstrate that they have become desensitised to prosocial values and seem to have suppressed feelings of empathy towards the bullied peer so that the distress of a fellow pupil has become a source of fun and enjoyment. This raises questions about individual qualities of vulnerability and resilience on the part of victims as well as the nature of the social contexts where the bullying behaviour takes place. These research findings are linked to interventions designed to promote positive values in the school community as a whole. The ideas are further explored in chapter 2 where Pörhölä considers continuities from school bullying through to bullying at university and the workplace and investigates why some children and young people escape victimisation while for others the bullying persists. She argues that, in order to develop means to prevent the continuities of bullying over time, more theoretical and empirical research is needed to better understand *why* the roles of bullies and victims tend to follow some individuals from one social context to another. Pörhölä suggests that more attention should be paid to social relationships between bullies and victims. She also considers the important role of the bystanders and their influence on whether the bullying continues or is prevented. To this end, she presents four explanatory theories that take account of the complex interactions among children and young people in their peer groups.

Chapter 1

What we know about school bullying

Helen Cowie and Carrie-Anne Myers

The nature and incidence of school bullying

This book is part of a series on the mental health and emotional well-being of children and young people. So, from the beginning, we emphasize the emotional risks that affect children who are involved in bullying, whether as victims or as perpetrators, or indeed as bystanders. School bullying is a major risk factor for children's emotional health and well-being, whether as targets of bullying, perpetrators or witnesses. Every day in our schoolyards and classrooms, thousands of children suffer the humiliation and shame of being bullied by their peers. Most recently, and with the upsurge in cyberbullying, the threat is with them day and night, in their homes, on their way to and from school and in their communities.

Bullying affects children's physical and mental health, their attendance at school, their educational attainment and their social relationships. The mental health consequences can be severe and long-lasting. For example, Lereya, Copeland, Costello, and Wolke (2015) found a strong relationship between being bullied as a child and mental disorders such as social anxiety and depression in adulthood; they also noted similar links to relationship difficulties in adulthood. The same research team (Lereya, Copeland, Zammit, & Wolke, 2015) found that the children most prone to mental health difficulties later on in their lives were the bully-victims – those children who bully others but who are themselves the targets of bullying in other contexts, whether in the family, the community or the school. Again, in a large ten-country study involving over 11,000 adolescents, Klomek et al. (2016) found a direct association between victimisation and self-injury, as well as depression and anxiety. In the present volume, in chapter 8, Luca presents case studies of adults whose mental health was badly affected by childhood bullying, while in chapter 10, Giovazolias and Malikiosi-Loizos investigate the moderating impact of fathers in alleviating depression in bullied children. Each of these chapters explores the mental health implications of bullying in some depth and offers insights to develop interventions to reduce the suffering of victims.

The authors in this book present current knowledge about the phenomenon of school bullying and the complex dialogues and debates that are involved in addressing the problem, with a particular emphasis on mental health. The overall aim of this book is:

- To collate in one volume current research evidence and theoretical perspectives about school bullying;
- To identify the nature and extent of bullying/cyberbullying at school and its impact on children's and young people's emotional health and well-being;
- To explore the interface between bullying and crime;
- To investigate social and cultural contexts which perpetuate bullying behaviour from childhood through adolescence and potentially to adulthood;
- To explore current interventions to prevent and reduce school bullying and to alleviate its negative effects on the mental health of children and young people;
- To discuss the implications for policy-makers, practitioners and researchers in this important field.

School bullying takes many forms and includes such behaviour as:

- Spreading nasty rumours on the grounds of age, race, sex, mental health, disability, sexual orientation and religion or belief;
- Physically attacking someone;
- Ridiculing or demeaning someone;
- Social exclusion;
- Unwelcome sexual advances;
- Posting embarrassing material online;
- Threatening someone, either directly on anonymously online.

Research into school bullying has traditionally focussed on the actual protagonists – the perpetrators and the targets. Consequently, we know a great deal about the psychological characteristics of bullies and victims and the consequences of bullying in undermining the emotional well-being of both targets and perpetrators. Pure bullies appear to show little empathy for others and have low levels of moral engagement with their community; they seem to have a cold callousness in their behaviour that allows them to perpetrate cruel acts towards targeted peers without feeling guilt or remorse, but they, like their victims, are also at risk of mental health and social difficulties, both in the short-term and the long-term. See chapter 9 where Cowie and Colliety explore the emotional needs of children who bully.

While an understanding of the personal aspects of the bully-victim relationship is important, it only addresses part of the issue. Bullying is experienced within a group of peers who adopt different participant roles and who experience a range of emotions. See chapter 2 where Pörhölä provides theoretical explanations of bullying in the complex world of peer relationships. Bullies do not act alone but rely on reinforcement from their immediate group of friends as well as the tacit approval of the onlookers. Most recently, there has been a concern to clarify the boundaries between bullying/cyberbullying and crime. This aspect is discussed in depth in Theme 2 of this book.

The most widely-used definition of school bullying is the one originally proposed by Olweus (1993) which identifies three core components:

1 There is an intent to harm or upset another student;
2 The harmful behaviour is done repeatedly over time;
3 The relationship between bully/bullies and victim/victims is characterised by an imbalance in power.

Since then, researchers have identified differences in how bullying is perceived and defined by children and young people (Currie et al., 2012) and by adults in the workplace (Jacobson, Hood, & van Buren, 2014) from which it appears that bullying is understood differently depending on the social context and the age of those involved. Smith, Cowie, Olafsson, and Liefooghe (2002) asked children from 14 different countries to look at 25 different stick figures illustrating situations that might be considered as bullying. Younger children had a less differentiated view of bullying than older children. There were also marked cultural differences, especially with regard to inclusion of indirect forms of bullying, such as ostracism and other forms of psychological bullying. Jacobson et al. (2014) argue that some of the ways in which individuals or groups interpret the phenomenon arise from cultural and situational differences in the construction of what it is to be bullied. Perceptions may vary widely depending on the amount of aggressive behaviour necessary for an act to be considered as bullying *in that context*. For example, bullying may be embedded in a child's family or community and that will have an influence on how the aggressive behaviour is interpreted. In a very authoritarian school, the threshold of behaviour that would be labelled as bullying would be higher than in a more person-centred school with a greater emphasis on nurturing good relationships among pupils. In some social contexts, the child who bullies may well not be aware of the destructive effect of his or her behaviour on targets. Particularly in situations where the young person is a bully-victim, their aggression towards vulnerable peers may be part of a protective mechanism to help them cope with negative experiences in their own lives.

Cyberbullying

We also need to take account of a more recent phenomenon. Bullying has not been limited to the offline world in the last decade. Rapid changes in electronic communication technologies have provided new tools for bullies, who benefit from the anonymity and ease that these methods of harassment provide. This new type of bullying is usually referred to as *cyberbullying*. Like traditional face-to-face bullying, cyberbullying involves the deliberate intent to hurt a person or persons through the electronic transmission of messages and images which target the victim(s) repeatedly over time. It is widely proposed that the reported reasons for attacking a person online involve the bullies' need for power and dominance within a group, the perceived vulnerability of the target, perceived provocativeness on the part of the target (usually as a justification for the aggression on the part of the bully) and interpersonal animosities (Kyriacou & Zuin, 2016).

The National Society for the Prevention of Cruelty to Children (NSPCC) (2015) estimates that, in the previous year, around 26,000 counselling sessions were provided by teachers to support students who had been cyberbullied. This gives an idea of the scale of the problem. Clearly schools face a huge challenge in dealing with this relatively recent phenomenon. In fact, Livingstone, Haddon, Vincent, Mascheroni, and Ólafsson (2014) found that young people in Britain are more likely to be bullied online than face-to-face in the playground.

But there are some controversies in the research findings with conflicting evidence from different studies. On the one hand, some researchers have found a substantial overlap between traditional bullying and cyberbullying. From this evidence, they conclude that cyberbullies often target peers who are already being bullied in traditional, face-to-face ways (Perren, Dooley, Shaw, & Cross, 2010; Sourander et al., 2010). By contrast, Schultze-Krumbholz et al. (2015) found structural differences in cyberbullying when compared with traditional bullying. Most significantly, they found an absence of an exclusive victim class in their study of 6,260 school-age adolescents (mean age 14–8 years) from six European countries. Instead of the four traditional categories of bully, victim, bully-victim and bystander, they identified only three: bully-victims, perpetrators and uninvolved. In this study, the perpetrators of cyberbullying were likely to have been bullied themselves and, as the researchers hypothesise, perhaps the cyber-victims felt more free to fight back against their aggressors online than they would in the 'real', face-to-face world. The lack of a clear victim group in this study is consistent with other studies that document an overlap between victims and perpetrators in cyberbullying. Further research will unravel the differences between these two sets of findings.

Cyberbullying potentially reaches a much larger audience (through, for example, social networking sites) and postings can be viewed repeatedly, with extremely disturbing consequences for the targets, including insomnia, depression, anxiety, suicidal thoughts, self-harm and, in rare cases, suicide (Sourander et al., 2010). The anonymity of the cyberbully is a powerful component. Kyriacou and Zuin (2016) argue that this anonymity results in desensitisation of prosocial values and empathy towards another person and ultimately in a process of moral disengagement since the cyberbully does not meet face-to-face with his/her target. Thus, there is less likelihood that the cyberbully will experience social disapproval or intervention on the part of bystanders.

Bystanders and witnesses

As Salmivalli (2010) points out, the original conception of bullying as proposed by Olweus (1978) was *mobbing* – a group phenomenon in which a group of peers 'gang up' on another child and repeatedly torment and harass that child. Salmivalli took this idea further by identifying the range of participant roles within the group, each driven by different emotions and motives. She also took account of the school or classroom ethos which, she argues, has a crucial influence on the ways in which individual characteristics interact with the social context where the bullying act takes place. The deeper insights that Salmivalli's approach offers contribute positively to the process of developing interventions, such as peer support, that help to counteract bullying within its particular context.

Within the school or classroom setting, the bystanders and witnesses of the bullying respond in a range of ways. The *assistants* to the bully actively join in the attacks of the ringleader bully; the *reinforcers* of the bully may not directly attack the victim but they provide strong encouragement for the ringleader and his/her cohort of followers by laughing and jeering at the discomfort and humiliation of the victim; *outsiders* ignore what is going on and claim to have nothing to do with it, even though their presence and inaction reinforce the behaviour of the bully and his/her supporters. Finally, *defenders* demonstrate their empathy for the victim's situation by offering support or by seeking out adult help.

Bystanders' behaviour has a powerful effect on whether the bullying continues or ceases. In classrooms where bystanders typically reinforce the bullies in some way, victimised children show the highest levels of social anxiety and peer rejection (Kärnä, Voeten, Poskiparta, & Salmivalli, 2010). Conversely, where classmates defend the victim, that child is less anxious, less depressed and has higher self-esteem than victims without defenders (Sainio, Veenstra, Huitsing, & Salmivalli, 2010).

But why do some bystanders intervene to help the victim while others simply stand back and enjoy the spectacle? In their classic study, Latané and Darley (1970) identified the impact of *bystander apathy* in the face of a disturbing event. They noted that the more witnesses are present in a potentially dangerous situation, the less likely it is that an individual witness will step forward to take action. This *diffusion of responsibility* can be explained by fear or embarrassment on the part of the individual about stepping out of line in the face of perceived inaction by the group. Related to this is the extent to which the bystander feels competent to intervene. They may calculate that others are better equipped to deal with the perceived threat or danger. However, diffusion of responsibility also represents the denial of moral obligation to others. As Clarkson (1996, p. 15) writes: "Metaphorically, bystanders wash their hands, as did Pontius Pilate, knowingly condemning an innocent to harm while publicly claiming guiltlessness".

In the school context, there is definitely an element of fear on the part of bystanders in that, by defending the often unpopular and socially isolated victim, the potential defender runs the risk of becoming a victim in the future. It may well be more expedient to keep on the right side of the powerful bully and his/her henchmen. It may also be easier simply to blame the victim for somehow bringing all this misery on themselves. Particularly in the context of cyberbullying, the bystander may not physically witness the bullying but view the episode via uploaded material so enabling a distancing of the witness from the target. In these circumstances, there is more likelihood that the bullying episode may be seen as a form of entertainment. Kernaghan and Elwood (2013) use Goffman's (1959) framework on the presentation of self in everyday life as a way of thinking about bullying as a type of performance where the bystanders are in the role of audience to a drama.

If we fail to understand the complexity of peer group relationships and the dynamics of the social settings where bullying flourishes, then interventions will remain largely ineffective. Initiatives that involve young people themselves have much more potential to address the problem of bullying. Dialogue is essential here to challenge the inaction of the bystanders. Young people in focus groups in the study by Purdy and York (2016) reported that often the issue of cyberbullying was 'a closed-door subject' and they also admitted that during an episode of bullying it is often easier to 'go with the crowd' since they were afraid that the bullies would turn on them. As against such sentiments of hopelessness, Salmivalli (2014) argues that a proportion of young people *do* wish to take positive action against bullying – the *defenders*. So, a key element in the process of developing interventions to address bullying must involve understanding of the ethos of the particular school (and even the surrounding community) as well as a willingness to develop interventions in consultation with all members of the school community, including the children and young people themselves.

Understanding the causes of moral disengagement

As we have seen, the children who bully, as well as their assistants and reinforcers, are characterised by a lack of empathy for the feelings of their victims. This becomes even more pronounced when there is a distancing between perpetrator and victims, as happens in the course of cyberbullying. This lack of direct face-to-face communication appears to promote in bystanders a lack of sensitivity to the plight of the victim. Through this process, the bullies as well as the bystanders increasingly view it as acceptable to laugh at the suffering of a fellow pupil. This *moral disengagement* perpetuates the view that there is no need to intervene to prevent the bullying or to support the victim.

Jones, Manstead, and Livingstone (2011) argue that group-based emotions have a strong influence on how children react to a bullying episode. *Pride* in taking part leads to a tendency to boast about one's achievement in humiliating another child; *anger* is more likely to lead to some form of action against the aggressors; *guilt* leads to a tendency to make amends to the victim; *shame* leads to a tendency to distance oneself from the disturbing situation. All of these group-based emotions can be observed in the behaviour of the children in the various participant roles during and after a bullying episode. The more that fellow pupils identify with the victim, the more likely they are to engage in some form of action to defend that person. Conversely, the more that children identify with and admire the bully and his/her cohort of supporters, the more likely they are to condone feelings of pride in attacking a vulnerable peer. In fact, Mazzone, Camodeca, and Salmivalli (2016) found that low levels of guilt correlated with bullying behaviour and concluded that this makes it easier for bullies to violate moral standards; they also found that low levels of guilt and high levels of moral disengagement reduced the likelihood of offering help to the victim. Furthermore, Schultze-Krumbholz, Schultze, Zagorscak, Wölfer, and Scheithauer (2016) found that perpetrators of cyberbullying display lower feelings of empathy towards their victims. Similarly, Meter and Bauman (2016) argue that those who show moral disengagement about cyberbullying are more likely to be perpetrators which, in turn, could transfer to traditional bullying as well. These findings are also supported by Tognetta, Avilés, and Rosário (2016) in their study of 2600 students in Brazil in which, using stories about bullying with a series of moral choices that the participants in the research could take, they found that bullies scored significantly higher on measures of moral disengagement.

Such studies indicate that a large part of the solution to the problem lies with the peer group itself. The success or otherwise of interventions to prevent bullying depends on the extent to which pupils respect the values of their school and have regular opportunities to discuss why bullying happens, what motivates people to engage in it and why bystanders find it amusing to witness the humiliation and distress of a peer. So, as Arthur and Harrison (2012), Tognetta et al. (2016) and Kyriacou and Zuin (2016) recommend, it is essential for schools to teach and demonstrate prosocial values right across the curriculum with a strong specific emphasis on considering why and where young people become morally disengaged from others. Interventions such as *Media Heroes* (Schultze-Krumbholz et al., 2016) specifically target cyberbullying at different levels – individual, classroom and family. At the individual level, training enhances personal and social skills, such as empathy and perspective-taking, as well as self-protection strategies, such as understanding how to manage privacy settings effectively; at classroom level, training focusses on fostering positive class norms and challenging bystander apathy; at family level, students educate their parents on modern communication technologies. Outcomes for *Media Heroes* have been very encouraging in terms of decreases in both traditional and cyber bullying; those with increased scores in perspective-taking decreased their cyberbullying behaviour. Studies such as these indicate that it is crucial to give children and young people many opportunities to listen to one another, to practise taking the perspective of others, to develop empathy for the feelings of others and to learn about alternatives to violence and aggression. In view of the continuities of bullying across time, it is essential to take action to challenge cruel, anti-social behaviour when it appears so that it does not persist from childhood through adolescence into adulthood.

In the present volume, and in line with the recommendations of Mazzone et al. (2016) and Meter and Bauman (2016) and Schultze-Krumbholz et al. (2016), we present a number of interventions that aim to challenge moral disengagement and that actively promote positive values in the school community as a whole. See chapter 16 where O'Higgins Norman and Sullivan propose a whole-school approach and chapter 17 where Avilés presents evidence to document the value of promoting *convivencia* in schools as an antidote to bullying. See also chapter 12 where Cefai describes a project designed to promote resilience in vulnerable children, and chapter 14 where Hanif and Zaheer explore the impact of participant roles on a school's culture. In chapter 18, Kimber discusses the impact of Social and Emotional Training (SET) in challenging bullying in two contrasting cultures – Sweden and Palestine. Such interventions illustrate evidence-based practice designed to improve students' capacity for moral reasoning, for reflecting on their own behaviour, for developing empathy for the emotions of others and for making amends when moral codes are violated.

References

Arthur, J., & Harrison, T. (2012). Exploring good character and citizenship in England. *Asia Pacific Journal of Education, 32*, 489–497.

Clarkson, P. (1996). *The bystander.* London: Whurr.

Currie, C., Zanotti, C., Morgan, A., & Currie, D. (2012). *Social determinants of health and well – Being among young people.* Geneva, Switzerland: World Health Organisation.

Goffman, E. (1959). *The presentation of self in everyday life.* London: Penguin Books.

Jacobson, K. J. L., Hood, J. N., & van Buren, H. J. (2014). Workplace bullying across cultures: A research agenda. *Journal of Cross Cultural Management, 14*, 47–65.

Jones, S. E., Manstead, A. S. R., & Livingstone, A. G. (2011). Ganging up or sticking together? Group processes and children's responses to text-message bullying. *British Journal of Psychology, 102*, 71–96.

Kärnä, A., Voeten, M., Poskiparta, E., & Salmivalli, C. (2010). Vulnerable children in varying classroom contexts: Bystanders' behaviours moderate the effects of risk factors on victimization. *Merrill-Palmer Quarterly, 56*(3), article 4. Retrieved from http://digitalcommons.wayne.edu/mpq/vol56/iss3/4

Kernaghan, D., & Elwood, J. (2013). All the (cyber) world's a stage: Framing cyberbullying as a performance. *Journal of Psychosocial Research on Cyberspace: Cyberpsychology*, 7(1), 1 – 11.

Klomek, A. B., Snir, A., Apter, A., Carli, V., Wasserman, C., Hadlaczky, G., Hoven, C. W., Sarchiapone, M., Balazs, J., Bobes, J., Brunner, R., Corcoran, P., Cosman, D., Haring, C., Kahn, J.-P. et al. (2016). Association between victimization by bullying and direct self-injurious behaviour among adolescence in Europe: A ten-country study. *European Child and Adolescent Psychiatry, 25*(11), 1183–1193.

Kyriacou, C., & Zuin, A. (2016). Cyberbullying and moral disengagement: An analysis based on a social pedagogy of pastoral care in schools. *Pastoral Care in Education, 34*(1), 34–42.

Latané, B., & Darley, M. (1970). *The unresponsive bystander: Why doesn't he help?* New York: Appleton Century Crofts.

Lereya, S. T., Copeland, W. E., Costello, E. G., & Wolke, D. (2015). Adult mental health, consequences of peer bullying and maltreatment in childhood: Two cohorts in two countries. *Lancet Psychiatry, 2*(6), 524–531.

Lereya, S. T., Copeland, W. E., Zammit, S., & Wolke, D. (2015). Bully/victims: A longitudinal population-based cohort study of their mental health. *European Child and Adolescent Psychiatry, 24*(12), 1461–1471.

Livingstone, S., Haddon, L., Vincent, J., Mascheroni, G., & Ólafsson, K. (2014). *Net children go mobile: The UK report.* London: London School of Economics.

Mazzone, A., Camodeca, M., & Salmivalli, C. (2016). Interactive effects of guilt and moral disengagement on bullying, defending and outsider behaviour. *Journal of Moral Education, 45*(4), 419–432.

Meter, D. J., & Bauman, S. (2016). Moral disengagement about cyberbullying and parental monitoring: Effects on traditional bullying and victimization via cyberbullying involvement. *Journal of Early Adolescence, 3*, 1–24. doi:10.1177/0272431616670752.

National Society for the Prevention of Cruelty to Children (NSPCC). (2015). *Share aware.* Retrieved from www.nspcc.org.uk/preventing-abuse/keeping-children-safe/share-aware/

Olweus, D. (1978). *Aggression in schools: Bullies and whipping boys.* Washington, DC: Hemisphere.

Olweus, D. (1993). *Bullying: What we know and what we can do.* Oxford: Basil Blackwell.

Perren, S., Dooley, J., Shaw, T., & Cross, D. (2010). Bullying in school and cyberspace: Associations with depressive symptoms in Swiss and Australian adolescents. *Child and Adolescent Psychiatry and Mental Health, 4*, 28–38.

Purdy, N., & York, L. (2016). A critical investigation of the nature and extent of cyberbullying in two post-primary schools in Northern Ireland. *Pastoral Care in Education, 34*(1), 13–23.

Sainio, M., Veenstra, R., Huitsing, G., & Salmivalli, C. (2010). Victims and their defenders: A dyadic approach. *International Journal of Behavioural Development, 35*(2), 144–151.

Salmivalli, C. (2010). Bullying and the peer group: A review. *Aggression and Violent Behaviour, 15*, 112–120.

Salmivalli, C. (2014). Participant roles in bullying: How can peer bystanders be utilized in interventions? *Theory Into Practice, 53*, 286–292.

Schultze-Krumbholz, A., Göbel, K., Scheithauer, H., Brighi, A., Guarini, A., Tsorbatzoudis, H., Barkoukis, V., Pyżalski, J., Plichta, P., Del Rey, R., Casas, J. A., Thompson F., & Smith, P. K. (2015). A comparison of classification approaches for cyberbullying and traditional bullying using data from six European countries. *Journal of School Violence, 14*(1), 47–65.

Schultze-Krumbholz, A., Schultze, M., Zagorscak, P., Wölfer, R., & Scheithauer, H. (2016). Feeling cybervictims' pain – The effect of empathy training on cyberbullying. *Aggressive Behaviour, 42*, 147–156. doi:10.1002/ab.21613.

Smith, P. K., Cowie, H., Olafsson, R. F., & Liefooghe, A. P. D. (2002). Definitions of bullying: A comparison of terms used, and age and gender differences, in a fourteen-country international comparison. *Child Development, 73*, 1119–1133.

Sourander, A., Brunstein, K. A. B., Ikomen, M., Lindroos, J., Luntamo, T., Koskelainen, M., Ristkari T, & Helenius, H. (2010). Psychosocial risk factors associated with cyberbullying among adolescents. *Archives of General Psychiatry, 67*, 720–728.

Tognetta, L. R. P., Avilés, J. M., & Rosário, P. J. S. (2016). Bullying, a moral issue: Representations of self and moral disconnections. *Revista de Educación, 373*(3), 9–32.

Chapter 2

Theoretical perspectives on the continuities of bullying over time

Maili Pörhölä

Introduction

Although previous research has clearly demonstrated the existence of different participant roles in which individuals can be engaged in bullying incidents (e.g. Salmivalli, 2010; Salmivalli, Lagerspetz, Björkqvist, Österman, & Kaukiainen, 1996), we still do not have much understanding of the interaction processes in which these roles of bullies, victims, their assistants and defenders, and bystanders are formed and maintained. What we know, however, is that, after the roles of bullies and victims have been established in preschool (Barker, Boivin et al., 2008), they tend to remain stable through elementary school (Biggs et al., 2010; Boivin, Petitclerc, Feng, Barker, & Delgadillo, 2010) to middle and high school (Barker, Arseneault, Brendgen, Fontaine, & Maughan, 2008; Bauman & Newman, 2013; Rosen, Beron, & Underwood, 2016; Schäfer, Korn, Brodbeck, Wolke, & Schulz, 2005; Sourander, Helstelä, Helenius, & Piha, 2000; Sumter, Baumgartner, Valkenburg, & Peter, 2012).

Evidence also exists to suggest that the roles of bully and victim tend to remain stable from childhood and adolescence to adulthood and from school contexts to higher education and even to workplace contexts. For example, Chapell et al. (2006) found in the US that 54% of individuals who admitted to having bullied as adults had also bullied during childhood and adolescence. Similarly, in Canada, Curwen, McNichol, and Sharpe (2011) detected that most of the bullies among undergraduate university students had a history of bullying at school. Bauman and Newman (2013) examined a sample of university students in the US and found that of the 3.7% of students who had been bullied at university, 84.6% reported that they had been bullied in junior high school as well, and 80.8% reported that they had been victimised in high school; 73% had been victimised at both school levels. Further, a representative sample of university students in Finland revealed that 51% of those individuals who had bullied their fellow students at university had also bullied their schoolmates, while 47% of those who had been victimised during higher education had previously been subjected to school bullying (Pörhölä, 2011). Furthermore, in a retrospective study among British working adults, Smith, Singer, Hoel, and Cooper (2003) found a positive relationship between having been bullied at school and being bullied in their workplace. Those who had been in both roles, bullying others and being victimised, were even more likely to be bullied as adults at work.

In order to develop means to prevent the continuities of bullying in individuals' lives and minimise the negative consequences on individual's well-being which can result from having these experiences, more theoretical and empirical research is needed to better understand *why* the roles of bullies and victims tend to follow some individuals from one social context to another. As Pörhölä, Karhunen, and Rainivaara (2006) emphasise, more attention should be paid to the social relationships between bullies and victims, and, in this research, bullying should be envisioned as an ongoing interaction process consisting of a continuous flow of exchanging and appraising messages. The parties involved in this interaction, particularly those who bully or witness the bullying, have a significant role in changing the course of this interaction and preventing the negative outcomes of bullying for all parties.

This chapter aims at extending our understanding of interaction processes in which the different participant roles are produced, maintained and reproduced, to enable the development of such self-concepts, perceptions of peers and social-cognitive schemas about peer relationships which then nourish the continuation of these participant roles. Four theories are discussed in order to gain better understanding of these interaction processes. Firstly, *positioning theory* by Harré and colleagues (e.g. Harré & van Langenhove, 1999; Harré & Moghaddam, 2003b) is used to better understand how social positions of bullies, victims, bully-victims and their supporters are produced and maintained in the interaction of a peer group. Secondly, *symbolic convergence theory* by Bormann (1972, 1983, 1996) is used to illuminate how storytelling can be used within a peer group as an interactive tool for generating the exclusion of some individuals from the peer group and encouraging their bullying. Third, *attribution theories* (e.g. Heider, 1958; Manusov & Spitzberg, 2008; McDermott, 2009; Seibold & Spitzberg, 1982; Weiner, 2000) bring further understanding of the social cognitive processes in which individuals try to make sense of their bullying experiences. Finally, the outcomes of these interaction and social cognitive processes for the individual are discussed by means of *peer community integration theory* (Pörhölä, 2009, 2016), to shed further light on the impact of different types of peer relationships on individuals' ability to integrate with peers in various peer communities from childhood to adulthood. The chapter concludes by seeking means to change the course of destructive trajectories in peer relationships, which tend to follow some individuals.

Positioning of individuals within a peer group

Positioning theory by Harré and colleagues (e.g. Harré & van Langenhove, 1999; Harré & Moghaddam, 2003b) can help us to understand how the social positions of bullies, victims, bully-victims and bystanders are created and maintained in the interaction processes of peer groups and why these positions have a tendency to follow individuals from one social context to another. In this theory, positioning is seen as a way of building and rebuilding one's own and others' social positions and identities through interaction. Positions are shared patterns of beliefs in the members of a relatively coherent social group such as a school class. A person can either appropriate a particular position within a social group, or it can be given to him or her. However, positions are jointly produced and reproduced, meaning that, in order to gain a position that a person pursues to appropriate or be pushed into a particular position, others must approve that the person has this position. Eventually, the members of the group internalise the positions of each individual, and these positions start to affect the ways in which they behave and see things (Davies & Harré, 1999; Harré & van Langenhove, 1999; Harré & Moghaddam, 2003a).

Associated with each position is a set of *rights and duties* which delimit the possibilities of behaviour and implicitly determine how much and what the person in that position can say and do, in a particular context and to specific interaction partners (Davies & Harré, 1999; Harré & Moghaddam, 2003a). For example, individuals in more legitimate positions are presumed to produce more relevant and worthy ideas, and, therefore, are more entitled to speak and to be heard, make decisions and be obeyed. Those in low positions have more duties than rights. In each social group there is a kind of realm of positions in which individuals can strive to locate themselves, be pushed into, be displaced from or be refused access or recess themselves from, through interaction processes. The theory differentiates categories of positioning, including the distinction between *selfpositioning* and the *positioning of others*, both of which can be either *deliberate* or *forced* (e.g. Harré & Moghaddam, 2003a; van Langenhove & Harré, 1999). Bullying can be used as a tool to raise one's own position and lower the target's position.

In these interaction processes, the bullies learn to position themselves as the authority above their peers. By means of their communication behaviour and physical acts they appropriate the right to choose other peers to be included in, or excluded from the group, and to decide on their rights and duties. Those who bully have gained the right to set standards for others, for example for physical appearance and acceptable behaviour, such as dressing, hair style, hobbies and the company they keep. As outsiders in the peer group, victims of bullying can have a hard time keeping up with these standards and how they change. This might explain for example, why, after having been mocked for any kinds of clothes they wore, some victims choose to wear only black clothes year after year. They may have learned that their dressing would be mocked anyway, so why bother to give new excuses for their bullies by changing their style. Furthermore, according to their own academic interests and capacities, bullies can even gain the right to determine how much effort should be put on school work and how successful peers are allowed to be in school assignments. As bullies tend to have lower school attendance and achievements than those uninvolved in bullying (e.g. Feldman et al., 2014), this could explain why they often choose targets who are academically skilled and therefore do not reach their standards.

The position of the victims is determined in repeated bullying situations, for example by ignoring their suggestions, criticising their ideas and achievements, refusing to collaborate with them on school work or prohibiting them from joining others for lunch or a play. By accusing the victim of lying or something that they deny having done, the bully would show that this person is unreliable and does not have the right to be believed; and by mocking the target person, for example by calling the person dumb, stupid or an idiot, the bully shows others that, due to the target person's characteristics, they do not have anything to say worth listening to and should not have the right to be heard. Physical violence, stealing or destroying subjects' property or school works, can be used to show that this person does not have the right to physical integrity, their own property or to acknowledgement of their achievements. Eventually, most of the victims' rights can be taken away while their duties are increased, and their position can be made so low that they barely have the right to talk in the peer group, or join the group. They can even be denied the right to their own intellectual capacity, for example by being told to do the bullies' school assignments (Pörhölä, 2016).

While most victims do not have the power or means to affect the position given to them, some victims can try to reposition themselves by bullying someone else. Sometimes students, who bully in order to raise their position within the peer group, are not given the position they desire, and other members of the group start bullying them instead. These individuals who struggle in dual roles (bully-victims) tend to be positioned quite low and can have minor rights and major duties in the peer group.

In addition to bullies and victims, bullying also determines other students' positions in the peer group. By giving their support to either the bully or victim, students make choices that affect their own position. The supporters of bullies gain some rights that victims' defenders do not have, while the duties of victims' defenders can be increased almost to the same level as the victims. Knowing this, the majority of peer group members end up in accepting the bullying of someone, by this way reinforcing the positions of the bullies and victims.

Creation of stories within a peer group

Positioning of the victims can occur also in their absence, by means of indirect forms of bullying, such as spreading nasty rumours about the person or their families, criticising them unjustifiably and causing damage to their peer relationships. The targets can be totally unaware of this interaction and they might not be afforded any logical situations to defend or protect themselves. Although they clearly experience the consequences of bullying, they might not even know the identity of their bullies (Pörhölä et al., 2006).

Symbolic convergence theory by Bormann (1972, 1982, 1983, 1996) can help understand this kind of interaction within a peer group. The theory assumes that, through interaction, groups of people share and interpret human symbols or messages, developing a common consciousness or *shared reality*. In this way, they create the basis to a community for discussing their common experiences and achieving mutual understanding of events. The cornerstone of this theory is the *fantasy*, a term that refers to a creative and imaginative shared interpretation of events outside the current time or place. Sharing these fantasies results in *fantasy chaining*, a process in which group members contribute to the fantasy and, with their own stories, increase the excitement and involvement around the fantasy. Integration of several similarly toned fantasies creates a composite drama that draws group members into a common symbolic reality.

As such, this interaction is constructive by nature, as it increases the cohesion of the group. For outsiders of the group, however, it can be destructive. A group of students can together develop a fantasy chain around a class mate, and the story they develop turns into their shared reality. Fantasies about the target could be related, for example, to their personality, physical appearance, behaviour, home, friends, school work or talks. Group members contribute to the story by adding elements, perceptions and interpretations, to confirm and extend the shared fantasy. Driven out of the context where something happened, was said or done, the target persons can be made to look stupid, odd, ridiculous or mean, or guilty of something they have not done.

As an example we can imagine how a student loses his wallet and then blames a particular classmate for stealing it. He shares his suspicion with others in the peer group. Another student continues the fantasy by reminding the others that her wallet also disappeared from her coat pocket a few days ago. A third student recalls having seen the target person many times in the school hallway where students' coats were hanging, after others had got into classrooms. Somebody adds to the story by telling that he saw the target person buying candies with a lot of money. After the group has finished the fantasy chain, all members would share an understanding that the target person stole the wallets, and whenever someone loses something, they would extend the fantasy chain by blaming this person for stealing. As questioning the accuracy of the fantasy would provide a threat to the cohesion of the group, it would be difficult for any member to suggest that the victim might have been waiting in the hallway for others to get into the classroom first, in order to avoid being bullied. And the money spent for candies was probably his or her own.

Attributions for bullying and victimisation

Attribution theory or theories (e.g. Heider, 1958; Manusov & Spitzberg, 2008; McDermott, 2009; Seibold & Spitzberg, 1982; Weiner, 2000) describe how people constantly try to explain the behaviour of others and themselves, in order to understand the outcomes of this behaviour and what is happening around them. The theory suggests that our attributions are based on two crucial concepts: *internal (dispositional)* attributions are made when a person's behaviour is explained to be caused by something about the person (e.g. characteristics or personality); while *external* (*situational*) attributions are used when the behaviour is seen to be caused by the circumstances or the situation. Weiner (2000) suggests that all attributions can be located within a three-dimensional framework consisting of: (a) *locus*, which refers to the location of a cause (internal or external factors); (b) *stability*, which refers to the duration of the cause (constant or temporary); and (c) *controllability*, which refers to the subject's perceived control over the causes of behaviour. As attributions are based on subjective interpretations, they vary according to the person making them. While bullies could perceive the causes of their bullying behaviour as temporary and controllable (e.g. "because we were just having fun"), victims might see their victimisation as a constant state of affairs and impossible for them to control (e.g. "because I am who I am").

One of the key concepts in attribution theory is *fundamental attribution error*. It refers to the tendency of people to overemphasise internal causes (e.g. personal characteristics) when they interpret other people's negative behaviour or failures, and situational causes when they interpret others' positive behaviour or outcomes. The direction of this attribution error is reversed when people come to judge their own behaviour. Thus, when they want to account for their own success, they tend to attribute the positive outcomes to internal causes, and when they explain their failures and negative outcomes of their behaviour, they ascribe them to external causes (e.g. the situation).

This aspect of fundamental attribution error is called the *self-serving bias* (e.g. Manusov & Spitzberg, 2008; McDermott, 2009).

Implementing the self-serving bias, those who bully could have a tendency to attribute their own behaviour to external causes, such as something in the situation or the behaviour of the victim, and the victims' failure to defend themselves to internal causes, such their inability to use physical or verbal power. However, for the victims, who tend to have a lowered self-esteem (Juvonen, Nishina, & Graham, 2000; Kaltiala-Heino, Rimpelä, Rantanen, & Rimpelä, 2000; Schäfer et al., 2004), the fundamental attribution error might work in the opposite direction. Serving rather as 'self-attacking bias', they might attribute their victimization to their own characteristics, which they perceive as stable and uncontrollable. If the victimisation continues from one social context to another, with different peers being involved, it can further reinforce the victims' tendency to self-blame.

Continuities in peer group positions

The peer group positions that are taken by or given to individuals have an inevitable impact on how these individuals see themselves among peers, that is, their self-positioning, which can be long-term by nature. Those who have occupied the bully's position have learned to see peer relationships as social battlefields on which individuals must fight for their position, in order to gain social power over others. They might have learned to make use of fantasies in order to affect the shared social reality of the peer group, and attribute their own harmful behaviour in the peer group to situational causes or the characteristics of the subjects who they hurt. Since the establishment of new peer relationships is not difficult for the bullies (Pörhölä, 2009), they would quickly be able to gather a new group of peers around them and take on a leading position within any new peer community. After having previously gained social power by bullying others, the risk of them repeating the same strategy is high. Indeed, empirical studies indicate that those who bully at school are most likely to continue to engage in various kinds of abusive behaviours in their social relationships; for example males who bully at school have a heightened risk for sexual harassment (De Souza & Ribeiro, 2005; Pellegrini, 2002) and dating violence (Connolly, Pepler, Craig, & Taradash, 2000; Pepler, Craig, Connolly, & Henderson, 2002).

With regard to the victims of bullying, they may have created quite a permanent way to see themselves in subordinate position in relation with peers. Due to their possible tendency to attribute their victimisation to their own stable and uncontrollable personal characteristics, they would expect and accept to be positioned in a similar way also by new peers in any social context they enter. Positioning themselves repeatedly as outsiders in any peer group, without a right to be heard, believed, valued or cared about would presumably result in avoiding or defensive interaction behaviour when they enter a new peer community. Instead of eagerly joining others, making friends with them, and displaying the kind of self-disclosure that is needed for building social relationships, these persons would most likely withdraw from social interaction, limit their self-closure and even show defensiveness in these situations. Building a vicious circle, this kind of behaviour would further increase the probability of their being again positioned as outsiders and put them at risk of further victimisation and abuse.

Indicating the variety of issues that victims have in their peer relationships, a study in Finland among 872 seventh and eighth graders showed that victimised students reported the most peer relationship problems, including having fewer or no close friends; not feeling valued and being disliked by peers; having few contacts with classmates; being unsuccessful in the establishment of peer relationships; and being afraid of peers in general. These problems occurred less for bullies and bully-victims, while students uninvolved in bullying reported the highest quality in their peer relationships and acceptance in peer community (Pörhölä, 2009). Furthermore, in a longitudinal study within a representative community sample of 1,273 young adults, Wolke, Copeland, Angold, and Costello (2013) found that the most heightened risk for victims and particularly bully-victims in young adulthood was impaired quality of social relationships (e.g. problems making or keeping friends, being engaged in violent relationships); the chronically bullied subjects (i.e. victims at two or more time points during schooldays) had the highest levels of these problems.

Conclusions

Based on the assumptions of positioning theory, symbolic convergence theory and attribution theory discussed above, I argue that, instead of coming into being coincidentally, the participant roles of bullies, victims, bully-victims, their supporters and bystanders are formed in complicated interaction processes in which the positions of each individual of a peer group are divided. In these interaction processes, some students have more power and means to determine their own and others' positions, while other students with less power and means are pushed into positions which they would never voluntarily choose. Through self-positioning and self-serving (in bullies) or self-attacking (in victims) attributions, these peer group positions are internalised by individuals, increasing the risk for the adopted participant role to follow the individual from one social context to another.

Peer community integration theory by Pörhölä (2009, 2016) can be used to illustrate the outcomes of the interaction and social cognitive processes discussed in this chapter. In a nutshell, the theory describes how different types of peer relationships in childhood and adolescence either promote or prevent individuals from integrating into various peer communities throughout their lives.

Successful integration into one's peer community (i.e. the crowd of peers with whom an individual has, or could have, an interpersonal relationship) is seen as a reciprocal interaction process through which the individual feels accepted, liked and valued by peers; as well as shows acceptance, care and respect for peers; and, consequently, feels an equal member of the peer community.

The basic assumption in this theory is that individuals become integrated into social communities through their interpersonal relationships. On the basis of the impact (*weight*) these relationships have on the integration process, five kinds of dyadic peer relationships are distinguished in descending order from the most beneficial to the most harmful ones: (1) *friendships* in which partners show mutual commitment, trust, support, valuation, love and care; (2) *companionship*, which is characterised by a substantial amount of time spent in shared activities; (3) *neutral relationships*, which can be characterised by a mutual lack of interest to the company of the other; (4) *enemy relationships*, characterised by mutually hostile verbal, nonverbal or physically hurtful behaviour and manifested as repeated conflicts; and (5) *abusive relationships*, such as bullying relationships, typical of which is an imbalance of power, unilateral subjection and hurtful behaviour, and the victim's inability to affect the nature of the relationship or to terminate it (Pörhölä, 2009, 2016).

Peer community integration theory suggests that the nature of individuals' peer relationships determines how well they succeed in integrating into the peer community. While friends and companions pull an individual toward the centre of the peer community, enemy relationships and abusive relationships push them away from the centre of the peer community, with neutral relationships having no particular impact on the integration. The more enemy relationships, and particularly abusive relationships, individuals have, the less successful the integration process will become for them; and the more companionship and friendships they have, the more successful they will be in integrating into the surrounding peer community. Furthermore, the theory assumes that the level of an individual's integration into their peer community during childhood and adolescence is reflected in later life in their ability to integrate into other peer communities (for a more detailed description of the theory, see Pörhölä, 2009, 2016; Pörhölä & Kinney, 2010). The issues discussed in this chapter have shed light on the question of why these trajectories occur in individuals' peer relationships.

As Cowie and Colliety (2016) recently argued, although there are a number of effective interventions to address bullying, none of them provides a quick and easy solution to change the long-term behaviour of children and young people who bully; or the faith of those who are repeatedly victimised by their peers in various social contexts. We should remember that once these young persons have learned to see themselves in particular positions within their peer group, even entering a new social environment (e.g. new school or school class) or meeting with new peers (e.g. through hobbies), would not automatically enable a new self-positioning and suddenly make them perceive themselves as accepted/accepting, valued/valuing and cared/caring individuals with similar rights and duties to their peers. Something needs to happen to make a repositioning possible.

As bullies have taken, and been given the right to, position and reposition individuals with respect to others, they can use this right to return some or all of the rights to the victims, or to release them from their duties. This repositioning could result from, for example, an intervention by teachers, parents or other classmates, an event, or a change in the relationship between the bully and victim or by a change in the peer group dynamic that would motivate a re-evaluation of the victim's position. Also, in a new social environment, new peers might not accept bullying, or could refuse to give a leading position to a person who used to bully. By limiting the rights of the bully and extending the rights of the victim, peers could reposition both parties. Repositioning could also take place between the bully and victim if the power relationship between them and the resources available to the parties changes for some reason, for example due to individual development in physical strength or attractiveness, competences or social skills and networks.

For those who have been bullied and pushed to a low position, friends and companions would be in a significant role, being able to affect their self-positioning among peers and by this way contributing to their future peer group positioning. When these persons perceive that they can have equal rights and duties in a peer relationship, this perception could change their expectations of future peer relationships and encourage a more positive view of themselves as insider of a peer group, which in turn, could affect their behaviour when entering a new peer group. Having friends would also provide opportunities for practicing peer interaction skills. Indeed, it has been shown that some victims have managed to escape their role as victim by acquiring new friends (Smith, Talamelli, Cowie, Naylor, & Chauhan, 2004).

As a number of students tend to be engaged in bullying in different participant roles, they would all share the same social reality in which fantasy chains are developed about the victims. As these stories tend to be shared in the absence of adults or, for example, online, identifying the fantasies around victims would be difficult for them. While students should be guided to identify imagined stories, differentiate between truth and fantasies and unravel destructive story telling about peers, also teachers, parents, siblings, friends and school health care professionals should be alert to listen to what and how students talk about their classmates. These conversations might reveal shared fantasies about someone who is bullied or excluded.

Furthermore, family members, teachers, friends and health care professionals are in a position to be able to affect the attributions given by individuals to their bullying experiences. Instead of using internal attributions by blaming stable and uncontrollable personal characteristics either of themselves or peers, it would be beneficial for victims to be guided to attribute their victimisation rather to external factors such as circumstances that can change in the future (e.g. young age and thoughtlessness of peers), and even be affected, for example, by teachers' intervention and parental guidance, or themselves by learning new skills and finding supportive friends. For those who bully it would be important to identify the attributions they use to justify their behaviour and understand that there is no justification for bullying.

References

Barker, E. D., Arseneault, L., Brendgen, M., Fontaine, N., & Maughan, B. (2008). Joint development of bullying and victimization in adolescence: Relations to delinquency and self-harm. *Journal of the American Academy of Child and Adolescent Psychiatry*, *47*, 1030–1038.

Barker, E. D., Boivin, M., Brendgen, M., Fontaine, F., Arseneault, L., Vitaro, F., Bissonette, C, & Tremblay, R. E. (2008). Predictive validity and early predictors of peer-victimization trajectories in preschool. *Archives of General Psychiatry*, *65*, 1185–1192.

Bauman, S., & Newman, M. L. (2013). Testing assumptions about cyberbullying: Perceived distress associated with acts of conventional and cyber bullying. *Psychology of Violence*, *3*, 27–38.

Biggs, B. K., Vernberg, E. M., Fonagy, P., Twemlow, S. W., Little, T. D., & Dill, E. J. (2010). Peer victimization trajectories and their association with children's affect in late elementary school. *International Journal of Behavioural Development*, *34*, 136–146.

Boivin, M., Petitclerc, A., Feng, B., Barker, E. D., & Delgadillo, S. S. (2010). The developmental trajectories of peer victimization in middle to late childhood and the changing nature of their behavioural correlates. *Merrill Palmer Quarterly*, *36*, 231–260.

Bormann, E. G. (1972). Fantasy and rhetorical vision: The rhetorical criticism of social reality. *Quarterly Journal of Speech*, *58*, 396–407.

Bormann, E. G. (1982). Fantasy and rhetorical vision: Ten years later. *Quarterly Journal of Speech*, *68*, 288–305.

Bormann, E. G. (1983). Symbolic convergence: Organizational communication and culture. In L. Putnam & M. E. Pacanowsky (Eds.), *Communication and organizations: An interpretive approach* (pp. 99–122). Beverly Hills, CA: Sage.

Bormann, E. G. (1996). Symbolic convergence theory and communication in group decision making. In R. Y. Hirokawa & M. S. Poole (Eds.), *Communication and group decision making* (2nd ed., pp. 81–113). Thousand Oaks, CA: Sage.

Chapell, M. S., Hasselman, S. L., Kitchin, T., Lomon, S. N., MacIver, K. W., & Sarullo, P. L. (2006). Bullying in elementary school, high school, and college. *Adolescence, 41*, 633–648.

Connolly, J., Pepler, D., Craig, W., & Taradash, A. (2000). Dating experiences of bullies in early adolescence. *Child Maltreatment, 5*, 299–310.

Cowie, H., & Colliety, P. (2016). Who cares about the bullies? *Pastoral Care in Education, 34*(1), 24–33.

Curwen, T., McNichol, J. S., & Sharpe, G. W. (2011). The progression of bullying from elementary school to university. *International Journal of Humanities and Social Science, 1*(13), 47–54.

Davies, B., & Harré, R. (1999). Positioning and personhood. In R. Harré & L. van Langenhove (Eds.), *Positioning theory: Moral contexts of intentional action* (pp. 32–52). Oxford: Blackwell.

De Souza, E. R., & Ribeiro, J. (2005). Bullying and sexual harassment among Brazilian high school students. *Journal of Interpersonal Violence, 20*(9), 1018–1038.

Feldman, M. A., Ojanen, T., Gesten, E. L., Smith-Schrandt, H., Brannick, M., Totura, C. M. W., Alexander, L., Scanga, D., & Brown, K. (2014). The effects of middle school bullying and victimization on adjustment through high school: Growth modeling of achievement, school attendance, and disciplinary trajectories. *Psychology in the Schools, 51*(10), 1046–1062.

Harré, R., & Moghaddam, F. (2003a). Introduction: The self and others in traditional psychology and in positioning theory. In R. Harré & F. Moghaddam (Eds.), *The self and others: Positioning individuals and groups in personal, political, and cultural contexts* (pp. 1–11). Westport, CT: Praeger.

Harré, R., & Moghaddam, F. (Eds.). (2003b). *The self and others: Positioning individuals and groups in personal, political, and cultural contexts.* Westport, CT: Praeger.

Harré, R., & van Langenhove, L. (Eds.). (1999). *Positioning theory: Moral contexts of intentional action.* Oxford: Blackwell.

Heider, F. (1958). *The psychology of interpersonal relations.* New York: Wiley.

Juvonen, J., Nishina, A., & Graham, S. (2000). Peer harassment, psychological adjustment, and school functioning in early adolescence. *Journal of Educational Psychology, 92*, 349–359.

Kaltiala-Heino, R., Rimpelä, M., Rantanen, P., & Rimpelä, A. (2000). Bullying at school – An indicator of adolescents at risk for mental disorders. *Journal of Adolescence, 23*, 661–674.

Manusov, V., & Spitzberg, B. (2008). Attribution theory: Finding good cause in the search for theory. In L. A. Baxter & D. O. Braithwaite (Eds.), *Engaging theories in interpersonal communication: Multiple perspectives* (pp. 37–49). Thousand Oaks, CA: Sage.

McDermott, V. M. (2009). Attribution theory. In S. W. Littlejohn & K. A. Foss (Eds.), *Encyclopedia of communication theory* (pp. 60–63). Los Angeles, CA: Sage.

Pellegrini, A. D. (2002). Bullying, victimization, and sexual harassment during the transition to middle school. *Educational Psychologist, 37*(3), 151–164.

Pepler, D., Craig, W., Connolly, J., & Henderson, K. (2002). Bullying, sexual harassment, dating violence, and substance use among adolescents. In C. Wekerle & A. M. Wall (Eds.), *The violence and addiction equation: Theoretical and clinical issues in substance abuse and relationship violence* (pp. 153–168). Philadelphia: Brunner/Mazel.

Pörhölä, M. (2009). Psychosocial well-being of victimized students. In T. A. Kinney & M. Pörhölä (Eds.), *Anti and pro-social communication: Theories, methods, and applications* (Language as Social Action, Vol. 6, pp. 83–93). New York: Peter Lang.

Pörhölä, M. (2011). Kiusaaminen opiskeluyhteisössä [Bullying in university community]. In K. Kunttu, A. Komulainen, K. Makkonen, & P. Pynnönen (Eds.), *Opiskeluterveys* (pp. 166–168). Helsinki, Finland: Duodecim.

Pörhölä, M. (2016). Do the roles of bully and victim remain stable from school to university? Theoretical considerations. In H. Cowie & C.-A. Myers (Eds.), *Bullying among university students: Cross-national perspectives* (pp. 35–46). Abingdon: Routledge.

Pörhölä, M., Karhunen, S., & Rainivaara, S. (2006). Bullying at school and in the workplace: A challenge for communication research. In C. S. Beck (Ed.), *Communication yearbook 30* (pp. 249–301). Mahwah, NJ: Erlbaum.

Pörhölä, M., & Kinney, T. A. (2010). *Bullying: Contexts, consequences, and control.* Barcelona, Spain: Editorial Aresta.

Rosen, L. H., Beron, K. J., & Underwood, M. K. (2016). Social victimization trajectories from middle childhood through late adolescence. *Social Development.* 26, 227–247. doi:10.1111/sode.12185.

Salmivalli, C. (2010). Bullying and the peer group: A review. *Aggression and Violent Behaviour, 15*, 112–120.

Salmivalli, C., Lagerspetz, K., Björkqvist, K., Österman, K., & Kaukiainen, A. (1996). Bullying as a group process: Participant roles and their relations to social status within the group. *Aggressive Behaviour, 22*, 1–15.

Schäfer, M., Korn, S., Brodbeck, F. C., Wolke, D., & Schulz, H. (2005). Bullying roles in changing contexts: The stability of victim and bully roles from primary to secondary school. *International Journal of Behavioural Development, 29*, 323–335.

Schäfer, M., Korn, S., Smith, P. K., Hunter, S. C., Mora-Merchán, J. A., Singer, M. M., & van der Meulen, K. (2004). Lonely in the crowd: Recollections of bullying. *British Journal of Developmental Psychology, 22*, 379–394.

Seibold, D. R., & Spitzberg, B. H. (1982). Attribution theory and research: Review and implications for communication. In B. Dervin & M. J. Voigt (Eds.), *Progress in communication sciences, vol. 3: An annual review* (pp. 85–125). Norwood, NJ: Ablex.

Smith, P. K., Singer, M., Hoel, H., & Cooper, C. L. (2003). Victimization in the school and the workplace: Are there any links? *British Journal of Psychology, 94*, 175–188.

Smith, P. K., Talamelli, L., Cowie, H., Naylor, P., & Chauhan, P. (2004). Profiles of non-victims, escaped victims, continuing victims and new victims of school bullying. *British Journal of Educational Psychology, 74*, 565–581.

Sourander, A., Helstelä, L., Helenius, H., & Piha, J. (2000). Persistence of bullying from childhood to adolescence: A longitudinal 8-year followup study. *Child Abuse & Neglect, 24*, 873–881.

Sumter, S. R., Baumgartner, S. E., Valkenburg, P. M., & Peter, J. (2012). Developmental trajectories of peer victimization: Off-line and online experiences during adolescence. *Journal of Adolescent Health, 50*, 607–613.

van Langenhove, L., & Harré, R. (1999). Introducing positioning theory. In R. Harré & L. van Langenhove (Eds.), *Positioning theory: Moral contexts of intentional action* (pp. 14–31). Oxford: Blackwell.

Weiner, B. (2000). Intrapersonal and interpersonal theories of motivation from an attributional perspective. *Educational Psychology Review, 12*, 1–14. doi:10.1023/A:1009017532121.

Wolke, D., Copeland, W. E., Angold, A., & Costello, E. J. (2013). Impact of bullying in childhood on adult health, wealth, crime, and social outcomes. *Psychological Science, 24*, 1958–1970.

Theme 2

The interface between bullying and crime

The authors in this theme propose that there is a very fine line between 'bullying' and 'criminal' behaviours, as indicated, amongst other things, in the complexities of the language and labels that are used to understand bullying. For example, when headline news stories claim that a situation evolved due to 'racist' bullying, 'sexist' bullying or 'homophobic' bullying, Myers, in chapter 3, poses the question as to whether it is bullying that is occurring, or crime. In chapter 5, Lee discusses the issue of sexual violence in schools – behaviour that in other settings would be considered a crime such as a serious sexual assault or rape. In chapter 6, Aziz continues this debate by exploring the nature of hate crime in schools, which would in a different setting or adult age-group, be considered as a criminal act, as would harassment, stalking and physical violence. This theme raises questions about individual qualities of vulnerability and resilience as well as the nature of the social contexts where this bullying behaviour takes place, specifically where there is a predominant 'laddish' culture that promotes homophobia, as discussed by Rivers in chapter 4 and prejudice towards minority groups like asylum seekers as argued by Aznar, Tenenbaum and Ruck in chapter 7.

The authors in this theme are not suggesting that school bullying should be criminalised. However, they are aware that bystander apathy, moral disengagement and lack of intervention, key problems within the criminal justice system, are also salient when tackling these forms of extreme bullying among children and young people.

Chapter 3

Boundaries of bullying

When does bullying behaviour become criminal?

Carrie-Anne Myers

Introduction

As this volume has documented, bullying is very distressing for those who are involved as bullies, victims or bystanders. Due to the emotional nature of incidents of bullying and cyberbullying, there will undoubtedly be times when there are calls for more to be done and in some cases recourse to the law being demanded. However, the law is applied on fact, not emotion, and this chapter will document the legal position within the UK, draw the differences between bullying and cyberbullying within a criminal context and consider whether bullying should ever be considered as a crime.

What is 'the law' with regard to bullying, what do schools have to do and why does it matter?

According to the UK Government, some forms of bullying are illegal and should be reported to the police. These include:

- violence or assault
- theft
- repeated harassment or intimidation, for example: name calling, threats and abusive phone calls, emails or text messages
- hate crimes (www.gov.uk/bullying-at-school/the-law)

Outside of these criminal acts, bullying in and of itself is not a criminal offence. Furthermore, the blurred boundaries of responsibility and policing add to the confusion on where to go for help, or to report serious incidents. Should a victim tell a parent? A teacher? The police? No one? And then who is responsible for 'getting something done'? Nonetheless, there have been a number of key pieces of legislation that have been introduced in the UK which determine how bullying is to be dealt with which will be discussed here: The School Standards and Framework Act (1998), The Education and Inspections Act (2006) and The Equality Act (2010). These pieces of legislation are the key laws which schools have an obligation to uphold. However, it has to be remembered that there are differences within the UK. England, Wales, Scotland and Northern Ireland since each has subtle variations within their governing systems. So the specific laws discussed within this chapter are enforceable within English schools only (although the other regions may have adopted some of the practices described). Furthermore, it has to be considered that these laws only apply to State-funded and maintained schools. They are not enforceable in the private education system.

The School Standards and Framework Act 1998

For many researchers and campaigners in the anti-bullying field the School Standards and Framework Act of 1998 was the key piece of legislation which gave schools certain statutory obligations regarding behaviour, and more specifically bullying. Section 61 mandates a school's governing body and head teacher to draw up policies to tackle discipline.

Key was section 61 (4) which made it a legal requirement for schools to produce an anti-bullying policy within the context of a discipline and behavioural policy:

> The head teacher shall determine measures (which may include the making of rules and provision for enforcing them) to be taken with a view to –
>
> (a) promoting, among pupils, self-discipline and proper regard for authority;
> (b) encouraging good behaviour and respect for others on the part of pupils and, in particular, preventing all forms of bullying among pupils;
> (c) securing that the standard of behaviour of pupils is acceptable; and
> (d) otherwise regulating the conduct of pupils.
>
> (School Standards and Framework Act 1998, (c. 31) p. 48)

What is crucial about this piece of legislation is that this policy had to be available for anyone to consult as stated in S.61 (7):

> The measures determined by the head teacher under subsection (4) shall be publicised by him in the form of a written document as follows –
>
> (a) he shall make the measures generally known within the school and to parents of registered pupils at the school; and
> (b) he shall in particular, at least once in every school year, take steps to bring them to the attention of all such pupils and parents and all persons employed, or otherwise engaged to provide their services, at the school.
>
> (School Standards and Framework Act 1998 (c. 31) p. 49)

Therefore, for the first time there was a legal requirement for behavioural and anti-bullying policies to be produced by every state-maintained school and the transparency of these documents was clearly set out. There was also an expectation that these documents would be revisited and updated as and when required. Although many would not see this as 'doing enough' in terms of the victims of bullying, from a practitioner point of view this is very significant as the school is setting the policy, the boundaries of what is and is not acceptable and has the power to react. Furthermore, the sharing of this policy as essentially a public document is useful in terms of accountability. A parent, guardian or pupil has the right to see this policy.

The Education and Inspections Act 2006

Building on existing legislation, the Education and Inspections Act 2006 gave schools further clear responsibilities with regard to behaviour and responding to bullying. The crucial section in this Act is 89 (1):

> The head teacher of a relevant school must determine measures to be taken with a view to –
>
> (a) promoting, among pupils, self-discipline and proper regard for authority,
> (b) encouraging good behaviour and respect for others on the part of pupils and, in particular, preventing all forms of bullying among pupils,
> (c) securing that the standard of behaviour of pupils is acceptable,
> (d) securing that pupils complete any tasks reasonably assigned to them in connection with their education, and
> (e) otherwise regulating the conduct of pupils.
>
> (Education and Inspections Act 2006 (c. 40). p. 71)

Therefore, every school must have measures to encourage good behaviour and *prevent all forms of bullying* amongst pupils which means that expansion and consideration of forms of bullying, such as cyberbullying, are legislated against. In practice this means that cyberbullying would now have to be included in any policy tackling bullying. Again, these measures should be part of the school's behaviour policy which must be communicated to all pupils, school staff and parents. What is also of note for this Act is that it gives head teachers the ability to discipline pupils for poor behaviour that occurs even when the pupil is not on school premises or under the lawful control of school staff:

> (5) The measures which the head teacher determines under subsection (1) may, to such extent as is reasonable, include measures to be taken with a view to regulating the conduct of pupils at a time when they are not on the premises of the school and are not under the lawful control or charge of a member of the staff of the school.
>
> (Education and Inspections Act 2006 (c. 40). p. 71)

Consequently, incidents that occur on the journey to and from school, or in cyber space, can be disciplined by the relevant authority at the school. This can relate to any bullying incidents occurring anywhere off the school premises, such as on school or public transport, outside the local shops, or in a town, village centre or recreation ground. Where bullying outside school is reported to school staff, it should be investigated and acted on. The headteacher should also consider whether it is appropriate to notify the police (or Anti-Social Behaviour Co-ordinator in their local authority) of the action taken against a pupil, for example exclusion from the school. If the misbehaviour could be criminal or poses a serious threat to a member of the public, the police should always be informed.

Thus, it can be stated that by law, all state (not private) schools, must have a behaviour policy in place that includes measures to prevent all forms of bullying among pupils. That is it though. That is all schools are legally required to do with regard to bullying and it is not surprising that this leaves some victims and their families feeling as though not enough is being done. However, in terms of accountability, transparency and the ability to deal with the problem of bullying it does mean that a good manager and head teacher would be able to design a 'tailor made', specific to the school, policy. Such whole-school approaches have been demonstrated to be very advantageous in research (see Cowie & Jennifer, 2007). Furthermore, it has been shown that schools that do not have coherent policies, positive relationships with the wider community and clear disciplinary procedures to deal with bullying are often synonymous with fostering bullying behaviour, have crime problems on the school premises, such as links to drugs and gangs, and high levels of victimisation (Wynne & Joo, 2011; Jeong, Kwak, Moon, & San Miguel, 2013).

The Equality Act 2010

As documented in chapters 4, 5 and 6 by Rivers, Lee and Aziz, there are real concerns in tackling and preventing bullying that has occurred over sexuality, sexual violence or hate crime. Additionally, research is emerging that documents levels of victimisation amongst disabled students and highlights the importance of understanding levels of victimisation amongst this group of pupils (Chatzitheochari, Parsons, & Platt, 2016). Such incidents come under the remit of the Equality Act 2010. This replaced key anti-discrimination laws including the Sex Discrimination Act 1975, the Race Relations Act 1976 and the Disability Discrimination Act 1995 with a single piece of legislation. A key requirement is a new *Public Sector Equality Duty*, which came into force on 5 April 2011. It replaced the three previous public sector equality duties for race, disability and gender, and covers age, disability, gender reassignment, pregnancy and maternity, race, religion or belief, sex and sexual orientation (DfE, 2014).

The Duty has three aims. It requires public bodies to have due regard to the need to:

- Eliminate unlawful discrimination, harassment, victimisation and any other conduct prohibited by the Act;

- Advance equality of opportunity between people who share a protected characteristic and people who do not share it;
- Foster good relations between people who share a protected characteristic and people who do not share it.

(DfE, 2014, p. 4)

Schools and all public sector organisations are required to comply with the new Equality Duty. The Act also makes it unlawful for the responsible body of a school to discriminate against, harass or victimise a pupil or potential pupil in relation to admissions, the way it provides education for pupils, provision of pupil access to any benefit, facility or service, or by excluding a pupil or subjecting them to any other detriment. In England and Wales the Act applies to all maintained and independent schools, including Academies and Free Schools, and maintained and non-maintained special schools (DfE, 2014). Therefore, the climate of the school is of key relevance here and there is a clear intolerance of discriminatory behaviour, which in turn should foster a positive learning environment. However, as the research demonstrates the bullying continues and as mentioned is not viewed as 'doing enough', especially if a tragic event unfolds which results in a pupil taking their own life, a 'bullycide'.

Criminal law – is bullying ever a crime?

Although bullying in itself is not a specific criminal offence in the UK, it is important to bear in mind that some types of harassing or threatening behaviour – or communications – could be a criminal offence, for example under the Protection from Harassment Act 1997, the Malicious Communications Act 1988, the Communications Act 2003, and the Public Order Act 1986. Furthermore, if staff believe that an offence has been committed, they are able to seek advice from the police. But school staff usually deal with the bullying problem 'in house' in a number of ways, and it usually is dependent on how 'serious' the bullying is perceived to be.

What is also interesting to note is that existing legislation is able to deal with incidents of cyberbullying and the virtual world fractionally more easily than the real world (see Myers & Cowie, 2017, in press, for a discussion of this debate). Additionally, as criminal acts need facts and evidence to prove an incident has occurred, it is often relatively straightforward to keep, for example, a number of abusive text messages or derogatory social network posts, which can be used to demonstrate the extent and severity of cyberbullying behaviour.

The boundaries between what is bullying and a criminal act have also been clarified on a new website launched by the Metropolitan Police service. Aimed at 11- to 16-year-olds, 'Safe' went live on July 29 2016. This new site informs young people about crime and safety issues which matter to them, and it covers a range of subjects including bullying, cybercrime, drugs, alcohol, gangs and knife crime (http://safe.met.police.uk/index.html).

This is an innovative tool and resource for young people in London, and indeed the factual information could help children and young people all over the UK. What is interesting is the Metropolitan Police Force's line on bullying and what can be done:

> No matter how bad bullying can seem, many incidents of bullying are not actually crimes, and therefore might not be a matter for the police. The best people to deal with them are parents, teachers or other responsible adults.
>
> ***But some types of bullying are illegal and should be reported to us***
>
> This includes bullying that involves:
>
> - harassment and intimidation over a period of time including calling someone names or threatening them, making abusive phone calls, and sending abusive emails or texts (one incident is not normally enough to get a conviction)
> - anything involving hate crimes.
>
> (http://safe.met.police.uk/bullying/*consequences_and_the_law.html*, emphasis in the original)

Thus, the legal position is very clear on what can and cannot be done with regard to the policing and criminalisation of bullying, yet some would argue it is not enough. This chapter will now briefly consider the victimology literature as a possible reason to why the legal position of bullying is never seen as adequate.

Victimisation, dissatisfaction and the law

There are often cases, reported in the media, about young victims who have taken their own life as a consequence of being bullied. One of the most recent cases in the UK, at the time of writing, was a young Polish girl, Dagmara Przybysz, 16, who committed suicide after complaining of being a victim of racist bullying at a Cornish school. Such cases, rightly, get covered across all media platforms and detail the potential consequences of bullying. However, from this one incident it is not clear cut. The victim alleges that she was being bullied on the grounds of racism. As we have seen in the chapter by Aziz, racism is a criminal offence and falls under the umbrella of hate crime. It also contravenes The Equality Act (2010). But the victim has also taken her own life, so who would justice be 'done' for? Her family? The school? The bully? In this one example the complexities of considering criminalisation are opened up. The racist bullying has to be 'proved' and those involved investigated. At the time of the tragedy Devon and Cornwall police were not treating the incident as suspicious but they were attempting to establish the circumstances surrounding her death.

When cases, such as Dagmara's, are reported, there is the usual call that not enough is being done in schools to tackle the problem. However, as has been documented the legal position is very clear. Schools have to have an anti-bullying and behavioural policy which has to be readily available. "Bullying" has no criminal legal definition (although there are notable exceptions and cyberbullying appears to have more specific existing criminal laws to prosecute incidents if they are brought to the attention of the police). So what is it that people actually want? And would bullying becoming a criminal offence help resolve the problem?

Research demonstrates a huge difference in prevalence rates of bullying, but the reality is what would happen if all of those cases were criminal? Is the criminal justice system equipped any more than the education system to deal with the problem of bullying? The needs of the victims and the bullies have been considered in this volume; but if those individuals were put into the criminal system, would their needs be met any more efficiently? Furthermore, some children who bully are also themselves bullied in other contexts and therefore suffer as victims. These bully-victims are the most at risk of mental health problems.

Victimological research highlights that the plight of the victim is seldom heard in a criminal situation and the victim often feels displaced within the criminal justice process, to the point that the legal system 'takes over' and the victim often feels as though they have lost control of their situation. Nils Christie (1977) argues that the state has 'stolen' the conflict and crime from the victim and it becomes a matter for the State against the offender. To add the 'crime' of bullying, which affects many people, would not ease this concern, nor the plight of the victims or the mental health and well-being of the children and young people involved in the bullying incident.

Furthermore, the complexities of the victim/offender cycle need to be considered. A number of bullies are often victims themselves and play out their frustrations and concerns when they are in the role of 'bully'. Indeed research argues that the bully-victim should be treated as a distinct subgroup due to the complexities and overlap between being a victim and a bully at the same time (Solberg, Olweus, & Endrensen, 2007). Another point to consider is that the mental health needs of the bully can be just as significant as the victim, and those individuals who are bully-victims are at an increased risk for maladjustment (Piquero, Piquero, & Underwood, 2016). Therefore, when tasked with safeguarding the emotional and mental health needs of pupils within a school setting, would criminalisation of the issue help? As mentioned, law is not argued on emotion, but fact, so one could assume with some level of accuracy making bullying a crime would not help the needs of the victim or the bully.

As the school has a duty of care for all of its pupils, it cannot discriminate against any of them as we have seen in the previously discussed legislation; so it is a complicated balancing act to look after and ensure the emotional health and well-being of everyone in the school setting. Furthermore, in contrast to the criminal justice system, the victim-centred approaches that have been discussed in this volume have shown how the victim does have a voice. Perhaps what is needed is not more prosecution or criminalisation, but that more best practice is shared. In line with this observation, restorative practices are very popular within the school setting and research demonstrates it can be successfully implemented (Russell & Crocker, 2016). Extreme cases and unfortunately bullycides will occur; nonetheless, there is the legislation and practice in place. It certainly is not perfect and bullying still exists. But on balance making bullying a criminal offence would not help the victims, the bullies nor their emotional health and well-being. It would also just add to the workload of an already overstretched criminal justice system, and probably result in even less satisfaction that the bullying problem was being dealt with, tackled and taken seriously.

References

Chatzitheochari, S., Parsons, S., & Platt, L. (2016). Doubly disadvantaged? Bullying experiences among disabled children and young people in England. *Sociology*, *50*(4), 695–713.

Christie, N. (1977). Conflicts as property. *British Journal of Criminology*, *17*, 1–19.

Cowie, H., & Jennifer, D. (2007). *Managing violence in schools: A whole-school approach to best practice*. London: Sage.

DfE. (2014). *The Equality Act 2010 and schools departmental advice for school leaders, school staff, governing bodies and local authorities*. Retrieved from www.gov.uk/government/uploads/system/uploads/attachment_data/file/315587/Equality_Act_Advice_Final.pdf (accessed 10 December 2016) http://safe.met.police.uk/bullying/consequences_and_the_law.html (accessed 10 December 2016) www.antibullyingworks.co.uk/resources/dutiesresponsibilities (accessed 10 December 2016) www.gov.uk/bullying-at-school/the-law (accessed 10 December 2016).

Jeong, S., Kwak, D.-H., Moon, B., & San Miguel, C. (2013). Predicting school bullying victimization: Focusing on individual and school environmental/security factors. *Journal of Criminology*, *2013*, 1–13.

Myers, C.-A., & Cowie, H. (2017 in press). Bullying at university: The social and legal contexts of cyberbullying among university students. *Journal of Cross-Cultural Psychology*. doi:10.1177/0022022116684208

Piquero, A. R., Piquero, N. L., & Underwood, M.K. (2016). Correlates of – and consequences for bully-victims in a sample of serious adolescent offenders. *Youth Violence and Juvenile Justice*. doi:10-1177/1541204016657396

Russell, S., & Crocker, D. (2016). The institutionalization of restorative justice in schools: A critical sensemaking account. *Restorative Justice: An International Journal*, *4*(2), 195–213.

Solberg, M. E., Olweus, D., & Endrensen, I. M. (2007). Bullies and victims at school: Are they the same pupils? *British Journal of Educational Psychology*, 77(2), 441–464.

Wynne, S. L., & Joo, H.-J. (2011). Predictors of school victimization: Individual, familial, and school factors. *Crime and Delinquency*, *57*(3), 458–488.

Chapter 4

Homophobic, biphobic and transphobic bullying in schools

Ian Rivers

Introduction

Research on the bullying and social exclusion of lesbian, gay, bisexual and transgender (LGBT) pupils in schools is now into its third decade. For over 20 years, studies have catalogued the daily torments many LGBTs have faced and continue to face going to school (Rivers, 2011). The wealth of evidence collected has prompted several governments to take action to address the homophobia that has long been apparent in the classrooms, corridors and on the playing fields of our schools. However, despite this wealth of evidence, some politicians, religious leaders and members of the teaching profession remain opposed to the delivery of curricula that acknowledge the diversity that exists within our schools, preferring to remain silent (at best) or overtly discriminate (at worst) against those young people who identify as other than heterosexual, or those who identify as members of the opposite sex.

The existence of homophobic, biphobic and transphobic (HBT) bullying is a mark of shame for many educational systems. There are probably few people reading this chapter who do not recall a peer in their class or year group being bullied mercilessly because of their actual or perceived sexual orientation, or because they were gender atypical:

> For almost a year of my school life I spent every break and every dinner break sitting in the back of the . . . of the toilet area reading because I knew I was safe there, that I was isolated, and no one would give me any hassle.
>
> (Rivers, 2011, p. 146)

HBT bullying is a feature of the majority if not all of the educational systems around the world (UNESCO, 2015). In Asia and the Pacific, societal expectations inform the ways in which those who do not adhere to cultural expectations are treated by others, and this begins at school: in many cultures, social order, family honour and sexual purity provide a longstanding foundation for what is considered to be acceptable behaviour. This includes societal expectations of heterosexual marriage, and the importance of having children to ensure care of elders and the family lineage. Research demonstrates that homophobia, biphobia, transphobia, intersex prejudice, heteronormativity and intolerance characterise peer interactions among many young people in schools of Asia-Pacific (UNESCO, 2015, p. 10).

HBT bullying has increasingly been cited as a priority for schools and, as noted earlier, national governments have begun to invest in the delivery of anti-bullying programmes that claim to tackle this form of abuse. However, there remains little independent evidence of the success of the majority of these programmes in terms of reducing bullying directly and, more importantly, whether any reported reduction is cost effective and, ultimately, sustainable (Rivers, 2014).

HBT bullying in schools: the evidence

Although reference to the bullying of LGB young people appeared in reports published in the 1980s (see Trenchard & Warren, 1984) in the United Kingdom (UK), the first detailed investigation of the nature, correlates and long-term effects of what became known as 'homophobic bullying' was conducted in the early 1990s with a sample of LGB adults recalling their experiences at school (Rivers, 2001). This research demonstrated that homophobic bullying was deliberate and systematic, often perpetrated by groups of peers rather than by individuals. While some participants in this study had overcome their experiences at schools, others had not. Overall 53% reported that they had thought about ending their own lives when they were at school with 40% attempting suicide once and three quarters of those more than once.

Following on from this early research, two further surveys sponsored by the UK charity Stonewall (Hunt & Jensen, 2007; Guasp, 2012) indicated that while homophobic bullying had decreased among their samples from 65% in 2007 to 55% in 2012, not enough was being done to combat it. In their 2012 survey, 58% of those who had been bullied were subjected to verbal abuse, 46% were the victims of gossip and 33% said they had received intimidating looks. Others reported being ignored (31%), being harassed via technology ('cyberbullying' 23%), physically hurt by others (16%), having property vandalised (11%), receiving hurtful telephone and text messages (9%), death threats (6%), being threatened with a weapon (3%) and being sexual assaulted (3%).

In the US, GLSEN (Gay, Lesbian and Straight Education Network) has undertaken biennial surveys (National School Climate Survey) of bullying and victimisation of LGBT young people since 1999. GLSEN's data have shown that, over the years, while there has been a significant decline in overt verbal harassment experienced by LGBT young people, rates of physical assault have remained stable. In terms of bullying and harassment arising from gender expression, once again GLSEN has shown a consistent decline in reports of overt verbal harassment but there has not been a concomitant decline in reported rates of physical assault.

One of the most detailed surveys of HBT bullying was undertaken between 2001 and 2002 by the California Safe School Coalition with researchers from the University of California-Davis. They surveyed 237,544 young people in grades 7–11 (ages 12 to 17 years) who were asked about their experiences of all forms of bullying. Overall they found that 7.5% of young people reported having been victims of HBT bullying and that two out of every three LGBT young people were bullied because of their actual or perceived sexual orientation (California Safe Schools Coalition & 4-H Centre for Youth Development, University of California, Davis, 2004). Additionally, those who were bullied because of their actual or perceived sexual orientation were more likely to receive lower grades at school (grade 'C' or below) when compared to those who were not bullied (24% versus 17%). They were also more likely to miss school because they reported feeling unsafe (27% versus 7%). Additionally, they were twice as likely to engage in health risk behaviours and were nearly six times more likely to be threatened or hurt by someone carrying a weapon (28% versus 5%). They were also four times more likely to carry a weapon themselves (19% versus 5%).

In terms of trans young people's experiences of bullying, data collected by the charity-gendered intelligence (n.d.) suggests it begins in primary school and can continue into college and university:

> Primary school; always got told by the older girls that I was in the wrong toilet. To the extent of physical bullying and being scared of being in the toilets. But obviously 'cause I'd been told from birth I'm a little girl, using those toilets. Going in to those toilets and actually missing classes 'cause I was hiding . . . in the cubicle 'cause I'd heard that the older girls or girls in my class were in the toilets chatting . . . for about 20 minutes or something, not caring – 'cause they're in like year 6 – that they're missing their class, but I was sitting there in year 4 thinking 'oh my god my teachers going to tell me off again . . . because I'm like 'oh well I can't leave this cubicle'.
>
> (p. 8)

For some trans youth the term 'bullying' does not convey adequately the violence they have experienced at the hands of peers which would, in any other situation, result in police action:

> I'd just like to record an objection to a word, 'bullying'. Because I think it continues to entrench the state of denial that schools and the government are in about what happens in schools. Which, in any other situation, would be called 'abuse', or 'harassment', and would be a criminal offence, which the police would deal with. But because it's in schools, it's just 'oh it's just kids being kids' and they need to get serious and start actually recognising when abusive crimes are happening and erm, you should have the same protection there as you would in the home.
>
> (p. 29)

There has been criticism of research on bullying and harassment and its mental health correlates due to its focus on negative experiences rather than taking a holistic view of young people's development (see Savin-Williams, 2005). Additionally, some researchers have argued that we need a much more nuanced understanding of young people's discourses and the dynamics of their relationships with others to determine whether phrases such as "that's so gay" are in fact homophobic (see, for example, McCormack, 2013). For some the argument is that the phrase "that's so gay" has become part of the young people's discourse and in environments that are supportive it is something *other* than homophobic; there is no intent to marginalise or discriminate, rather there is a desire to bond or to identify with the speaker. Thus, in a school where there are high levels of intolerance towards LGBTs the intent behind a comment such as "that's so gay" may be entirely different from a school where there is support for LGBT pupils and staff. Of course, it should be noted that this argument does not apply to the use of all LGBT-themed epithets – many of which are clear in their intent to cause harm or otherwise denigrate the target (see Thurlow, 2001).

Mental health correlates of HBT bullying

According to Hatzenbuehler (2011), the social spaces and political environments LGBT young people occupy play a significant part in their mental health and well-being. In the absence of visible support mechanisms such as LGBT groups, public figures and clubs, increased levels of emotional disturbance and suicide ideation appear. Using pooled data from the 2005 and 2007 Youth Risk Behaviour Surveillance (YRBS) surveys (N = 55,559, aged 13–18 years), Haztenbuehler, Birkett, Wagenen, and Meyer (2014) found that suicide ideation among LGB young people was lower in counties and cities where sexual minority students reported feeling more protected and less isolated (e.g. they had identified safe spaces to go to, or their schools had a Gay-Straight Alliance). In developing his Minority Stress Theory, Meyer (2003) argued that invisibility and experiences of discrimination – which he described in terms of proximal factors (personal fear of rejection, further isolation or experiences of prejudice) and distal factors (societal prejudice and discrimination) – influence well-being and, ultimately, impact upon proactive engagement with society.

To date, numerous studies suggest that there are long-term and life-threatening effects associated with HBT bullying (see, for example, Poteat, Rivers, & Scheer, 2016). In addition to the reports of suicide ideation reported in Rivers' (2001) study, in its 2012 study, Stonewall reported that 41% of LGB respondents had deliberately self-harmed as a result of homophobic bullying (biphobic and transphobic bullying were not considered). GLSEN's (2011) report indicated that high rates of depression and low-esteem were correlated with HBT bullying for the LGBT young people who participated in its survey. Additionally, in California, 55% of those who were bullied because of their actual or perceived sexual orientation reported that they had experienced depression for at least two weeks over the last 12 months (compared to 23% among peers who were not bullied). Over two-fifths (45%) had seriously considered suicide (compared to 14% among peers who had not been bullied at school), and 35% had made a suicide plan (compared to 9% of non-bullied peers, California Safe Schools Coalition & 4-H Centre for Youth Development, University of California, Davis, 2004). However, Rivers (2011) reported that, when compared to heterosexual and LGB adults who were bullied at school *for other reasons*, those who experienced HBT bullying did not differ significantly in terms of rates of depression or anxiety. However, among 13- to16-year-olds, Rivers and Noret (2008) reported that those who were attracted to members of the same-sex (N = 53) scored higher on measures of negative affect when compared to a group of matched controls who were attracted to members of the opposite-sex. Overall, this research suggests that there are both acute/immediate and chronic/long-term correlates of HBT bullying. Both have repercussions for schools and require appropriate interventions that address the mental health distress caused by bullying as well as the behaviour it entails.

Why does HBT bullying exist?

Ultimately HBT bullying exists because many cultures condemn homosexuality and bisexuality, or perceive people who are trans to be deviant or dangerous. This was clearly demonstrated in recent legislation introduced in the US to ban trans people from using gender appropriate lavatories.

The hysteria associated with fears of assault or voyeurism has been translated into prohibitive legislation for elementary and secondary schools, colleges and universities. For example, the now infamous House Bill 2 (HB2) introduced in North Carolina states that:

> Local boards of education shall require every multiple occupancy bathroom or changing facility that is designated for student use to be designated for and used only by students based on their biological sex.
>
> (General Assembly of North Carolina, 2016, pp. 1–2)

Within this particularly pernicious piece of legislation, biological sex refers to, "the physical condition of being male or female, which is stated on a person's birth certificate." For many people, such a legislative bill may seem entirely appropriate and the bill contains an exemption allowing for the provision of a single occupancy bathroom or changing facility, "that has been temporarily designated for use by that person's biological sex." However, it is the inference and meaning underpinning the use of the term "biological sex" and the failure of North Carolina's legislature to consider the needs of minorities, preferring to use language that promotes assumptions and beliefs about deviation from biological 'norms'. This has resulted in a number of heterosexual men entering women's public restrooms claiming that they believed a trans person was using the facility illegally.

In order to understand why HBT bullying or, indeed, any form of bullying exists, it is necessary to understand the psychological processes that underpin the decision to bully or intimidate another. Figure 4.1 provides a graphic representation of a five-stage model of bullying perpetration entitled **PAPER** (***P***recipitation, ***A***ssessment, ***P***rovocation, ***E***scalation and ***R***esponse). This model was first proposed in the *Times Educational Supplement* in 2012 (see Rivers, 2012). It builds upon research drawn from social and developmental psychology and proposes that there are both moderating and mediating factors that can impact upon the decision whether a person bullies another (moderators), or the severity of that behaviour if enacted (mediators).

The starting point (***P***recipitation) begins with an assumption or belief about a person or group of people. In his ground-breaking text, *The Nature of Prejudice*, Gordon W. Allport (1954) demonstrated how assumptions or beliefs, many of which are untrue, influence the prejudices we have against other groups in society. Beliefs that certain ethnic or cultural groups are 'smelly' or 'sly' and 'tricky' underpin the ways in which we engage with members of those communities: when something goes wrong (the catalyst), they are to blame or when something goes right, they have had an unfair advantage or have been prioritised above others. Consequently, they do not deserve praise, reward or, as history has shown, equality.

The allocation of blame resulting from an unfavourable outcome constitutes Stage 2 of the model (***A***ssessment). Here expectations of success or failure are moderated by the outcome. If the outcome is favourable to the minority, then ***P***rovocation (Stage 3) is likely to follow together with emotional escalation. If the outcome is favourable to the majority, then the likelihood of emotional escalation subsides (at least on the part of the potential perpetrator). In terms of bullying behaviour, Galvan, Hare, Voss, Glover, and Casey (2007) study of risk-taking behaviour provides useful support for Stage 3 of the PAPER model. This research suggests that, in terms of frontal cortex development, many young people are unable to engage a so-called emotional 'braking system' and are, therefore, unable to down-regulate negative reactions to events, resulting in faulty logic and a poor assessment of a given situation. In principle, it seems that the ability to stem negative emotional reactions and challenge those faulty beliefs or assumptions is the key to tackling bullying and especially bullying related to prejudice.

Where the outcome leads to a strong negative emotional reaction, ***E***scalation follows. At this stage, two factors come into play – status and proximity. How perpetrators view themselves relative to the target of their aggression is very important. Violence becomes a means to sustain or enhance personal status within the school-yard hierarchy. If that status cannot be sustained or enhanced, then the repercussions may be less severe for the target. Similarly the proximity of the target (same class, same year group, sibling, friend, team mate) may also play a role in the decision to perpetrate bullying. Tajfel (1972) argued that an individual's identity with a particular group of peers (social identity) is related

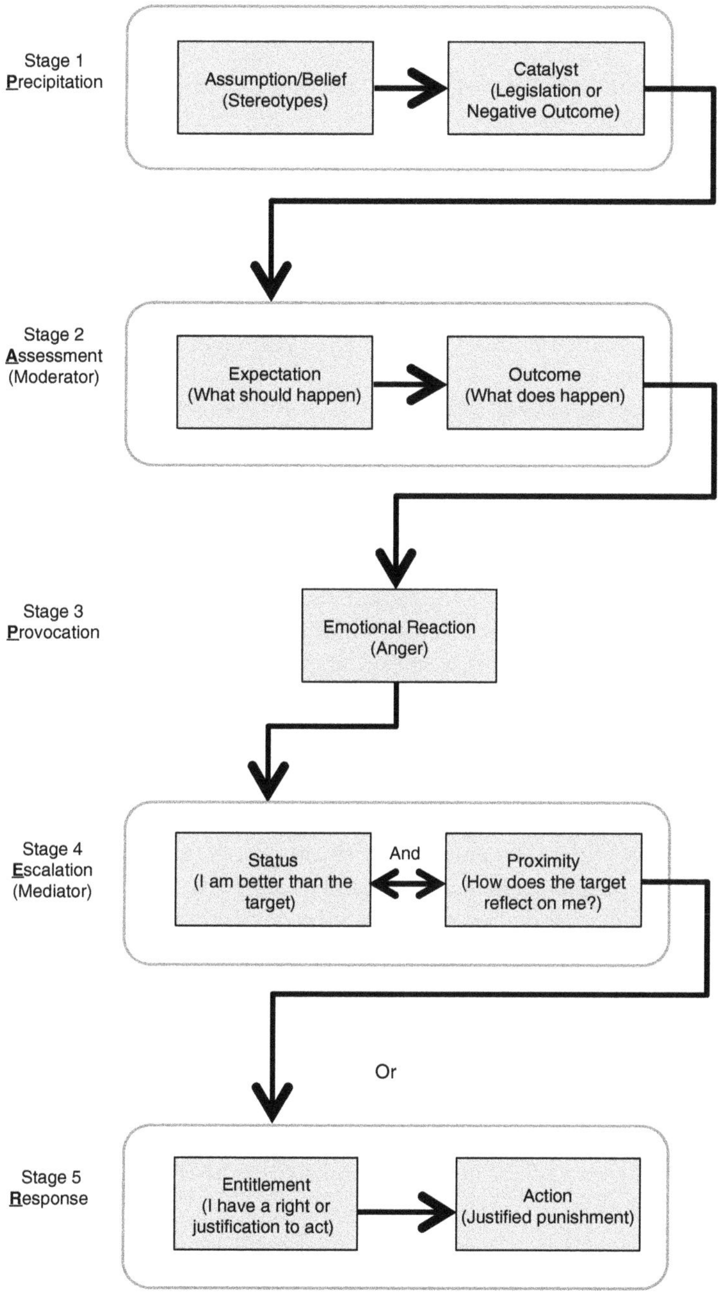

Figure 4.1 Five stage model of bullying perpetration (PAPER)

to the emotional and evaluative significance membership of that group offers. Through membership of that social group, a person's status within the social hierarchy is determined. Self-worth thus becomes inextricably linked to the way in which one person or group is perceived relative to another person or group. Once again, cognition and motivation are central to understanding why discrimination occurs:

> It is cognitive insofar as the categorization process leads the subjects to overestimate intergroup differences and to underestimate ingroup differences. It is motivational insofar as what motivates discrimination is the need for self-esteem and self-respect.
>
> (Deschamps & Devos, 1998, p. 6)

From the perspective of the perpetrator, a positive assessment of personal status relative to that of the target, and a desire to create distance (in terms of identity) from that target creates both a sense of entitlement to discriminate together with a desire *and* a need to take action to underscore those differences (Stage 5, ***R***esponse). The acceptability of discriminatory actions may be based upon those social and cultural factors described in UNESCO's (2015) report (i.e. social order, family honour, sexual purity and societal expectations of heterosexual marriage and having children to care for elders and the family lineage). It can also be the result of the sanitisation of language (describing behaviour as justifiable punishment rather than unjustified aggression) and the use of expedient historical examples to justify behaviour (e.g. condemnation of particular groups from history or significant cultural or religious texts, see Bandura, 1999; Wiens & Dempsey, 2009).

Of course, as society changes and there is greater acceptance of LGBT people, so there should be a concomitant decline in HBT bullying, particularly among young people. Indeed, this argument supports the evidence presented by Savin-Williams (2005) and, to a degree, by McCormack (2013). However, as we have seen, there can also be a conservative challenge to those changes which can result in an escalation in violent action either by individuals or by groups. Engaging young people in discussions relating to acts of violence perpetrated against LGBT people is becoming increasingly important. Indeed, the absence of any discussion in the classroom allows misinformation and prejudice to take hold. Teachers ultimately have to be able to talk with confidence about the reasons why some groups are opposed to LGBT equality, and to be able to talk openly and objectively about the different views that people hold and why they hold them.

What works in challenging HBT bullying?

In 2014 Public Health England commissioned a rapid topic overview of research and interventions associated with homophobic and transphobic bullying (see Rivers, 2014). The resulting report identified a number of interventions, including curriculum-based programmes that were promising in terms of the impact upon rates of bullying. Many of these intervention programmes involved the training of teachers on equality and diversity issues and the use of historical examples to demonstrate to young people the contribution LGBT people have made and continue to make in society. One key intervention that showed a significant long-term impact upon rates of sexual and HBT bullying was a curriculum-based intervention called Second Step© which focusses on social-emotional learning and encouraged young people in school to understand the impact of HBT bullying collectively (Committee for Children, 2008). Among 6th and 7th grade school students, Espelage, Low, Polanin, and Brown (2015) found that there was a reduction in homophobic name-calling of 56% two years following the introduction of the programme for middle schools. The programme included sessions on social-emotional skills development (i.e. empathy, assertive communication skills, emotional regulation and problem-solving skills). With young people in 6th grade, sessions also covered issues such as recognising bullying and bystander intervention. For those in 7th grade, sessions included advice on responding to bullying, cyberbullying and sexual harassment (with a reported reduction of 39% after two years). Additionally, there was a 42% reduction in physical violence within the first year (Espelage, Low, Polanin, & Brown, 2013).

There are three important features of Second Step© that explain its success. Firstly, it breaks down those social identity barriers that promote bullying, teaching empathy and understanding. Secondly, it promotes emotional regulation and, with an eye to Galvan et al.'s (2007) findings, provides potential perpetrators with an opportunity to 'engage' at important emotional breaking points. Finally, it promotes communication skills and equips young people with the language necessary to challenge bullying when they encounter it. Comparable with Espelage et al. (2013, 2015), Richards, Rivers, and Akhurst (2008) noted that following a nine-week positive psychology intervention in one school that included teaching communication skills, rates of bullying declined and self-reports of well-being improved among 11-year olds.

Summary

Despite evidence that, for some LGBT young people, school experiences have improved immensely, for others HBT bullying remains a problem. Since those very early studies conducted in the 1990s, there has been significant legislative change, and a commitment by governments to make schools, colleges and universities safe for all young people regardless of their sexual orientation or gender identity. Issues such as marriage equality have proven divisive and the conservative backlash has, unfortunately, impacted upon schools directly. HB2 is one such example. However, LGBT young people are coming out earlier than before and primary/elementary schools are increasingly reporting that they actively support the trans students in their care. While there will always be challenges to LGBT equality, one key lesson that must guide our thinking and practice now and in the future has to be a recognition of the fact that what we teach today will, ultimately, influence the actions of tomorrow.

References

Allport, G. W. (1954). *The nature of prejudice.* Reading, MA: Addison-Wesley.

Bandura, A. (1999). Moral disengagement in the perpetration of inhumanties. *Personality and Social Psychology Review, 3*(3), 193–209.

California Safe Schools Coalition and 4-H Centre for Youth Development, University of California, Davis. (2004). *Safe place to learn: Consequences of harassment based on actual or perceived sexual orientation and gender non-conformity and step for making schools safer.* San Francisco: California Safe Schools Coalition and 4-H Centre for Youth Development, University of California, Davis.

Committee for Children. (2008). *Second Step: Student success through prevention programme.* Seattle, WA: Committee for Children.

Deschamps, J.-C., & Devos, T. (1998). Regarding the relationship between social identity and personal identity. In S. Worchel, J. F. Morales, D. Pàez, & J.-C. Deschamps (Eds.), *Social identity: International perspectives* (pp. 1–12). London: Sage.

Espelage, D. L., Low, S., Polanin, J. R., & Brown, E. (2013). The impact of a middle-school programme to reduce aggression, victimization, and sexual violence. *Journal of Adolescent Health, 53*(2), 180–186.

Espelage, D. L., Low, S., Polanin, J. R., & Brown, E. C. (2015). Clinical trial of Second Step© middle-school programme: Impact on aggression and victimization. *Journal of Applied Developmental Psychology, 37*(1), 52–63.

Galvan, A., Hare, T. A., Voss, H., Glover, G., & Casey, B. J. (2007). Risk-taking and the adolescent brain: Who is at risk? *Developmental Science, 10*(2), F8–F14.

General Assembly of North Carolina. (2016). *House bill 2.* Retrieved from www.ncleg.net/Sessions/2015E2/Bills/House/PDF/H2v4.pdf (accessed 26 July 2016).

GLSEN. (2011). *The 2011 national school climate survey: The experiences of lesbian, gay, bisexual, and transgender youth in our nation's schools.* New York: GLSEN.

Guasp, A. (2012). *The school report: The experiences of gay young people in Britain's schools in 2012.* London: Stonewall.

Hatzenbuehler, M. L. (2011). The social environment and suicide attempts in a population-based sample of LGB youth. *Pediatrics, 127*(5), 896–903.

Haztenbuehler, M. L., Birkett, M., Wagenen, A. van, & Meyer, I. H. (2014). Protective school climate and reduced risk for suicide ideation in sexual minority youths. *American Journal of Public Health, 104*(2), 279–286.

Hunt, R., & Jensen, J. (2007). *The school report: The experiences of gay young people in Britain's schools.* London: Stonewall.

McCormack, M. (2013). Mapping the boundaries of homophobic language in bullying. In I. Rivers & N. Duncan (Eds.), *Bullying: Experiences and discourses of sexuality and gender* (pp. 91–104). London: Routledge.

Meyer, I. H. (2003). Prejudice, social stress, and mental health in lesbian, gay, and bisexual populations: Conceptual issues and research evidence. *Psychological Bulletin, 129*(5), 674–697.

Poteat, V. P., Rivers, I., & Scheer, J. R. (2016). Unique mental health concerns, LGBTQ youth. In M. K. Holt & A. E. Grills (Eds.), *Critical issues in school-based mental health* (pp. 105–117). New York: Routledge.

Richards, A., Rivers, I., & Akhurst, J. (2008). A positive psychology approach to tackling bullying in secondary schools: A comparative evaluation. *Educational and Child Psychology, 25*(2), 72–81.

Rivers, I. (2001). The bullying of sexual minorities at school: Its nature and long-term correlates. *Educational and Child Psychology, 18*(1), 33–46.

Rivers, I. (2011). *Homophobic bullying: Research and theoretical perspectives.* New York: Oxford University Press.

Rivers, I. (2012). Bully and victims: Busting the myths. *Times Educational Supplement, TESpro*, 29 June, 8–9.

Rivers, I. (2014). *Homophobic and transphobic bullying: Rapid topic overview.* London: Public Health England.

Rivers, I., & Noret, N. (2008). Well-being among same-sex and opposite sex attracted youth at school. *School Psychology Review, 37*(2), 174–187.

Savin-Williams, R. C. (2005). *The new gay teenager.* Cambridge, MA: Harvard University Press.

Tajfel, H. (1972). La catégorisation social. In S. Moscovici (Ed.), *Introduction à la psychologie sociale* (Vol. 1, pp. 272–302). Paris: Larousse.

Thurlow, C. (2001). Naming the 'outside within': Homophobic pejorative and the verbal abuse of LGB high-school pupils. *Journal of Adolescence, 24*(1), 25–38.

Trenchard, L., & Warren, H. (1984). *Something to tell you.* London: London Gay Teenage Group.

UNESCO. (2015). *From insult to inclusion: Asia-Pacific report on school bullying, violence, and discrimination on the basis of sexual orientation and gender identity.* Paris and Bangkok: UNESCO. Retrieved from http://unesdoc.unesco.org/images/0023/002354/235414e.pdf. (accessed 29 June 2016).

Wiens, B. A., & Dempsey, A. (2009). Bystander involvement in per victimization: The value of looking beyond aggressors and victims. *Journal of School Violence, 8*(3), 206–215.

Chapter 5

Contested and complex terrain

Sexual violence in UK schools

Kerry Lee

Introduction

Over the last few months the issue of sexual violence in schools has achieved prominence in the United Kingdom (UK). In March 2016 the UK Government announced £3.85 million in funding for a new awareness campaign and educational resources to raise awareness and understanding of consent, sexting and relationship abuse amongst teenagers (HM Government, 2016). This was followed in April, with the initiation of a cross governmental inquiry by the Women and Equalities Select Committee, which, as I write this chapter, is in the process of collating evidence on sexual violence and harassment in schools (Parliament UK, 2016). Both build on the creation of a taskforce focussing on sexual violence and harassment in UK universities and the Higher Education sector (HM Government, 2016).

The catalyst for the inquiry is a small evidence base which suggests sexual violence and harassment in schools is an 'everyday' reality, particularly for girls (EVAW, 2010; Fixers, 2015). In response to figures demonstrating that police forces recorded over 5,000 sexual offence allegations in schools, including over 600 allegations of rape, one senior officer commented the figures were only the "tip of the iceberg" and "while I cannot prove this – I believe more child abuse is taking place" (BBC, 2015).

Not all accept that sexual violence and harassment in schools is a significant problem however. The Department for Education (DfE), the Government department responsible for all aspects of primary and secondary education in England, has presented evidence contesting the scale of the problem. The department's written submission to the inquiry (DfE, 2016a) started with the definitive statement that 'Schools are safe places and crime in schools is very rare', before drawing on two sources: school exclusion figures for sexual misconduct and a recent Teacher Voice Survey (NFER, 2015) which asked about pupil behaviour and the most common forms of bullying. Sexual violence, sexual harassment and sexual bullying were not an explicit focus of the survey, but 74% of respondents identified verbal abuse as the most common form of bullying, followed by cyberbullying and physical abuse (45% and 26% respectively).

Citing that these three forms of bullying would include behaviours that could be considered sexual harassment, the DfE claimed:

> We can say with a good level of certainty that this type of bullying is seen as common around 5% of schools on average.
>
> (DfE, 2016a)

It is what can or cannot be said with any degree of certainty that is the focus of this chapter. After providing an overview of the UK school system and the current policy context, the chapter will discuss what is currently known about sexual violence in schools before concluding with reflections on what can be currently be said with a 'good degree of certainty' and what requires further exploration.

A brief overview of the UK school system

It is something of a misnomer to refer to the 'UK school system'. The UK comprises England, Wales, Scotland and Northern Ireland, each with differing degrees of devolved responsibility for the education sector. This results in some variations in school policy between the countries. In England, the DfE is responsible for education policy, whilst in Scotland it is the Scottish Executive, the Welsh Government in Wales and the Department for Education and Training in Northern Ireland.

Education is compulsory between the ages of 5–16, with the exception of Northern Ireland which has a starting age of 4-years-old. Children from ages 4/5 begin primary school based education moving to secondary education at approximately age 11 (12 in Scotland). However, in some areas in England there are also middle schools catering for ages 8–11. Further differences in school policy and governance relate not to country but to the type of school (see www.gov.uk/types-ofschool/overview) with a key distinction between publicly and privately funded schools. Privately funded or Independent primary and secondary schools charge fees to attend and do not have to follow the National Curriculum as set by Government. There are a number of different types of publicly funded secondary schools in England. Comprehensives are the most common type of publicly funded secondary school, admitting all pupils regardless of ability whereas Grammar schools are selective and pupils have to pass an entrance exam. Pupil Referral Units (PRUs) cater for pupils who have been excluded or unable to attend mainstream schools and a more recent form of secondary school – Academies – are publicly funded but Independent. They have the freedom to set their own pay, length of school year and some freedoms regarding the curriculum.

Schools are independently inspected by a number of different inspection bodies. In England the Office for Standards, Children's Services and Skills (OFSTED, n.d.) is responsible for inspecting the majority of schools with the exception of some Independent (private) schools, which are inspected by one of two other bodies, the Independent Schools Inspectorate (ISI, n.d.) and the School Inspection Service (SIS, n.d.). In Wales all schools are inspected by Estyn (Estyn, n.d.), in Scotland it is Education Scotland (Education Scotland, n.d.) and in Northern Ireland the Education and Training Inspectorate (ETINI, n.d.).

Children, sexual violence and policy – disconnected terrain

Knowledge about children and young people as both victims and perpetrators of sexual violence has increased significantly over the last three decades. From recognition of Child Sexual Abuse (CSA) either at the hands of adult strangers or family members in the 1980s (Morgan & Zedner, 1992), the scope of enquiry has developed over time to include Child Sexual Exploitation (CSE) (Beckett & Schubotz, 2014) including gang-associated sexual violence (Firmin, 2013). Whilst prevalence rates vary, a large scale survey by the NSPCC (Radford et al., 2011) found that a quarter of 18–24-year-olds experienced some form of sexual abuse in childhood; that the victimisation rate was higher for girls (31%, 17.4% for boys), and that girls aged 15–17 reported the highest 'previous year' rates of sexual abuse. Further, two-thirds of the 'contact' sexual abuse was perpetrated by children under the age of 18 and the majority of perpetrators (both adult and peer) were known males. Overall, 11.3% had experienced a form of 'contact' sexual abuse that is defined as a criminal offence. More recently, recognition of so called Teen Relationship Abuse (TRA) (Barter, McCarry, Berridge, & Evans, 2009) has revealed that a third of girls and 16% of boys report some form of sexual violence from an intimate partner.

Thus, we currently know a significant amount about some of the types of sexual violence both experienced and perpetrated by children and young people, as well as some of the specific contexts within which it occurs (family, peer groups/gangs and intimate relationships). As noted by Firmin (2013) each has tended to become associated with specific policy domains, with practical implications for how peer on peer sexual violence is understood and responded to. Whilst school may be implicated in any of the above, either as a location for specific incidents or because pupils from the same school are involved, it is largely absent as a specific site of sexual violence.

At the same time, school is widely recognised as a specific site of some forms of violence, namely bullying. Knowledge about bullying in the UK has increased exponentially (see Cowie and Myers chapter 1 of this volume), focussing on 'new' forms such as cyber-bullying, different 'types' of bullying such as homophobic bullying and relatively new behaviours such as sexting. As in the US (Gruber & Fineran, 2016), bullying has also become a significant policy concern. All schools are now expected to develop a policy on bullying and examination of these policies are part of the school inspections framework. However, somewhat paradoxically, whilst some homophobic bullying and sexting can also be sexual violence (although the inclusion of sexting in definitions of sexual violence is not without challenge, see Ringrose, Gill, Livingstone, & Harvey, 2012), most bullying research does not explicitly include sexual violence and harassment.

The recently revised Keeping Children Safe in Education guidance from the DfE (2016b), which applies to all schools irrespective of funding status in the UK, largely reflects this paradox. It contains specific mention of different forms of bullying and different forms of sexual violence such as sexual abuse and CSE. However, sexual abuse by peers or children is briefly referenced on only three pages in the 75-page document, resulting in guidance that predominantly situates sexual violence as something that is done by adults and which happens outside of school rather than within it.

Sexual violence in schools

To achieve any degree of 'certainty' about the scope and nature of sexual violence in UK schools, we need evidence or research data that allows us to specify at least four things: who the victim is, who the perpetrator is, sexual violence and the school as either a site or context. Whilst this may seem rather obvious, the review of the evidence reveals that we currently have different pieces of the puzzle. There are three potential sources of information about the prevalence of sexual violence in schools: 'official' statistics such as crime statistics and school exclusion data, large scale victimisation surveys and smaller research studies.

School data

As perhaps highlighted by the DfE submission to the inquiry, there is a distinct lack of data collected by schools to inform debates about the scale and nature of sexual violence experienced on their premises. There is currently no mandatory requirement to report incidents to the government or other central body (such as the Inspectorates) and statistics on allegations of abuse or proceedings against school staff are not collated centrally. The only indicator is the number of pupil exclusions due to sexual misconduct which is defined as – lewd behaviour; sexual abuse, sexual assault, sexual bullying, sexual graffiti and sexual harassment, and collected as part of the School Census. Whilst the figures look encouraging (see Table 5.1), with less than 1% of all exclusions due to sexual misconduct, they are a grossly unreliable indicator for several reasons.

Only state (publicly funded) schools are required to complete the School Census and no information is collected from private or Independent schools. A further drawback is that each country reports school exclusion figures separately and at the time of writing, only England and Wales have publicly available exclusion statistics which include the category of 'sexual misconduct' as a reason for exclusion.

Nor do the figures reveal anything about the number of pupils excluded (one pupil may be excluded multiple times) or who has been excluded. Anecdotal

Table 5.1 Exclusions due to sexual misconduct in England and Wales, 2011–14

Year	*England*		*Wales*	
	N	*% of all*	*N*	*% of all*
2011/12	2,800	0.9	81	0.5
2012/13	2,550	0.9	54	0.4
2013/14	2,200	0.8	89	0.7

Figures compiled from: www.gov.uk/government/collections/statistics-exclusions and http://dera.ioe.ac.uk/24422/1/150929-permanent-fixed-term-exclusions-from-schools-2013–14-en.pdf

evidence suggests that in some cases it may be the victim rather than the alleged perpetrator. A recent case illustrates this – the school initially excluded the alleged victim for breach of school rules regarding sex on school premises after staff presumed the sexual activity was consensual (BBC, 2013).

Police data

A second source of 'official data' is recorded crime or police statistics. Crime statistics do not routinely publish figures based on location or age of perpetrator/victim (Walby, Towers, & Francis, 2014), but a recent Freedom of Information (FOI) request by a UK national broadcaster, the British Broadcasting Corporation (BBC) obtained information from police forces in all four countries (BBC, 2015).

Asked how many sexual offences were recorded at schools, police forces in England, Wales and Northern Ireland provided figures for 2012 to 2015, Scotland for 2011 to 2013. Over 5,500 allegations were recorded, with approximately 4,000 physical sexual assaults and over 600 rapes. Not all forces provided information about the age of the alleged perpetrator, but where this was available approximately a fifth were children. Similarly, the age of victims was not provided so it is not possible to determine how many victims or perpetrators were children/pupils or adult staff members.

Like school exclusion figures, police-recorded crime data is not an accurate indicator of prevalence due to under-reporting (Walby et al., 2014). However, analysis of police case files can yield useful information about the nature of sexual violence in schools. No published studies have used police data to specifically explore school-based sexual violence, but one unpublished source provides some partial information. The focus of the study was multiple perpetrator rapes (MPR – defined as three or more perpetrators) in one London borough. It found that of 78 MPR cases one in six (15.4%) occurred in school and that the suspects were fellow school pupils in 14.3% of the MPR cases, 4.8% of cases with two (duos) and 5.1% of lone perpetrator cases. Whilst it is not possible to determine from the figures the overall proportion of recorded rape allegations occurring in school, cases where one or more fellow pupils were the suspects account for approximately 5% of all recorded allegations (Young & Choudary, 2014).

Victimisation surveys – 'early surveys'

Two Scottish victimisation surveys provided some of the earliest prevalence estimates of school children's experiences of behaviours which the survey authors categorised as 'sexual harassment'. The first conducted in Edinburgh with 1,150 young people aged 11–15, asked whether adult males had 'touched or tried to touch you', 'asked you to touch him', 'tried to get you to go somewhere with him' and 'indecently exposed himself to you' (Anderson, Kinsey, Loader, & Smith, 1990). Just over a quarter (26%) of girls and 9% of boys reported at least one incident in the past 9 months, with 4% of boys and 17% of girls reporting that an adult male had touched them. For boys victimisation decreased with age but increased for girls.

The second conducted in Glasgow with 208 schoolchildren aged 12 to 14, found almost identical rates of sexual assault (5% boys and 17% girls reported being touched by adult males) but much higher overall prevalence rates – 49% girls and 17% boys experienced at least one incident of sexual harassment in the past year. This could in part be due to the longer time frame included and the slightly older age of the sample (Hartless, Ditton, Nair, & Phillips, 1995).

Whilst both surveys provided useful 'early' estimates of the extent of sexual violence and harassment experienced by children and young people, and demonstrated the gendered nature of victimisation, both excluded incidents occurring at school, perpetrated by fellow pupils or by females.

These gaps were acknowledged to some degree in two surveys both using the same behavioural questions as the Edinburgh Study. The first was the British Crime Survey (now called the Crime Survey for England and Wales – CSEW). It is a crime victimisation survey which in the 1992 sweep included a booster sample of 1,350 12–15-year-olds resident in private households in England and Wales. As with the Scottish surveys, respondents were asked to report incidents perpetrated by adult men (defined as aged 16 and over). Far lower prevalence estimates were obtained with 6% of respondents (2% of boys and 10% of girls) reporting at least one incident of sexual harassment in the preceding period of 6–8 months. Results for each separate behaviour were not published so it is not possible to draw comparisons with the two Scottish surveys. However, the BCS respondents were asked the location of the 'last' incident. Results were not analysed by gender, but overall 14% reported it as occurring at school and 13% near school (Aye Maung, 1995).

The Children and Young Peoples Safety Survey (CYPSS) was conducted with 2,420 children aged 9- to 16-years-old from 26 primary and secondary schools in the North West of England (Deakin, 2006). The author categorised the behaviours as 'sexual intrusions' rather than sexual harassment. Overall, just over a fifth (21.8%) of children reported at least one incident of 'sexual intrusion'. Unlike the other three surveys, questions about perpetrators were not restricted to adult males. Most perpetrators were male, but 14% of respondents cited a female and 6% both a male and female as the perpetrators. Just over half of perpetrators were children (56%) and sexual victimisation by adults was most common in the 9–10-year-old age group. Respondents were also asked the location of the incidents. 'Sexual intrusion' was most likely to occur in the street (28%) but school was the second most common location (18%).

Whilst these four early surveys provide something of a baseline measurement from which to assess changes over time, each only provides a partial account by either focussing only on male adult perpetrators and excluding school as a location, or including school but excluding peers as perpetrators. This partial picture is sustained as much by reporting practices as it is by what is included or excluded in the surveys. However, the survey instruments do signal a gradual move away from the 'stranger danger' agenda and an increased recognition of schools as locations and children as perpetrators of sexual violence.

Contemporary surveys and research studies

Unfortunately, this recognition has not been sustained, and the current version of the BCS – the Crime Survey for England and Wales (CSEW) has failed to replicate the questions asked of the 12–15-year-olds in 1992. Although 10 to 15-year-olds are now routinely included in the survey, questions about sexual violence are asked only of those aged 16- to 59-years-old, with respondents asked to report victimisation experiences since age 16. Thus, whilst results consistently confirm that those aged 16 to 19 are at higher risk for different forms of sexual violence (9% of women and 1.4% of men in the last year – ONS, 2016), including partner sexual violence and stalking, it is an unsuitable prevalence source for sexual violence in schools.

In the contemporary context it is largely NGOs or charitable organisations that have commissioned surveys with an explicit focus on sexual harassment and violence in school. Samples vary in size, age range and respondent sex. There are also differences in which specific behaviours have been included, and in how results have been analysed and reported. In total, four surveys have been commissioned in the last six years.

An online survey of 788 16- to 18-year-olds in the UK (EVAW, 2010) explored the extent of sexual harassment and sexual violence within schools. Sexual name calling was found to be common with 71% of 16- to18-year-olds reporting they had heard terms such as slut or slag directed at girls in school daily or a few times per week. Just over a fifth (21%) reported unwanted sexual touching from someone at school, with girls far more likely to experience this (29%, 14% boys). Overall, 28% had seen sexual pictures on mobile phones at school a few times a month or more with more boys reporting this (31% – girls 25%). This is a similar proportion to an EU wide survey conducted in 2010 where 24% of 9- to 16-year-olds in the UK reported seeing sexual content (on or offline). Whilst a repeat of the survey in 2014 found a significant decrease in exposure to sexual images and sexting, this was far less pronounced for girls (Livingstone, Haddon, Vincent, Mascheroni, & Ólafsson, 2014).

Two further surveys, one with a large representative sample of 3,710 adults aged 18 years and over in England, Scotland and Wales found that just under a quarter (22%) of women experienced sexual touching, groping, flashing, sexual assault or rape in or around school (Plan UK, 2015), and one with a smaller (188 school/college students 16 years and older) found 27% reporting pressure to engage in sexual activity or sexting in and around school; just under a fifth (18%) reporting sexual harassment and 12% a sexual assault (Fixers, 2015).

It is a survey commissioned in 2014 by charity Girlguiding (2014) that provides the most extensive and detailed information to date, although the one rather significant drawback is that the sample only includes females. Comprising a sample of 1,405 girls and young women aged 7 to 21 from across the UK, the survey featured a number of questions on sexism, different forms of sexual violence and harassment and most importantly, specifically asked about school as a location. This survey also asked how teachers responded to reports of sexual violence and harassment.

Findings were reported by age group. For those aged 13 to 21 just under two-thirds (59%) experienced some form of sexual harassment at school, university or workplace in the past year.

- 37% reported jokes or taunts of a sexual nature (22% of those aged 7–12)
- 25% reported seeing sexually explicit pictures and videos
- 20% reported unwanted sexual attention
- 19% unwanted touching (10% of those aged 7–12)
- 18% reported seeing rude or obscene graffiti about girls/women (12% of those aged 7–12)
- 15% experienced sexual abuse on social media
- 14% reported frequent unwanted behaviour

Younger girls were more likely to report incidents to school staff (81% of 7–10 year olds report but only 54% of 17–21 year olds). Overall, two-fifths (42%) report that staff always take their reports seriously, but two-thirds (64%) of girls aged 11–16, secondary school age, reported that staff 'sometimes or always' respond by telling girls to ignore it. Overall, just over half of girls (of all ages) reported staff as 'always or sometimes' dismissing sexual harassment as boys 'mucking' around or as banter.

Perhaps unsurprisingly given the high levels of sexual harassment reported, the majority of girls responding to the survey were in favour of improved education about harassment and consent and the implementation of better prevention and support processes.

So what can be said with a 'good' level of certainty?

There are obvious deficiencies in the current evidence base. Most of the evidence reviewed above does not permit consideration of 'who' the perpetrator is or allow differentiation between types of school. Schools are places where sexual violence may be pupil to pupil, pupil to teacher, teacher to pupil or teacher to teacher, and any consideration of sexual violence in schools needs to consider all possible dyads.

Jimmy Savile, a famous UK DJ and television personality, was knighted on 1990 for his extensive contributions to charity and his widely-publicised voluntary work in hospitals. However, soon after his death in 2012, serious allegations were made about his prolific sexual abuse of children and young people over a very long period of time. Since the Savile scandal in the UK, reporting of sexual assault and abuse, some of which occurred many years ago, has increased significantly and a number of schools, particularly Independent and Boarding schools across the UK, are implicated (The Times, 2014). Whilst there are many media reports of pupils sexually victimised by teachers or other school staff, there is no way of knowing the scale of the problem or if the scale and nature of sexual violence differs depending on the type of school. Similarly, we know very little about the extent and ways in which boys are victimised (and type of school may well be relevant here) or girls may be involved as perpetrators of sexual violence and harassment at schools.

However, from the surveys discussed above, it is clear that sexual harassment, particularly in the form of verbal abuse and comments is relatively commonplace in UK schools. Similarly, verbal forms of bullying, much of which may be 'sexual' in intent and nature, are reported as most common in the UK (see Chapter 1).

The surveys above have also included a range of different behaviours (e.g. groping, unwanted sexual touching, through to rape), that outside of the school context would be considered criminal sexual assaults. Perhaps unsurprisingly given the different sampling methods, types of behaviours included and age range of respondents, there is some variation in the prevalence rates produced. However, drawing together findings, it would appear that between a fifth and a just under a third of girls and young women experience some form of behaviour in school that could be considered a criminal sexual assault. This behaviour is also not limited to secondary schools, given that 10% of girls aged 7–12 (the majority would be in primary school until age 11) reported unwanted sexual touching.

Opening up the scope of enquiry – adopting a lens of acknowledgement

There is clearly much we need to know to enable development and implementation of appropriate policies, prevention and support mechanisms, and the introduction of a mandatory reporting mechanism across all schools and countries of the UK would be a welcome step. But what the available data does establish is that schools are sites where sexual harassment and assaults, some of which are clearly very serious, can and do occur. Given that we know sexual violence and harassment occurs everywhere else in society, including in other educational settings such as universities (Cowie & Myers, 2016; NUS, 2011; Smith, 2012) perhaps a more realistic starting point is 'why wouldn't it happen in school?'

Starting from a lens of acknowledgement rather than one of denial is not to suggest danger lurks in every corridor, but aims to simply re-orient the debate to the lived reality of many school children throughout the UK. Acknowledging that sexual violence and harassment occur in schools is a vital step if a defensive reaction which too often results in disbelief or minimisation of victim reports and missed opportunities for prevention, is to be avoided.

There are signs that some schools in the UK are more willing to acknowledge and address sexual violence against women and girls, pre-dominantly through the implementation of 'whole-school approaches' (see for example, Welsh Government, 2015). However, whether this will culminate in national policies and guidance for recognising and responding specifically to peer on peer sexual violence and harassment *in* rather than outside of schools remains to be seen.

References

Anderson, S., Kinsey, R., Loader, I., & Smith, C. (1990). *Cautionary tales: A study of young people and crime in Edinburgh: A summary of findings*. Aldershot: Avebury Press.

Aye Maung, N. (1995). *Young people, victimisation and the police: BCS findings on experiences and attitudes of 12 to 15 year olds*. London: Home Office Research and Planning Unit Report, HMSO.

Barter, C., McCarry, M., Berridge, D., & Evans, K. (2009). *Partner exploitation and violence in teenage intimate relationships*. London: NSPCC.

BBC. (2013). *Hampshire school criticised for failing to protect vulnerable pupil*. Retrieved from www.bbc.co.uk/news/uk-england-hampshire-21129310

BBC. (2015). *School sex crime reports in UK top 5,500 in three years*. Retrieved from www.bbc.co.uk/news/education-34138287

Beckett, H., & Schubotz, D. (2014). Young people's self-reported experiences of sexual exploitation and sexual violence: A view from Northern Ireland. *Journal of Youth Studies, 17*(4), 430–445.

Cowie, H., & Myers, C. A. (2016). What we know about bullying and cyberbullying among university students. Chapter 1. In H. Cowie & C. A. Myers (Eds.), *Bullying among university students: Cross-national perspectives* (pp. 3–14). Oxon: Routledge.

Deakin, J. (2006). Dangerous people, dangerous places: The nature and location of young people's victimisation and fear. *Children and Society, 20*(5), 376–390.

Department for Education. (2016a). *Evidence of the scale of the problem*. Retrieved from http://data.parliament.uk/writtenevidence/committeeevidence.svc/evidencedocument/women-andequalities-committee/sexual-harassment-and-sexual-violence-in-schools/oral/34251.pdf

Department for Education. (2016b) *Keeping children safe in education: Statutory guidance for schools and colleges*. London: Department for Education. Retrieved from www.gov.uk/government/uploads/system/uploads/attachment_data/file/526153/Keeping_children_safe_in_education_guidance_from_5_September_2016.pdf

EducationScotland. (n.d.). Retrieved from www.educationscotland.gov.uk/inspectionandreview/

Estyn. (n.d.). Retrieved from www.estyn.gov.wales/about-us

ETINI. (n.d.). Retrieved from www.etini.gov.uk/

EVAW. (2010). *End violence against women poll results*. London: EVAW. Retrieved from www.endviolenceagainstwomen.org.uk/data/files/Schools_Safe_4_Girls/YouGov_poll_for_EVAW_on_sexual_harassment_in_schools_2010.pdf

Firmin, C. (2013) Something old or something new: Do pre-existing conceptualisations of abuse enable a sufficient response to abuse in young people's relationships and peer groups? In M. Melrose & J. Pearce (Eds.), *Critical perspectives on child sexual exploitation and related trafficking*. Basingstoke: Palgrave Macmillan.

Fixers. (2015). *Fixers investigates: The trouble . . . with sex in school*. Retrieved from www.parliament.uk/documents/commons-committees/women-and-equalities/FixersSS.pdf

Girlguiding. (2014). *Girls Attitudes Survey 2014*. Retrieved from http://new.girlguiding.org.uk/girlsattitudes-survey-2014

Gruber, J., & Fineran, S. (2016) Sexual harassment: Bullying and school outcomes for high school girls and boys. *Violence Against Women, 22*(1), 112–133.

Hartless, J. M., Ditton, J., Nair, G., & Phillips, S. (1995). More sinned against than sinning: A study of young teenagers experience of crime. *British Journal of Criminology, 25*(1), 114–133.

HM Government. (2016). *Ending violence against women and girls: Strategy 2016–2020*. London: HMSO.

ISI. (n.d.). Retrieved from www.isi.net/about/what-we-do

Livingstone, S., Haddon, L., Vincent, J., Mascheroni, G., & Ólafsson, K. (2014). *Net children go mobile: The UK report*. London: London School of Economics and Political Science.

Morgan, J., & Zedner, L. (1992). *Child victims: Crime, impact and criminal justice*. Oxford: Clarendon Press.

National Foundation for Educational Research. (2015). *NFER teacher voice omnibus: Questions for the Department for Education – June 2015. Research brief*. London: Department for Education. Retrieved from www.gov.uk/government/uploads/system/uploads/attachment_data/file/483275/DFE-RR493_Teacher_voice_omnibus_questions_for_DfE_-_June_2015.pdf

NUS. (2011). *Hidden marks: A study of women students' experiences of harassment, stalking, violence and sexual assault*. London: NUS. Retrieved from www.nus.org.uk/Global/NUS_hidden_marks_report_2nd_edition_web.pdf

Office for National Statistics. (2016). *Focus on violent crime and sexual offences: Year ending March 2015*. Retrieved from www.ons.gov.uk/peoplepopulationandcommunity/crimeandjustice/compendium/focusonviolentcrimeandsexualoffences/yearendingmarch2015/chapter1overviewofviolentcrimeandsexualoffences

OFSTED. (n.d.). Retrieved from www.gov.uk/government/organisations/ofsted

Parliament UK. (2016). *Sexual harassment and sexual violence in schools inquiry launched*. Retrieved from www.parliament.uk/business/committees/committees-a-z/commons-select/women-and-equalitiescommittee/news-parliament-2015/sexual-harassment-and-sexual-violence-in-schools-launch-15–16/

Plan UK. (2015). Retrieved from www.plan-uk.org/because-i-am-a-girl/learn-without-fear/

Radford, L., Corral, S., Bradley, C., Fisher, H., Bassett, C., Howat, N., & Collishaw, S. (2011). *Child abuse and neglect in the UK today*. London: NSPCC.

Ringrose, J., Gill, R., Livingstone, S., & Harvey, L. (2012). *A qualitative study of children, young people and 'sexting'*. London: NSPCC.

SIS. (n.d.). Retrieved from www.schoolinspectionservice.co.uk/

Smith, G (2012). Violence against women students in the UK: Time to take action. *Gender and Education, 24*(4), 357–373.

The Times. (2014). *130 Private schools in child abuse scandal.* Retrieved from www.thetimes.co.uk/tto/news/uk/article3980201.ece

Walby, S., Towers, J., & Francis, B. (2014). Mainstreaming domestic and gender-based violence into sociology and the criminology of violence. *The Sociological Review, 62*(2), 187–214.

Welsh Government. (2015). *Good practice guide: A whole education approach to violence against women, domestic abuse and sexual violence in Wales.* Retrieved from http://gov.wales/docs/dsjlg/publications/commsafety/151020-whole-education-approach-good-practice-guide-en.pdf

Young, T., & Choudary, N. (2014). *An investigation into the sexual abuse and exploitation of females by gang-affiliated youth.* Unpublished report, London Metropolitan University.

Chapter 6

Exploring the nature and extent of hate crime in schools and interventions to combat it

Rashid Aziz

Introduction

Other chapters have explored the nature of various forms of discrimination and violence as part of the everyday experiences of children in schools. For example, chapter 4 explores the nature of homophobic bullying and chapter 7 explores the role that religion and ethnicity can play in bullying in schools. What is clear from these examples is that young people are being targeted not only because of age, but other factors such as race, ethnic identity and sexual orientation. They are being made victims of bullying and violence because they are perceived to be 'different' from others. Homophobic bullying, disablist bullying and bullying due to race, gender or religion are technically, according to legal definitions, 'hate crimes'. Hate crime, whilst a relatively new phenomenon in terms of criminal law, has been a way of demonising those considered 'different' throughout history, marginalising those who are perceived to be different from a more accepted, or mainstream, culture. As has already been discussed in this theme, children are both victims and perpetrators of this kind of violence or bullying. If such behaviour were to take place outside of the school setting and by those who are over the age of criminal responsibility, there would be legal consequences and official records of these incidents. However, as these occurrences are generally dealt with by the school, there is a lack of understanding of the nature and extent of the problem. This chapter will explore this further using information from a range of sources.

In academic terms, Hate Crime is defined in a number of different ways. Ray (2011) defines hate crime as one in which the victims are chosen because of particular characteristics, for example race, ethnicity, disability, gender, sexuality and religion. Therefore, these crimes are biased towards those with these characteristics, hence this type of crime should be referred to as 'bias crime'. Petrosino (2003, p. 10) takes into consideration the victim in her definition of hate crime; 'the victimisation of minorities due to their racial or ethnic identity by members of the majority'. Sheffield (1995) considers the political element of hate crime and argues that hate crimes are a consequence of the political culture and the right it gives to certain groups of people based on their biological or social characteristics.

Whilst academic definitions of hate crime focus on the characteristics of the victim, official definitions of hate crime focus on the legal aspect of the incident. The Association of Chief Police Officers states that a hate incident is: 'any incident, which may or may not constitute a criminal offence, which is perceived by the victim or any other person, as being motivated by prejudice or hate' (Association of Chief Police Officers, 2005, p. 9). Although the term 'hate' is used, it is argued that the offender targets the victim because they are part of a different social group, and not because they hold any feelings of 'hate' or resentment to them personally (Horvath & Kelly, 2007). It should then be considered that when children are perpetrators of hate crime, it is not because they hold any contempt for their victim, but because they have been conditioned to react in a way to people who are perceived to be different from them. This suggests that children *learn* this behaviour; whom they learn it *from* is important (see chapter 7 by Aznar et al.).

In the UK, there were 52,258 hate crimes recorded by the police in 2014/15 which was an increase on 18% compared with the previous year (Corcoran, Lader, & Smith, 2015). Table 6.1 shows that of these, racist hate crimes make up the largest number of recorded incidents.

This chapter will consider to what extent this apparent rise in hate crime has meant that it has also entered into schools and the classroom. It will also consider the steps being taken in order to prevent hate crime in schools. Firstly, this chapter will explore racist and religious hate crime, focussing on the experience of Asians and Muslim post September 11 2001. It will be argued that the rise of Islamophobia in the national context (Tell MAMMA, 2016) is mirrored in British schools. It will also consider the effect of key incidents in the UK, including the EU referendum in Britain in 2016, and the effect that this has had on hate crime in and around schools. Secondly, this chapter will explore the nature and extent of lesbian, gay, bisexual and transgender (LGBT) bullying in school and this is compared with LGBT hate crime outside of schools. Finally, this chapter will explore how much is known about disability hate crime and its presence in British schools and what measures are in place to combat it. It will be argued that lack of available data on hate crime in schools is the biggest obstacle in understanding this phenomenon.

Table 6.1 Hate crime by type 2014/15

Type of Hate Crime	*Number*	*Percentage of total*
Race Hate	42,930	**82%**
Sexual Orientation Hate	5,597	**11%**
Religious Hate	3,254	**6%**
Disability Hate	2,508	**5%**
Transgender Hate	605	**1%**

Adapted from Corcoran et al. (2015, p. 1)

As we see in chapter 3, legally, state schools are required to have an anti-bullying policy in place which covers prevention and reduction of bullying and they must also adhere to anti-discrimination law (Gov.uk, 2016). This means that they must have policies in place which ensure that all children are not being discriminated against or being targeted because of their race, religion, gender, sex or sexual orientation. However, schools are not required to record all incidents where children have been victims of bullying due to the characteristics mentioned above, which makes it difficult to gauge the extent of the hate crime problem in schools.

Racist and religious hate crime

Official definitions of racism include "conduct or words or practices which disadvantage people because of their colour, culture or ethnic origin. In its more subtle form, it is as damaging as in its overt form" (Macpherson, 1999, p. 20). A racist incident "is any incident which is perceived to be racist by the victim or any other person" (Macpherson, 1999, p. 328). However academic definitions consider both the biological and cultural characteristics of an individual (for example Kundnani, 2001). It is the outward characteristics of an individual that are likely to be targeted in both racist and religiously motivated attacks, which is why both race and religion will be considered in this section with a focus on Islamophobia in the UK. The Department for Children, Schools and Families (2006) conducted a survey of 34,428 pupils and found that almost all of the respondents had been verbally abused because of their ethnicity. What were the reasons behind this?

A number of high profile incidents in the United Kingdom and around the world have formed the hate crime agenda in the UK. Whilst Muslims have been viewed as a threat in the West for centuries, more recently, in the months following the September 11th 2001 attacks in New York there was a fourfold increase in the number of racist and religiously motivated attacks experienced by British Muslims and those who 'appear' to be Muslim, namely Sikhs and Hindus (McGhee, 2005). Furthermore, the 7th July 2005 bombings in London as well as more recent terrorist attacks in Paris have led to the increased suspicion of Muslim communities in the UK. Greer (2012, p. 36) sums up this feeling of suspicion towards British Muslims: "In a post-September 11th world of heightened 'Islamophobia', fear and suspicion of Asian youth are exacerbated by news reports which crudely, but commonly, marry the terms 'Asian' and 'Muslim', on the one hand, and 'Islam' and 'Islamic fundamentalism', on the other".

We now consider to what extent this racism and religious hate has entered schools in the United Kingdom. Tell MAMA (2016), an organisation set up to monitor Islamophobia in the UK, reported a 326% increase in incidents of anti-Muslim hate in 2015 with 11% of incidents taking place in schools or colleges. This increase in Islamophobia in the national context appears to have been mirrored in schools. In 2012–13 the NSPCC (2013) reported a 69% increase in racist bullying with more than 1,400 children contacting them regarding racist incidents compared with 802 in 2011. This included children being called 'terrorist' or a 'bomber' or being told to 'go back home'. What this indicates is that young people are aware of news reports and are picking up on the language being used to describe the perpetrators of terrorist incidents. The rhetoric of the media (e.g. reporting the former Prime Minister David Cameron calling migrants and asylum seekers 'a swarm' (Daily Express, 2015) appears to be present in the classroom.

There have also been reports of an increase in racist and religious hate crime following the outcome of the British EU referendum "Brexit" in June 2016. There have been reports of xenophobic leaflets being distributed outside primary schools and through letterboxes of Polish people living in the UK, telling them to 'go home' (Agerholm, 2016). It must also be added that racism in schools is not only constrained to peer on peer violence. In 2014 a 14-year-old boy was sentenced to 11 years in prison for stabbing his teacher in what was said to be a racially motivated attack (Andrews, 2015). Andrews (2015) argues that it is the culture of allowing racist language in schools, which mirrors that of wider society, which allows such attacks to take place. It is this rhetoric that must be addressed in order to protect young children from becoming victims of racially or religiously motivated hate crimes.

There is also a concern regarding the government's *Prevent* strategy, part of the wider counterterrorism initiative, *Contest*, which, some propose, disproportionately demonises Muslim students. The National Union of Teachers (NUT) argues that *Prevent* inhibits discussion around issues to do with extremism (NUT, 2016). As grooming of potential victims happens outside of school premises, an open discussion of such issues is necessary to combat this (NUT, 2016). Referral data also suggests that out of those referred as part of the *Prevent* initiative between April 2012 and March 2014, 56% were recorded as Muslim; however, Muslims make up just 5% of the UK population (Office for National Statistcs (ONS), 2011). Qurashi (2016) argues that *Prevent* restricts students from openly discussing normal Islamic ideas and cultural practices which could in turn have an effect on the mental well-being of young people. These examples are consistent with Sheffield's (1995) definition of hate crime as discussed earlier in this chapter. This also adds to the growing concern about Muslims and especially young Muslims who are seen as targets for radicalisation, further displaying them as 'different' from 'other' young people.

LGBT hate crime

McManus and Rivers (2001, p. 2) define homophobia as "a fear of same-sex attraction and LGB people. It is directed at people who are or are perceived to be lesbian, gay, bisexual or somehow sexually 'different'". This implies a deep-rooted fear of homosexual people, but as discussed earlier, hate crimes are not necessarily committed because of a hatred, but because victims are perceived to be different from the perpetrator. It can also be argued that perpetrators of homophobic crime are not fearful of the victim, but attack them because of this perceived 'difference' (Tomsen & Mason, 2001). What effect does this has on their mental health and well-being?

The Crime Survey for England and Wales (2013) revealed that in the years 2011/12 and 2012/13 there were an average of 39,000 sexual-orientation hate crimes per year. This is in comparison to just 4267 offences recorded by the police in 2012/13. Some 42% of these crimes involved violence against the person. Stonewall (2013) in The Gay British Crime Survey also revealed a higher number of sexual-orientation-motivated hate crimes than official recorded statistics. They found, based on a sample of 2544 LGB adults, that one in six LGB people had experienced a hate crime in the previous three years and that one in ten victims experienced a physical assault. They also found that more than 75% of victims did not report the crime to the police and two-thirds did not tell anyone that the incident had occurred.

Stonewall (2012) argues that harassment is a part of everyday life for gay men and lesbians and this appears to be the case for pupils who are also LGBT. Stonewall (2012, 2015) reports that 55% of lesbian, gay and bi pupils have been victims of bullying in schools. As with racist and religious hate crime, rhetoric is important, since 99% of gay young people reported hearing the phrases 'that's so gay' or 'you're so gay' in school and 96% reported hearing homophobic language (Stonewall, 2012, 2015). Again, as discussed earlier in this chapter, it must be questioned where this language is being learnt and also where this language is being used in a derogatory way. (See also chapter 4).

As well as verbal bullying and hearing homophobic slurs, almost a third of gay, lesbian and bi pupils reported that they were 'ignored' or 'isolated' by other pupils. This is bullying in the form of social exclusion and can have a direct effect on the mental health of young people. It is not surprising then that 41% of LGB pupils have attempted or contemplated suicide in the past and an equal number have deliberately self-harmed. Stonewall (2012, 2015) also reports that 59% of trans young people had self-harmed compared with 8.9% of all 16–24-year-olds.

Disablist hate crime

Academic definitions of disablism include: "discriminatory, oppressive or abusive behaviour arising from the belief that disabled people are inferior to others" (Miller, Parker, & Gillinson, 2004, p. 28). The Disability Discrimination Act (1994) defines someone as being disabled or having a disability as "someone with 'a physical or mental impairment which has a substantial and long-term adverse effect on his ability to carry out normal day-to-day activities'". Not all disabilities are physical and some may not be able to be seen. This makes this form of hate different from racist and religious hate. The Association of Chief Police Officers (2005, p. 11) define a disablist hate crime as: "Any incident which is perceived to be based upon prejudice towards or hatred of the victim because of their disability or so perceived by the victim or any other person".

Official Police Recorded Statistics in 2012/13 showed just 1814 incidents of hate crime which were motivated by disability; however, the Crime Survey in England and Wales revealed a much higher figure, estimating that in the years 2011/12 and 2012/13 there were around 62,000 incidents of hate crime motivated by disability on average per year. This is a startling difference between official recorded statistics and the CSEW. This suggests that victims are either not confident in reporting the crime to the police or that recording practises of crimes of this nature are not sufficient. Another problem with statistics is that there appear to be no official statistics for disability hate crime in schools. However, a number of studies can be used to gauge the extent of the problem.

Bullying due to disability in schools is commonplace according to a number of studies. MENCAP (2007) report that 56% of children who have a learning disability had cried because of bullying incidents. They also found that a third of children had used the private space of their bedroom in order to hide away from bullying. MENCAP also found that almost half of all children with a learning disability were victims of longer term bullying, some lasting for more than a year. Little (2002) found that more than 90% of parents of children with Asperger's Syndrome reported that their child had been bullied in the previous 12 months. The study found that children with Asperger's Syndrome were likely to be 'shunned' or socially excluded in terms of being invited to birthday parties or having to eat alone at lunch time. What should also be noted is that bullying can be detrimental to the mental health of the victim, as explored earlier in this chapter, and those with existing learning difficulties and mental health disorder may be more susceptible to the negative effects of name-calling and other forms of bullying. This may be why children with learning difficulties retreat to the safety of their bedrooms as a result of being isolated and victimised. MENCAP (2007) found that more than half of children who had a learning disability had been bullied and third of children with learning difficulties hid away in their bedrooms (see also Hebron & Humphrey, 2014).

What is being done to combat hate crime in schools?

In July 2016, the UK government released its updated plan for tackling hate crime entitled *Action Against Hate* (Home Office, 2016). This included measures to tackle hate crime on a national scale and includes initiatives to combat hate crime in schools by challenging the beliefs that lead to hate crime and by giving teachers the tools to engage in discussions around 'difficult' topics. One must wonder how this is going to work in line with the government's *Prevent* strategy (discussed earlier) which inhibits such discussions. Teachers will be provided with resource packs to help facilitate such discussions. The government also plans to conduct an assessment of Islamophobia, anti-Semitic, homophobic and racist bullying in schools, something which is required in order to fully understand the problem of hate crime amongst young people. The plan also includes an assessment on the level of hate crime in schools which may help in understanding the true extent of the problem. However, there still does not appear to be any guidance on reporting hate crime incidents in schools which will continue to hinder the understanding of the nature and extent of the problem. Whilst schools should be responsible for hate crimes that happen within the school setting, they have relatively fewer powers to challenge ideas and attitudes in the home setting. As demonstrated in this chapter, hate crime incidents in the UK are rising and this may be due to a growing distorted extremist sense of national identity; if this is transmitted to young people in the home, then combatting this in the classroom will be an even more difficult task. Myers (chapter 3) argues that criminalising young people is not the way forward, and whilst I agree, in order to fully understand the nature and extent that 'hate' has entered into schools, records of violent incidents in schools where race, religion, gender, disability and sexuality have been a motivating factor should be kept. This would allow us to understand the nature and extent of the problem. Schools should be allowed to deal with such incidents without referring children to the police, but require training in order to do so. Restorative practices may prove to be helpful in these situations. The victim would be able to explain the affect the incident has had on them and the perpetrator would gain some understanding of the harm caused. Research suggests that restorative practices are effective at reducing incidents of bullying (for example, London Borough of Barnet, 2008) and that restorative practices are viewed favourably by schools in the UK (Department for Education, 2014).

Conclusion

A number of conclusions can be drawn from this chapter regarding the various types of hate crime discussed. Firstly, the striking lack of information around the nature and extent of hate crime in schools makes it difficult to accurately paint a picture of the problem. From the information presented in this chapter, it can be concluded that national trends in hate crime influence peer on peer hate crime and bullying in schools in all aspects of hate crime. It can be deduced from this that young people are learning the rhetoric and culture of hate, which creates an 'otherness' of those who are perceived to be 'different'. Whether they are learning this from the media or from other influences in their lives remains to be seen and further research into this area is needed. It can also be concluded that hate crime in schools is having a negative effect on the mental health and well-being of pupils; as discussed earlier, some victims of disablist hate crime are hiding away in the privacy and safety of their rooms whilst victims of LGBT hate crimes are more likely to self-harm. This is clearly a problem that needs to be addressed through open dialogue and educational programmes.

A number of recommendations can be made based on these findings. Firstly, government initiatives to reduce hate crime incidents in schools should be adhered to in order to provide the correct preventative measures but there must also be procedures in place to record the nature of bullying incidents in order to accurately represent the problem. Without a full understanding of the problem, there is unlikely to be a solution. Secondly, restorative practices should be used in order to help the perpetrator to understand the harm caused by these incidents and to help the victim recover from them. Finally, as it is clear that incidents of hate which occur in our school are as common as they are outside of schools, reducing the number of hate crimes nationally would help to reduce hate crimes in schools.

References

Agerholm, H. (2016). Brexit: Wave of hate crime and racial abuse reported following EU referendum. *Independent Online*. 26th June 2016. Retrieved from www.independent.co.uk/news/uk/home-news/brexit-eu-referendum-racial-racism-abuse-hate-crime-reported-latest-leave-immigration-a7104191.html (accessed 30 September 2016).

Andrews, K. (2015). Why Britain's schools are failing to tackle racism. *Guardian Online*, 12th August 2015 [Online]. Retrieved from www.theguardian.com/commentisfree/2015/aug/12/racism-schools-government-reforms-targets (accessed 30 September 2016).

Association of Chief Police Officers. (2005). *Hate crime: Delivering a quality service, good practise and tactical guidance, home office police standards unit*. Retrieved from www.bedfordshire.police.uk/pdf/tacticalguidance.pdf (accessed 1 September 2016).

Corcoran, H., Lader, D., & Smith, K. (2015). *Hate crime, England and Wales 2014/15: Statistical bulletin 05/15*, London: Home Office. Retrieved from www.gov.uk/government/uploads/system/uploads/attachment_data/file/467366/hosb0515.pdf (accessed 1 July 2016).

Daily Express. (2015). Swarms of migrants are the norm in the UK in 2015. *Express Online*, 28th August 2015. Retrieved from www.express.co.uk/comment/expresscomment/601512/Swarms-migrants-are-the-norm-the-UK-2015?_ga=1.90213849.294594533.1469877790 (accessed 30 September 2016).

Department for Education. (2014). *Preventing and tackling bullying: Advice for headteachers, staff and governing bodies*, October 2014. Retrieved from www.restorativejustice.org.uk/sites/default/files/resources/files/Preventing%20and%20tackling%20bullying.pdf (accessed 30 September 2016).

Gov.UK. (2016). *Bullying at school*. Retrieved from www.gov.uk/bullying-at-school/the-law (Last updated 23 September 2016; accessed 30 September 2016).

Greer, C. (2012). News media, victims and crime. In P. Davies, P. Francis, & C. Greer (Eds.), *Victims, crime and society*. London: Sage.

Hebron, J. S., & Humphrey, N. (2014). Exposure to bullying among students with autism spectrum conditions: A multi-informant analysis of risk and protective factors. *Autism*, *18*, 618–630.

Home Office. (2016). *Action against hate: The UK Government's plan for tackling hate crime*, July 2016. Retrieved from www.gov.uk/government/uploads/system/uploads/attachment_data/file/543679/Action_Against_Hate_-_UK_Government_s_Plan_to_Tackle_Hate_Crime_2016.pdf (accessed 1 October 2016).

Horvath, M., & Kelly, L. (2007). *From the outset: Why violence should be a priority for the commission for equality and human rights – Ending violence against women*. London: London Metropolitan University.

Kundnani, A. (2001). In a foreign land: The new popular racism. *Race and Class*, *43*(2), 41–60.

Little, L. (2002). 'Middle-class mothers' perceptions of peer and sibling victimisation among children with Asperger's syndrome and non-verbal learning disorders. *Issues in Comprehensive Paediatric Nursing, 25*(1), 43–57.

London Borough of Barnet. (2008). *Restorative approaches in primary schools: An evaluation of the project co-ordinated by the Barnet Youth Offending Service.* Barnet. Retrieved from www.restorativejustice.org.uk/sites/default/files/resources/files/Restorative%20Approaches%20in%20Primary%20Schools%20An%20Evaluation%20of%20the%20Project%20Co-ordinated%20by%20the%20Barnet%20Youth%20Offending%20Service.pdf (accessed 30 September 2016).

McManus, J. & Rivers, I. (2001). *Without Prejudice.* London: NACRO

McGhee, D. (2005). *Intolerant Britain? Hate, citizenship and difference.* Berkshire: Open University Press.

MENCAP. (2007). *Bullying wrecks lives: The experiences of children and young people with a learning disability.* London: Mencap.

Miller, P., Parker, S., & Gillinson, S. (2004). *Disablism: How to tackle the last prejudice.* London: Demos [Online]. Retrieved from www.demos.co.uk/files/disablism.pdf (accessed 30 September 2016).

Nation Society for the Prevention of Cruelty to Children (NSPCC) (2013). How Safe Are Our Children? London: NSPCC

National Union of Teachers. (2016). *Prevent strategy: NUT Conference 2016.* Retrieved from www.teachers.org.uk/news-events/conference-2016/prevent-strategy (accessed 1 September 2016).

Office for National Statistic. (2013). *An overview of hate crime in England and Wales.* Home Office, Office for National Statistics and Ministry of Justice. Retrieved from www.gov.uk/government/uploads/system/uploads/attachment_data/file/266358/hate-crime-2013.pdf (accessed 30 September 2016).

Petrosino, C. (2003). Connecting the past to the future: Hate crime in America. In B. Perry (Ed.), *Hate crime and bias crime: A reader.* London: Routledge.

Qurashi, F. (2016). Prevent gives people permission to hate Muslims – It has no place in schools. *Guardian Online*, 4th April 2016. Retrieved from www.theguardian.com/commentisfree/2016/apr/04/prevent-hate-muslims-schools-terrorism-teachers-reject (accessed 1 July 2016).

Ray, L. (2011). *Violence and society.* London: Sage.

Sheffield, C. (1995). Hate violence. In P. Rothenburg (Ed.), *Race, class and gender in the United States.* New York: St. Martins Press.

Stonewall. (2012). *The school report: The experiences of gay young people in Britain's schools in 2012.* Stonewall. Retrieved from www.stonewall.org.uk/sites/default/files/The_School_Report__2012_.pdf (accessed 30 September 2016).

Stonewall. (2013). *Homophobic hate crime: The gay British crime survey 2013.* Stonewall. Retrieved from www.stonewall.org.uk/sites/default/files/Homophobic_Hate_Crime_2013_.pdf (accessed 30 September 2016).

Stonewall. (2015). *Unhealthy attitudes: The treatment of LGBT people within health and social care services.* Stonewall. Retrieved from www.stonewall.org.uk/sites/default/files/unhealthy_attitudes.pdf (accessed 30 September 2016).

Tell MAMMA. (2016). *The geography of anti-Muslim hatred: Tell MAMA annual report 2015.* Faith Matters, London. Retrieved from http://tellmamauk.org/wp-content/uploads/pdf/tell_mama_2015_annual_report.pdf (accessed 5 September 2016).

Tomsen, S., & Mason, G. (2001). Engendering homophobia: Violence, sexuality and gender conformity. *Journal of Sociology, 37*(3), 257–273.

Chapter 7

Bullying of religious minorities and asylum seekers

Ana Aznar, Harriet R. Tenenbaum and Martin D. Ruck

Introduction

In the final week of July 2016, the UK saw a 57% increase in xenophobic abuse *as reported widely in the national press.* Although the level of overt abuse is unprecedented, the attitudes underlying such abuse are not new. In this chapter, we are particularly focussed on how such attitudes may affect the bullying of asylum seeking and religious minority children, who typically come from ethnic and religious minority immigrant backgrounds.

Bullying, also known as peer victimisation or peer harassment (we follow the terminology used by authors of articles discussed) is an instrumental form of aggression, used to gain or keep a prominent position in a peer group and obtain higher levels of resource control (Peeters, Cillessen, & Scholte, 2010; Sijtsema, Veenstra, Lindenberg, & Salmivalli, 2009). Bullies use direct, indirect, physical, and relational aggression, including exclusion, physical and/or verbal violence (Olweus, 2012). Thus, bullying includes diverse acts ranging from racist name-calling (Whitney & Smith, 1993) to social exclusion and rejection (Boivin & Hymel, 1997; Salmivalli, Lagerspetz, Bjorkqvist, Osterman, & Kaukiainen, 1996).

What distinguishes bullying from typical conflict between peers is that there must be a power imbalance between the victim and perpetrator (Olweus, 2012). This power differential may stem from physical size, psychological, socioeconomic, or other factors. In relation to ethnicity, research from peer relations suggests that differences in ethnicity may also create power differentials (Cohen, Lotan, & Catanzarite, 1990).

Negative attitudes toward immigrants, ethnic and religious minorities, asylum seekers, and non-UK nationals are not uncommon amongst English children (Abrams, Rutland, Pelletier, & Ferrell, 2009; Cameron & Rutland, 2008; Cameron, Rutland, Brown, & Douch, 2006; MacDonald, Bhavnani, Khan, & John, 1989) or elsewhere. Indeed, English children prefer members of their own national group and show bias towards some outgroups by age 10 (Rutland, 1999). Similarly, Dutch adolescents are less tolerant of Muslim than non-Muslim residents wishing to set up religious schools or to hold a political demonstration (Verkuyten & Slooter, 2007, 2008). In addition, over a third of the Dutch adolescents were not accepting of Muslims' religious practices such as the wearing of a headscarf.

Not surprisingly, individuals also hold negative attitudes towards refugee and asylum seeking children. It has been reported that majority group members, and young people in particular, when given the opportunity, deny rights to members of minority groups, and hold negative attitudes toward asylum seekers (Cameron & Rutland, 2008; Ruck & Tenenbaum, 2014; Tenenbaum & Ruck, 2012). More specifically, British young people believed that asylum-seeking youth should not have the right to decide whether they should carry identification cards or choose where to live, rights that are routinely granted to the majority group (Ruck & Tenenbaum, 2014; Tenenbaum & Ruck, 2012). These findings suggest that British young people perceive themselves differently from the asylum-seeker population. Moreover, British adolescents rated their refugee peers more negatively than they did their British counterparts (Cameron & Rutland, 2008; Cameron et al., 2006). Such attitudes can easily give rise to different types of bullying, such as peer victimisation.

Past research on peer victimisation of ethnic minority young people also helps inform our thinking about the likelihood of bullying of these groups. However, these findings have been somewhat equivocal. For instance, when looking at bullying more generally, several studies have not found an increased risk of bullying for immigrant youth in Canada (McKenney, Pepler, Craig, & Connolly, 2006) or Austria (Strohmeier & Spiel, 2003). Similarly, there was no increased risk found for African-American or Latino/a children compared to White majority children in the US (Hanish & Guerra, 2001). Finally, in the Netherlands, ethnic minority children were less likely to be victimised than ethnic majority children after controlling for the ethnic composition of classrooms (Vervoort, Scholte, & Overbeek, 2010). In contrast, Strohmeir, Karna, and Salmivalli (2011) reported that first and second generation immigrant children were more likely than their native Finnish counterparts to suffer peer victimisation.

When examining ethnic peer victimization, in contrast, Monks, Ortega-Ruiz, and Rodriguez-Hidalgo (2008) found that ethnic minority children in England and Spain suffered more cultural verbal abuse (name-calling and exclusion based on ethnicity) than their ethnic majority counterparts with more than a third of the minority groups reporting such abuse. Similarly, in the Netherlands, racist name-calling and social exclusion is more common for children from Turkish, Surinamese and Moroccan backgrounds than those from Dutch backgrounds (Verkuyten & Thijs, 2002). Thus, it seems that although general bullying may not be increased for immigrant or ethnic minority children, ethnic peer victimisation may be elevated for these groups compared to their majority counterparts.

As noted above, social exclusion on the basis of group membership is another type of bullying. Children from ethnic (Killen & Stangor, 2001) and religious

(Abbotts, Williams, Sweeting, & West, 2004) minority backgrounds tend to be more at risk of suffering social exclusion than their mainstream counterparts (Killen, Mulvey, & Hitti, 2013). This is because intergroup attitudes and bias can influence children's chances of being bullied. However, both Swiss and non-Swiss children rated exclusion based on nationality as less legitimate than exclusion based on gender and personality traits. Nonetheless, non-Swiss children viewed exclusion based on nationality as less legitimate than their mainstream counterparts (Malti, Killen, & Gasser, 2012). Similarly, Møller and Tenenbaum (2011) found that Danish children thought it was worse to exclude a child from a Muslim religious background than one from a Danish majority background. Others, however, have found increased rejection of refugee children. For example, Dutch preadolescents rejected asylum seekers more frequently than their Moroccan counterparts. Rejection of asylum seekers was stronger the closer the participants lived near a centre for asylum seekers (Verkuyten & Steenhuis, 2005). In sum, the findings suggest that there may be increased risk for religious minority and asylum seekers to suffer from social exclusion, but the findings are equivocal.

The present study

The present study examines how children reason about the social exclusion of religious minority asylum seekers. As mentioned, social exclusion is a type of bullying. We specifically focussed on the reasoning of young people in the UK about asylum seekers because of the growing political and public concern associated with the asylum seeker population, many of whom come from Muslim backgrounds (International Business Times, 2016).

Our literature review suggests that religious minorities and asylum seekers might also be at a higher risk of being bullied than their mainstream counterparts. We consider bullying as a group process in which the bully (a high status figure) gains or maintains social power by intentionally inflicting harm in the victim (a low status figure). We focussed on young people's evaluation of the exclusion and rights of Muslim asylum seekers to examine more general attitudes toward this group.

Method

Participants

Participants were ten children (seven boys; three girls) between the ages of ten and 15 years. All children lived in the London metropolitan area (UK) and came from middle to upper middle-class backgrounds. A snowball technique was used to recruit participants. All were of white ethnic majority. Participants were recruited on a volunteer basis. All parents signed an informed consent form and children gave assent.

Materials and procedure

Based on Killen, Henning, Kelly, Crystal, and Ruck (2007), participants were read three hypothetical vignettes in which a child who is a Muslim asylum seeker is excluded. The three vignettes included a peer (friends going to the cinema), home (family party) and school (inviting a date to the school dance) contexts. The protagonists were matched to participants' gender. After the presentation of each vignette, participants were asked to evaluate how good or bad it was to exclude the target individual. Next, participants were asked to rate how good or bad it was to exclude the target individual because he/she was a Muslim asylum seeker and explain their judgement. For example, for the family context:

> Rachel/Mike is celebrating her birthday party at home. She/He wants to invite her/his friend, Fatimah/Mohammed who is a Muslim asylum seeker but she/he decides against it because she/he doesn't know if her/his parents would agree. How good or bad is it to exclude Fatimah/Mohammed? Why do you think that? How good or bad is it to exclude Fatimah/Mohammed because she/he is a Muslim asylum seeker? Why do you think that?

Next, participants were read six vignettes about the rights of Muslim asylum seekers, based on Tenenbaum and Ruck (2012). In these vignettes children were asked to decide whether Muslim asylum seekers should be allowed to have the same rights as British residents (e.g. right to housing, right to be educated, right to be granted asylum, right to access the National Health System). For each statement participants were asked to provide a justification for their response. For instance: "Fatimah is a Muslim asylum seeker who attends a school in London. Should she be allowed to wear her headscarf to school? Why?"

Recorded interviews took place in participants' homes and were conducted by the first author.

Transcription and coding

The interviews were transcribed verbatim and analysed qualitatively. We chose this type of analysis because it is an effective method to develop a good understanding of the culture underlying the group processes of bullying (Thornberg, 2011).

Results and discussion

Thematic analysis, which is the widest used form of analysis for qualitative data (Guest, Namey, & Mitchell, 2012), was conducted on the data set to identify and establish patterns in children's reasoning. To do so, we followed the steps as designed by Braun and Clarke (2006). Firstly, all interviews were transcribed verbatim. Secondly, each transcript was read through at least twice and provisional codes were generated based on topics that were recurrent. Third, the codes were compared and contrasted to create potential themes. Next, transcripts were read again and compared with the themes to establish that all identified themes were representative of the whole data set. Finally, themes were operationally defined and named. Seven themes emerged from this analysis: 1) empathy; 2) getting to know the person; 3) importance of parents' opinions; 4) fairness and practicality; 5) importance of friends' opinions; 6) mistrust and stereotypes; and 7) negative experiences and consequences. The interviews were then read again in light of the themes by the second author. Below we provide extracts from the transcripts to demonstrate the existence of these themes.

The first two themes, *empathy* and *getting to know the person*, suggest that some children would not show negativity towards Muslim asylum seekers.

Empathy

Some participants made reference to the feelings of the Muslim asylum seeker child should she or he be rejected. A 13-year-old girl explained, "Because then Munirah will feel lonely and upset, she needs to make friends because she is in a new country so they should let her join the group."

Getting to know the person

Many participants believed that it is important to get to know the Muslim asylum seeker child. For example, a 10-year-old boy explained "If Sam's friends don't know Ahmed they could get to know him a little bit better because he could be really nice but because he is from a different country and from a different religion they don't know him that much".

Some participants argued that it is good to get to know the Muslim asylum seeker child because you can have fun together and because he or she might help you in the future if you help them now. A 12-year-old boy said, "Because if we take them now and we get to know them maybe if England is at war they would take us as refugees because they owe us."

The following two themes, *Importance of Parents' Opinions* and *Fairness and Practicality*, were more mixed in the valence directed toward Muslim asylum-seekers.

Importance of parents' opinions

Participants also discussed whether parents should have the right to decide who you should be allowed to invite to your home and whether children should follow their parents' advice and opinions. The majority of the children interviewed believed that although parents should have the right to decide who they can invite to their home, they should also trust their children's judgments and get to know the person before making a decision.

A 13-year-old girl mentioned, "It is very bad if Rachel's parents don't want to invite her (Fatimah) because she is a Muslim but the parents have the right to decide whether she can invite Fatimah or not."

Fairness and practicality

The majority of participants suggested that Muslim asylum seekers should not be excluded and should be treated like their British peers because they all are the same. Children argued that both British and Muslim asylum seekers are human beings and as such they should all be treated fairly and equally. For example, a 10-year-old boy said, "Everyone is a human being, so Ahmed should be allowed to play because he is a human being like the others". Similarly, one 11-year-old boy argued, "It doesn't really matter what kind of religion you have because . . . because we are all humans at the end of the day".

Many participants reasoned that Muslim asylum seekers should not be excluded because they are not different from their British counterparts. However, when reasoning about their rights, participants did not believe that Muslim asylum seekers should have the same rights as they did. For example, when asked if a Muslim asylum seeker child should have the right to have surgery in the NHS, a 12-year-old boy replied: "It depends if they don't pay taxes then no, because the NHS is for people who pay taxes and if he gets surgery then the people who are paying taxes will get annoyed."

When asked if a Muslim asylum seeker child should have the right to go to school in the UK, a 13-year-old boy explained "I don't strongly agree because if he has just come to London you don't know how his family is, they might be at war or something." Or when asked if a Muslim asylum seeker child should be accepted as a refugee, a 14-year-old girl said, "There is so many people like Fatimah that we cannot help everyone. . . . It depends on the housing, the amount of food we have."

These two final examples about the rights of Muslim asylum seeker children seem to indicate that although negative attitudes toward Muslim asylum seekers may be more muted, many participants believed that the opinions and the needs of the majority group are more important and should prevail over the needs of the Muslim asylum seeker children.

Importance of friends' opinions

Participants were divided in their views as to whether they should worry or not about their friends' opinions. Some participants argued that friends' opinions are not important and that they should not influence the way one behaves or thinks. For example, a 14-year-old girl explained, "Because he (George, a British boy) shouldn't care about what his friends think and Jadiyah (a Muslim asylum seeker girl) could be very nice".

In contrast, other participants believed that friends' opinions are important and that they could influence one's opinions and behaviours. One 10-year-old boy indicated that, "George (a British boy) should care about what his friends think because if he does invite her (Jadiyah, a Muslim asylum seeker), and his friends oppose and they didn't want her to come they might say bad things about her".

This theme may have implications for bullying because children who do not conform to peer pressure might be less likely to support a bully and might be more likely to defend the victim should they found themselves in such a situation. For example, Rigby and Johnson (2006) found that 11– and 13-year-old children were more likely to help victims of bullying when they believed that their peers expected them to do so.

The final two themes, *Mistrust and Stereotypes* and *Negative Experiences and Consequences*, suggest that some participants were worried because of the lack of knowledge and understanding that they have of Muslim asylum seekers as a group. This finding is consistent with Allport's (1954) intergroup contact hypothesis, which posits that prejudice and discrimination are consequences of unfamiliarity with the outgroup. Extensive research suggests that prejudice and bias can be reduced through positive contact between members of different groups (Pettigrew, Tropp, Wagner, & Christ, 2011).

Mistrust and stereotypes

Some participants made reference to negative stereotypes associated sometimes with Muslims. An 11-year-old explained, "Because maybe you don't like Muslims because of something that you have heard or something like that, for example, wars. There are Muslim people who are in wars so maybe you don't want to be friends with them if their parents are at war or something like that."

They also suggested that it is difficult to trust people who you don't know or people who might be very different from you. When asked whether the family of the Muslim asylum seeker's child should have the right to live in government-provided housing in the UK, an 11-year-old boy stated, "No, because they (the state) can trust better those who live here".

Negative experiences and consequences

An 11-year-old boy argued, "Because if she does it (wear the headscarf) she probably won't stop wearing it (the headscarf) because she obviously she might not have enough friends and she might have like a different skin colour so people might start making fun of her so yeah."

Conclusion

The present study examined young people's reasoning about the exclusion of Muslim asylum seekers and the rights Muslim asylum seeker children should be granted as way of understanding attitudes towards this group. Participants were very mixed in their reasoning about Muslim asylum seeker children. Many of them argued that Muslim asylum seekers deserve fair treatment and should be treated in the same way as their British counterparts. These children's responses suggest that in some situations, this group may not experience an increased risk of being bullied more generally (Hanish & Guerra, 2001; McKenney et al., 2006; Strohmeier & Spiel, 2003).

Although many participants demonstrated positive attitudes, some did not. Indeed, a number of participants also displayed prejudice and referred to negative stereotypes about Muslim asylum seekers. Participants argued that they did not know what Muslim asylum seekers were like, and as a consequence were distrustful. In this way, the participants demonstrated ingroup biases. Bullying of ethnic minority children is more likely to take place in school settings when ethnic majority classmates evidence higher ingroup bias (Thijs & Verkuyten, 2014). Thus, intergroup processes in which one favours one's ingroup can lead to bullying of ethnic minority children (Schuman, Craig, & Rosu, 2013). Moreover, as we indicated earlier, bullying occurs as a result of a power imbalance between individuals or groups. Indeed, in the school setting, ethnicity may serve as a status variable (Cohen et al., 1990), and as a consequence, ethnic minority asylum seekers may be more likely to become victims if they are a numerical minority in classrooms (Thijs & Verkuyten, 2014). Finally, given that ethnic peer victimisation is elevated for ethnic minorities (Monks et al., 2008; Thijs et al., 2014; Verkuyten & Thijs, 2002), we would expect to see increased name-calling and social exclusion of these groups in peer or school settings.

Another prominent theme was the role of parents and friends. A recent meta-analysis found that children's and parents' attitudes are related throughout childhood and adolescence (Degner & Dalege, 2013). Although some children argued that parents' attitudes should not prevent the story characters from befriending Muslim asylum seekers, children's own behaviours may be closely aligned with their parents' attitudes whether these attitudes are positive or negative.

In addition to parents, friends increasingly play a prominent role in children's lives (Harris, 1995). Although the older child quoted in the results section argues that one should not listen to friends when they wish to exclude someone, research with larger samples finds that 15-year-olds perceive peer exclusion as more acceptable than 9– year-olds (Killen, Lee-Kim, McGlothlin, & Stangor, 2002) or 12-year-olds (Killen et al., 2002; Malti et al., 2012). These differences may arise because adolescents begin to weigh up considerations of group functioning and ingroup loyalty (Killen & Rutland, 2011) and have a greater understanding of group nous than younger children (Abrams et al., 2009). Thus, friends may play a pivotal role in children's peer groups and the specific role a child may play in a bullying situation.

In sum, the findings from the study conducted for this chapter suggest that some children from majority backgrounds may have prejudiced attitudes towards religious minorities and asylum seekers. One limitation of this study is that we did not examine how attitudes towards religious minority and asylum seeking children predict different types of bullying in the classroom and in peer groups. Only through an understanding of the root causes of such bullying, can we find ways of preventing the bullying of children who have already suffered trauma. We also need to find ways of teaching children to accept others from different backgrounds so that we can foster the emotional well-being of all children.

Acknowledgement

We would like to thank Leverhulme for funding the project.

References

Abbotts, J. E., Williams, R. G., Sweeting, H. N., & West, P. B. (2004). Is going to church good or bad for you? Denomination, attendance and mental health of children in West Scotland. *Social Science & Medicine, 58*(3), 645–656.

Abrams, D., Rutland, A., Pelletier, J., & Ferrell, J. M. (2009). Children's group nous: Understanding and applying peer exclusion within and between groups. *Child Development, 80*(1), 224–243.

Allport, G. W. (1954). *The nature of prejudice.* New York: Doubleday Anchor Books.

Boivin, M., & Hymel, S. (1997). Peer experiences and social self-perceptions: A sequential model. *Developmental Psychology, 33*(1), 135–145.

Braun, V., & Clarke, V. (2006). Using thematic analysis in psychology. *Qualitative Research in Psychology, 3*(2), 77–101.

Cameron, L., & Rutland, A. (2008). An integrative approach to changing children's intergroup attitudes. In S. Levy & M. Killen (Eds.), *Intergroup attitudes and relations in childhood through adulthood* (pp. 191–203). Oxford, UK: Oxford University Press.

Cameron, L., Rutland, A., Brown, R., & Douch, R. (2006). Changing children's intergroup attitudes toward refugees: Testing different models of extended contact. *Child Development,* 77(5), 1208–1219.

Cohen, E. G., Lotan, R., & Catanzarite, L. (1990). Treating status problems in the cooperative classroom. In S. Sharan (Ed.), *Cooperative learning: Theory and research* (pp. 203–230). New York: Praeger.

Degner, J., & Dalege, J. (2013). The apple does not fall far from the tree, or does it? A meta-analysis of parent-child similarity in intergroup attitudes. *Psychological Bulletin, 139*(6), 1270–1304.

Guest, G., Namey, E. E., & Mitchell, M. L. (2012). *Collecting qualitative data: A field manual for applied research.* London: Sage.

Hanish, L. D., & Guerra, N. G. (2001). The roles of ethnicity and school context in predicting children's victimization by peers. *American Journal of Community Psychology, 28*(2), 201–223.

Harris, J. R. (1995). Where the child's environment? A group socialization theory of development. *Psychological Review, 102*(3), 458–489.

International Business Times. *In 2016, Muslim population is more than 3M, expected to rise with more asylum seekers.* New York: Jess McHugh.

Killen, M., Henning, A., Kelly, M. C., Crystal, D., & Ruck, M. (2007). Evaluations of interracial peer encounters by majority and minority US children and adolescents. *International Journal of Behavioural Development, 31*(50), 491–500.

Killen, M., Lee-Kim, J., McGlothlin, H., & Stangor, C. (2002). How children and adolescents evaluate gender and racial exclusion. *Monographs of the Society for the Research in Child Development, 67*(4), serial no. 271.

Killen, M., Mulvey, K. L., & Hitti, A. (2013). Social exclusion in childhood: A developmental intergroup perspective. *Child Development, 84*(3), 772–790.

Killen, M., & Rutland, A. (2011). *Children and social exclusion: Morality, prejudice, and group identity.* New York: Wiley-Blackwell.

Killen, M., & Stangor, C. (2001). Children's social reasoning about inclusion and exclusion in gender and race peer group contexts. *Child Development, 72*(1), 174–186.

MacDonald, I., Bhavnani, R., Khan, L., & John, G. (1989). *Murder in the playground: The report in the Macdonald inquiry into racism and racial violence in Manchester schools.* London: Longsight.

Malti, T., Killen, M., & Gasser, L. (2012). Social judgements and emotion attributions about exclusion in Switzerland. *Child Development, 83*(2), 697–711.

McKenney, K. S., Pepler, D., Craig, W., & Connolly, J. (2006). Peer victimization and psychosocial adjustment: The experiences of Canadian immigrant youth. *Electronic Journal of Research in Educational Psychology, 9*(4), 239–264.

Merrell, K. W., Gueldner, B. A., Ross, S. W., & Isava, D. M. (2008). How effective are school bullying intervention programmes? A meta-analysis of intervention research. *School Psychology Quarterly, 23*(1), 26–42.

Møller S. J., & Tenenbaum H.R. (2011) 'Danish Majority Children's Reasoning About Exclusion Based on Gender and Ethnicity'. Wiley *Child Development*, 82 (2), pp. 520–532.

Monks, C. P., Ortega-Ruiz, R., & Rodriguez-Hidalgo, A. J. (2008). Peer victimization in multicultural schools in Spain and England. *European Journal of Developmental Psychology, 5*(4), 507–535.

Olweus, D. (2012). Invited expert discussion paper cyberbullying: An overrated phenomenon? *European Journal of Developmental Psychology, 9*(5), 520–538.

Peeters, M., Cillessen, A. H., & Scholte, R. H. (2010). Clueless or powerful? Identifying subtypes of bullies in adolescence. *Journal of Youth and Adolescence, 39*(9), 1041–1052.

Pettigrew, T. F., Tropp, L. R., Wagner, U., & Christ, O. (2011). Recent advances in intergroup contact theory. *International Journal of Intercultural Relations, 35*(3), 271–280.

Rigby, K., & Johnson, B. (2006). Expressed readiness of Australian schoolchildren to act as bystanders in support of children who are being bullied. *Educational Psychology, 26*(3), 425–440.

Ruck, M. D., & Tenenbaum, H. R. (2014). Does moral and social conventional reasoning predict British young people's judgments about the rights of asylum-seeker youth? *Journal of Social Issues, 70*(1), 47–62.

Rutland, A. (1999). The development of national prejudice, in-group favouritism and self-stereotypes in British children. *British Journal of Social Psychology, 38*(1), 55–70.

Salmivalli, C., Lagerspetz, K., Bjorkqvist, K., Osterman, K., & Kaukiainen, A. (1996). Bullying as a group process: Participant roles and their relations to social status within the group. *Aggressive Behaviour, 22*(1), 1–15.

Schuman, L., Craig, W., & Rosu, A. (2013). Minority in the majority: Community ethnicity as a context for racial bullying and victimization. *Journal of Community Psychology, 41*(8), 959–972.

Sijtsema, J. J., Veenstra, R., Lindenberg, S., & Salmivalli, C. (2009). Empirical test of bullies' status goals: Assessing direct goals, aggression, and prestige. *Aggressive Behaviour, 35*(1), 57–67.

Strohmeir, D., Karna, A., & Salmivalli, C. (2011). Intrapersonal and interpersonal risk factors for peer victimization in immigrant youth in Finland. *Developmental Psychology, 47*(1), 248–258.

Strohmeier, D., & Spiel, C. (2003). Immigrant children in Austria: Aggressive behaviour and friendship patterns in multicultural school classes. *Journal of Applied School Psychology, 19*(2), 99–116.

Tenenbaum, H. R., & Ruck, M. D. (2012). British adolescents' and young adults' understanding and reasoning about the religious and nonreligious rights of asylum-seeker youth. *Child Development, 83*(3), 1102–1115.

Thijs, J., & Verkuyten, M. (2014). School ethnic diversity and students' interethnic relations. *British Journal of Educational Psychology, 84*(1), 1–21.

Thornberg, R. (2011). She's weird! The social construction of bullying in school: A review of qualitative research. *Children & Society, 25*(4), 258–267.

Verkuyten, M., & Slooter, L. (2007). Tolerance of Muslim beliefs and practices: Age related differences and context effects. *International Journal of Behavioural Development, 31*(5), 467–477.

Verkuyten, M., & Slooter, L. (2008). Muslim and Non-muslim adolescents' reasoning about freedom of speech and minority rights. *Child Development, 79*(3), 514–528.

Verkuyten, M., & Steenhuis, A. (2005). Preadolescents' understanding and reasoning about asylum seeker peers and friendships. *Applied Developmental Psychology, 26*(6), 660–679.

Verkuyten, M., & Thijs, J. (2002). Racist victimization among children in the Netherlands: The effect of ethnic group and school. *Ethnic and Racial Studies, 25*(2), 310–331.

Vervoort, M. H. M., Scholte, R. H. J., & Overbeek, G. (2010). Bullying and victimization among adolescents: The role of ethnicity and ethnic composition of school. *Journal of Youth and Adolescence, 39*(1), 1–11.

Whitney, I., & Smith, P. K. (1993). A survey of the nature and extent of bullying in junior/middle and secondary schools. *Educational Research, 35*(1), 3–25.

Theme 3

Bullying

Its impact on emotional health and well-being

There are many negative consequences for the targets of bullying, such as long-term psychological problems, including increased levels of anxiety, depressive symptoms, poor self-worth, social isolation and loneliness, psychosomatic complaints, suicidal ideation and suicide attempts. In chapter 8, Luca discusses the role of the counsellor in providing emotional support for the victims of bullying and highlights the long-term consequences for the adult of being bullied at a young age. Research, however, demonstrates that there must also be a focus on the mental health of those who bully and attention given to their psychological needs. This aspect of bullying is often neglected but perpetrators of bullying have been found to be at heightened risk of anxiety, depression, psychosomatic symptoms and eating disorders, psychosocial problems, externalising behaviours and anti-social behaviour. Bully-victims are at the greatest risk for adversity. Cowie and Collliety, in chapter 9, discuss the mental health difficulties of children and young people who bully their peers. The research literature is beginning to explore the role of the family in bullying. Specifically, Giovazolias and Malikiosi-Loizos, in chapter 10, provide original data on the moderating effect of father acceptance in the relationship between bullying/victimisation and the presence of depressive symptoms in school-age children.

Chapter 8

The bullied child in the vulnerable adult

Therapeutic work with adults bullied in childhood

Maria Luca

Introduction

This chapter explores the vulnerabilities developed through childhood maltreatment, reinforced through bullying at school and manifested in mental health problems in adulthood. A brief review of the literature on bullying and mental health provides the context and foundation in understanding the negative impact of bullying on children and adolescents and, through clinical scenarios, highlights its long-term psychological effects. The chapter concludes with a summary on the consequences of childhood trauma and bullying on mental health.

Bullying is characterised by (1) aggressive behaviour or intentional harm-doing that is (2) carried out repeatedly over time in (3) an interpersonal relationship characterized by an imbalance of power. This aggressive behaviour may be verbal, physical or relational. Whereas verbal aggression is common among both girls and boys, physical aggression and taking of personal belongings tend to occur more frequently among boys, and rejection or isolation is more common among girls (Olweus, 1997; Olweus et al., 1999). The media have been recently reporting cases of bullying, particularly sexting and baiting out videos involving sexual domination, a form of bullying exercised mostly by young boys (Luca, M. Sky News, 25/03/2016, p. 11:42). These and other types of bullying have detrimental effects on young people's mental health. "Research indicates that victims of bullying constitute two distinct groups of children. On the one hand, pure victims are solely targets of bullies, and on the other hand, bully-victims are both victims of bullying and bully others. Findings show that these two groups have distinct risk factors and outcomes, with bully-victims being exposed to more risk factors than victims and showing the worst mental health outcomes in childhood"(Arseneault, Bowes, & Shakoor, 2010, p. 725).

Physical, emotional and sexual abuse, as well as neglect in childhood, "are related to risk for involvement in particular kinds of violence in adolescence and adulthood, as well as to intermediary mechanisms" (Davis et al., 2015, p. 1). The psychological impact of bullying has been well documented (see Cowie & Myers, 2016; Luca, 2016; Fisher et al., 2012). A study by Nansel et al. (2004) evaluating bullying in several countries, concluded that across countries "involvement in bullying was associated with poorer psychosocial adjustment. In all or nearly all countries, bullies, victims, and bully victims reported greater health problems and poorer emotional and social adjustment" (p. 730). Zhu, Chan Ling, and Chen (2015) used the data from a representative sample to investigate the association between family violence and child bullying victimisation in China and concluded that there is a strong association between family violence and the likelihood of an increasing risk of child bullying victimisation.

As Arseneault et al. (2010) state: "Research indicates that being the victim of bullying (1) is not a random event and can be predicted by individual characteristics and family factors; (2) can be stable across ages; (3) is associated with severe symptoms of mental health problems, including self-harm, violent behaviour and psychotic symptoms; (4) has long-lasting effects that can persist until late adolescence; and (5) contributes independently to children's mental health problems" (p. 217). A study by Barker et al. (2008) found that high levels of harsh and reactive parenting were specific to groups of children showing high and chronic levels of peer victimisation as opposed to other preschool trajectories. To progress our understanding of bullied schoolchildren, we need further research looking at the early home environment and whether this is a factor in being bullied later at school and in adult life so that early support can be provided.

Victims of bullying show increased symptoms of anxiety and depression (Hodges & Perry, 1999), low self-esteem and poor social skills (Egan & Perry, 1998) and eating disorders. One of the 'coping' mechanisms used among young people "to escape from a terrible state of mind" (Madge et al., 2008, p. 676), often precipitated by bullying, is self-harming. In the UK it is one of the top five reasons for acute medical admissions (NHS Centre for Reviews & Dissemination, 1998). Research also found that adolescents who are being bullied and those who are bullies are at an increased risk of suicide (Kaltiala-Heino, Rimpelä, Marttunen, Rimpelä, & Rantanen, 1999).

Krystal: hearing the voice of the vulnerable child

This vignette will highlight how giving birth became the catalyst of childhood trauma, manifesting in psychotic thoughts. Krystal, a 32-year-old teacher married with a 4-year-old child, came to therapy to help her with her depression, anxiety and, since the birth of her son, suicidal thoughts. She had seen a therapist when her son was a few months old, as she was flooded with images of knives flying around and of her unwittingly killing her baby. Her biggest anxiety was that she might harm her baby unintentionally, as she felt she had no control over the feelings of rage and the disturbing images. Her husband was having an affair during her pregnancy, which had a devastating impact on her life. She had been diagnosed by a psychiatrist with *postpartum psychosis* and found the brief therapy in the NHS helped her gain perspective and deal with rage she had suppressed linked to her husband's infidelity.

In her initial consultation with me she presented as pleasant, confident, highly articulate and sensitive. What precipitated her decision to seek therapy was an incident at work, which triggered insomnia, depression and anxiety. A male colleague 14 years her senior was making sexual remarks, on occasion winking at her and displaying what she felt was 'sexist behaviour'. She became frightened of him and tried to avoid him. She found him 'loathsome' and 'arrogant'. She was asking herself whether she had 'led him on' in any way, but assured herself that her approach to him had been friendly but not flirtatious. Her avoidance of him seemed to make him angry and her anxiety 'hit the roof'. Her sleep and levels of concentration had been adversely affected, she started taking time off work and she lost interest in her little boy and her husband. She said: "my life is empty. I am withdrawn, I don't want to see any of my friends, I don't want to go to work and I lost what little interest in sex I had. I worry about my little boy and losing my job, my marriage, everything that I have worked so hard for. My husband suggested I see a counsellor".

Krystal was the eldest of two children; she had a brother three years younger. Their parents ran their own business, a pub that afforded them a comfortable lifestyle. They were both educated at a local grammar school. Her mother was depressed and abused alcohol during Krystal's childhood, so she had very little time for Krystal or her brother. Krystal's relationship with her father was 'complicated'. She said, "Sometimes I loved him for paying me so much attention, sometimes I hated him for being aggressive towards my mother and sometimes I wanted him . . . dead!". The maternal grandparents lived in the same village so Krystal and her brother visited often. She loved her grandfather dearly for being kind and playing with her and her brother. The grandmother was remote and would tell the children off for being noisy.

I asked Krystal if there were any painful childhood memories she recalled; her demeanour changed dramatically and she cried. School, she said, was a living nightmare. She had been bullied by a group of girls in her year consistently, but she never told anyone about it, as she was afraid this might make the bullying worse. They called her names, stole items belonging to her, which got her into trouble at home and excluded her from the group. One of the girls had been friends with her before joining forces with the others. Krystal felt hurt and angry and swallowed up her feelings, until she found a way to relieve herself by cutting on her belly. Nobody could see the cutting she said, so it became a regular 'treatment for coping with the bullying'.

I began to realise that underneath her secure persona, there was an anxious, frightened and very angry person she learned to hide from others. It also made sense that becoming a mother had been a catalyst of severe anxiety due to her fear, that like her mother she would let her child down. The incident at work had also triggered childhood trauma in being bullied, resulting in Krystal regressing and feeling unable to stand up for herself.

Therapy focussed on helping Krystal work through early childhood trauma that impacted on her sense of self-worth and militated against her ability to protect herself from threats, or invite support from others which also presented in therapy, with Krystal's persona of confidence, finding it difficult to allow me to see her vulnerable side. We also worked in helping Krystal make sense of her reaction to becoming a mother and being bullied at work, enabling her to increase her self-esteem, so she could manage feelings triggered from witnessing violence and being emotionally starved at home. She worked on integrating the outer persona of a confident woman with the frightened child hiding from the world. The integration of different aspects of Krystal's self made dialogue between these parts possible, so that her adult part could mother her child part, by learning to soothe or seek out support, as opposed to suffering in silence.

Steven: the impact of sexual bullying in childhood

This scenario will raise issues on the debilitating effects of childhood sexual bullying and abuse, having lasting effects on the individual's ability to relate to others and form healthy, intimate relationships. Steven, a 26-year-old man, graduated in law from Oxford University and found work in a reputable firm in the city of London. He had difficulty forming intimate relationships despite being extremely good looking and intelligent. He felt there was something missing, 'a gap of some sort in my personality' and could not understand why, after a few dates, girlfriends would reject him. He sought private therapy to help him understand what was wrong with him so he could form a relationship and create the family he so longed for. He explained that at work he felt envious of his colleagues for being able to relate and banter with one another, whereas he felt always an outsider. Steven spoke in a gentle but controlled tone, making sure there was no space for me to say anything. I wondered whether the wall he created between us was a familiar pattern in his interactions with colleagues and women in which he was romantically interested.

Steven had gone to a boys' independent school and disclosed early on in our work that he had been sexually abused by the house master and another teacher who were sometimes abusing him together. He kept this a secret until now out of fear of stigmatisation. As he put it: "there was a bullying culture at the school, older boys bullied younger boys, stronger and more aggressive boys bullied shy, weaker boys and teachers used humiliation and shaming of boys to exert discipline. I was a shy and lonely boy, an easy target for bullying. My mother died from cancer when I was 7 (she was suffering for 3 years before her death) and my father married soon after. They were so loved up I suppose I was in the way. I suppose my mother's illness meant they could not have more children, so I grew up alone and lonely. Watching my neighbour's two children, they were brothers around my age, I felt sad and used to fantasise about having a little brother to play with. My mother's parents visited me regularly and I spent some of my holidays with them. Those were the only times I felt loved".

Steven was visibly upset in describing the loss of his mother and the rejection from his father, pushing back tears. The lonely, rejected and abused little boy in Steven was enveloped in shame. His traumatic experience evoked affection and the desire to help in me. However, the wall around him kept me at a safe distance. Not surprisingly Steven's attachments were ambivalent, not trusting anyone out of fear his safety would be compromised if people were to see how deeply ashamed he felt about himself.

It took Steven a year in therapy to let his guard down and to trust that I would not humiliate him as his teachers and peer group had done. His internalised attachments were crowding his psyche with bullying figures, so trust had to be earned. He was testing me through attempts to provoke anger in me and the anticipated rejection. At times he was persecuting, mocking my therapeutic efforts and my clinical approach, leaving me feeling rejected and humiliated. Often people who suffered from bullying and being persecuted reverse their trauma by embodying the bully, a copying mechanism for managing the fear of repeated trauma. This is a finding in studies mentioned earlier, e.g. Arseneault et al. (2010). I knew that if I became defensive it would become a self-fulfilling philosophy for Steven, adding me to his list of people who let him down. My approach was to contain my temptation to retaliate and use my understanding to help Steven develop insight into his internal world manifested in his relationship with me. My clinical focus was to help him understand the sources of his adult behaviour and provide him with an opportunity to experience a more benign attachment figure (in the therapist) so that his fragile self could be strengthened. I was well aware that his masculinity had received many knocks, so I was careful to moderate and pace out my need to nurture the frightened little boy in him. He needed to feel secure as a man first before he could develop the confidence to date and sustain intimate relationships. He seemed to be blasé and apathetic (rejecting) in his romantic endeavours, setting up the eventual rejection from girlfriends.

This had been challenging work. Steven's avoidance of emotional closeness had been established long ago when those in positions of authority did not seem to care. To soften rigid psychological defences requires patience and long-term therapy. Although Steven attempted to sabotage therapy, a part of him longed to be understood and respected. Therefore his motivation to address his problems kept the therapy alive for six years. During this time he met a woman at work five years his senior and he invited me to the wedding that took place six months before therapy ended. He understood that I could not accept his invitation and felt that both his mother and I would be there in spirit.

Marcella: the impact of being bullied at home

The scenario of Marcella will be used to highlight how childhood bullying by parents makes a child more prone to bullying at school with detrimental psychological effects, in this case sexualised behaviours, addiction and severe anxiety.

Therapy was, for Marcella, the last resort after years of psychological distress using her own coping mechanisms, which perpetuated rather than helped with her symptoms. She had been diagnosed with irritable bowel syndrome (IBS) at 16, became severely anorexic around 13 and started self-harming at 21. In her young adulthood she was depressed, coped with an array of physical symptoms and struggled to make sense of the meaning of life. She took an overdose at 23 after a five-month relationship with a man she met at university broke down. This disrupted her studies so she took a year out to recover, returning home to live with her parents and younger brother. She had some therapy in that year, but when she returned to university she stopped and sought no further help. Although bright, her psychological vulnerability impacted on her obtaining a classified degree. At the end of her studies she felt lost and could not imagine developing a career in anything. So she decided to travel, using the inheritance from her grandmother. She travelled to Australia where she met a woman at a party, became close to her and they started a sexual relationship that lasted three months. She then returned to the UK and found work in advertising. Pressure at work was causing her anxiety and affected her sleep, so she started taking sleeping pills she had obtained from the internet. She also started drinking alcohol at every possible opportunity, especially with colleagues at lunch and after work, until she realised she could not go to bed at night without consuming a bottle, sometimes two on her own. In her sexual encounters she turned herself into a 'flirtatious seductress', a strategy that proved successful in attracting men and women, but without being able to sustain a relationship lasting more than three months. Her clinginess, servile attitude and neediness frightened partners away. She felt confused about her sexual identity, had a very low sense of self and her external locus of evaluation was blocking her need for autonomy and confidence in herself. Others' views of her were paramount, but of course she only presented a persona of a capable, intelligent and self-assured woman to the world, so deep inside she never felt validated by positive views. She believed she was a fraud and if people knew who she was inside, they would reject her.

Her early childhood was characterised with relocation to different countries to suit her father's career as a business man. She always felt different from other children and had memories of feeling something was wrong with her. At home, father would have violent outbursts, chasing her around the house and having screaming matches with her. Mother was always attempting to appease father's aggression, but she was ineffective and anxious. At school she had been subjected to regular bullying by girls and boys, but kept quiet about it as she feared father would get angry and blame her. Anything that she felt was going wrong in her life she would blame herself for and cutting was her way of releasing what she described as this 'hideous, dirty' part of herself.

At 29 she had been to a rehabilitation clinic for addictions, stayed off alcohol for two months, then reverted back to her old habits. Her G.P. suggested therapy, so she came to see me. In the early phase of our work she did not disclose her alcohol addiction and focussed on her anxiety and insomnia. Exploration of her childhood evoked intolerable feelings which intensified her symptoms. Although I had pre-empted the possibility that she might feel worse before she could feel better during therapy, she became angry with me for not 'curing her of her symptoms', punished me through not paying her invoices on time, but continued attending her sessions. She was watchful and mistrusting of me, not allowing me to help her. The bullied child in Marcella presented itself as an adult bully, turning me into the bullied victim. We gradually began to understand how this therapy dynamic came about as an unconscious need to reverse the potential threat in being bullied by me (in the transference I became the sadistic, violent father), so she could protect herself from being traumatised again. It had taken a year before she could trust that I was there to help and for her to gradually reveal the bullied child in herself. In this phase of therapy she would curl up in her chair, cry for most of the sessions, looked lost and frightened and hoped I would rescue her. Each time she experienced emotional pain in therapy her drinking would escalate. We began to understand that alcohol represented a soothing tool for the frightened, lost child in her. She developed insights about herself which helped in embracing the bullied, vulnerable aspect, but found it hard to let go of the destructive mechanisms. The external aggressor/bully was still in operation through internalisation. I hoped that Marcella would begin to internalise a soothing aspect through therapy to militate against the bullying aspect. After two years of therapy Marcella was less persecutory and self-destructive and more ready to engage in intimate relationships. Her victim/persecutor/rescuer psychological strategy was therapeutically challenged so she could now function more autonomously of the dynamic that had sabotaged her need for a healthy relationship with herself and others.

The consequences of childhood trauma and bullying on mental health

Psychotherapy practice with bullied adults highlights the predicament in children and adolescents who grow up in a bullying home environment. Their sense of self is attacked, eroding a safe belonging and trust in the environment to be nurturing and safe. If the psychological resilience in children is affected through a hostile home environment, they are more likely to be targeted and bullied or become bullies at school. Research suggests that: "victimization correlates with psychosomatic complaints, anxiety and depression, as well as lowered self-esteem, loneliness, isolation, impaired concentration, fear of going to school and truancy among primary and secondary school children" (Kaltiala-Heino, Rimpela, Rantanten, & Rimpela, 2000, p. 661).

It is of particular concern that "Children who are victimized by an adult at home and by their peers at school may represent a particularly vulnerable subgroup that shows the most problematic behavioural and emotional profiles among all victimized children" (Arseneault et al., 2010, p. 725). Further, "The association of various mental health problems with all types of involvement in bullying, and the frequent co-occurrence of mental health problems among those involved emphasizes the importance of understanding involvement in bullying as an indicator of severe risk for mental disorders" (Kaltiala-Heino et al., 2000, p. 670). Naylor and Cowie (1999) found that "peer support systems in challenging bullying in U.K. (mainly English) secondary schools and colleges (n = 51) is effective in reducing the negative effects of bullying for victims" (p. 467).

Therapeutic work with adults bullied in childhood suggests an association between bullying and mental health problems in later life. Suicidal ideation, anxiety, depression, self-harm, sexualised behaviour, fear of intimacy and psychosomatic symptoms are some of the consequences. The scenarios presented earlier in this chapter capture the individual survival mechanisms adopted by three different clients to help them cope with the psychological trauma. Clinical work suggests that survival mechanisms chosen by bullied individuals are random and perhaps linked to personality and other factors, such as insecure attachments and type of early relationships with parents. Research shows "that for both sexes frequent peer victimization and low social support contributed significantly and independently to relatively poor mental health" (Rigby, 2000, p. 57). Early recognition of bullying, acknowledgement of its impact on mental health, prevention strategies as well as support systems for victims and perpetrators are fundamental in reducing the long-lasting effects of bullying.

The psychological impact of bullying on children is well documented in the literature, even though it is often un-reported and un-documented by schools. The trauma associated with early childhood bullying presents itself in therapy as a vulnerability and a compromised psychological resilience with the associated risk of being bullied as an adult.

References

Arseneault, L., Bowes, L., & Shakoor, S. (2010). Bullying victimization in youths and mental health problems: 'Much ado about nothing'? *Psychological Medicine, 40*, 717–729. doi:10.1017/S0033291709991383.

Barker, E. D., Boivin, M., Brendgen, M., Fontaine, N., Arseneault, L., Vitaro, F., Bissonnette, C., & Tremblay, R. E. (2008). The predictive validity and early predictors of peer victimization trajectories in preschool. *Archives of General Psychiatry, 65*, 1185–1192.

Cowie, H., & Myers, C. A. (Eds.). (2016). *Bullying among university students.* London: Taylor & Francis/Routledge.

Davis, K. C., Masters, N. T., Casey, E., Kelly, F., Kajumulo, K. F., Norris, J., William, H., & George, W. H. (2000). Effects of peer victimization in schools and perceived social support on adolescent well-being. *Journal of Adolescence, 23*, 57–68.

Egan, S. K., & Perry, D. G.(1998). Does low self-regard invite victimization? *Developmental Psychology, 34*(2), 299–309.

Fisher, H. L. et al. (2012). Bullying victimisation and risk of self-harm in early adolescence: Longitudinal cohort study. *British Medical Journal*, 344.

Hodges, E. V. E., & Perry, D. G. (1999). Personal and interpersonal antecedents and consequences of victimization by peers. *Journal of Personality and Social Psychology, 76*(4), 677–685.

Kaltiala-Heino, R., Rimpelä, M., Marttunen, M., Rimpelä, A., & Rantanen, P. (1999). Bullying at school – An indicator of adolescents at risk for mental disorders. *British Medical Journal, 319*, 348–351.

Luca, M. (2016). Sexting and bating out. *Sky News*, 25 March 2016; 11:42.
Luca, M. (2016). The role of the therapist in helping university students who have been bullied: A case study of sexual bullying. In Helen Cowie and Carrie-Anne Myers (Eds.), *Bullying among university students*. London: Taylor & Francis/Routledge.
Madge, N., Hewitt, A., Hawton, K., de Wilde, E. J., Corcoran, P., Fekete, S., van Heeringen, K., De Leo, D., & Ystgaard, M. (2008). Deliberate self-harm within an international community sample of young people: Comparative findings from the Child & Adolescent Self-harm in Europe (CASE) study. *Journal of Child Psychology and Psychiatry*, *49*(6), 667–677. doi:10.1111/j.1469-7610.2008.01879.x.
Nansel, T. R., Craig, W., Mary, D., Overpeck, M. D., Saluja, G. W., & Ruan, J. (2004). Cross-national consistency in the relationship between bullying behaviours and psychosocial adjustment. *Arch Pediatr Adolesc Med*, *158*(8), 730–736.
Naylor, P., & Cowie, H. (1999). The effectiveness of peer support systems in challenging school bullying: The perspectives and experiences of teachers and pupils. *Journal of Adolescence*, *22*, 467–479.
NHS Centre for Reviews and Dissemination. (1998). *Deliberate self-harm*. York: University of York.
Olweus, D. (1997). Bully/victim problems in school: Knowledge base and an effective intervention programme. *The Irish Journal of Psychology*, *18*(2), 170–190.
Olweus, D. (1999). Sweden. In P. K. Smith, Y. Morita, J. Junger-Tas, D. Olweus, R. Catalano, & P. Slee (Eds.), *The nature of school bullying: A cross-national perspective* (pp. 7–27). New York, NY: Routledge.
Rigby, K. (2000). Effects of peer victimization in schools and perceived social support on adolescent well-being. *Journal of Adolescence*, *23*, 57–68.
Zhu, Y., Chan Ling, K., & Chen, J. (2015). Bullying victimization among Chinese middle school students: The role of family violence. *Journal of Interpersonal Violence*, 1–20. doi:10.1177/0886260515621082.

Chapter 9

Addressing the mental health and emotional needs of children who bully

Helen Cowie and Pat Colliety

Introduction

People do not naturally empathise with the bully and any tendency to show concern for the bully's emotional state is understandably likely to be met with criticism on the part of the targets of bullying and by those who support and defend victims. In fact, expressions of vengeance are increasingly apparent in the media. Particularly in the context of cyberbullying, public shaming of bullies is becoming more common through such operations as OpAntiBully as a means of seeking justice for victims and revenge on the perpetrators. As Stroud (2016) proposes, such approaches demonstrate the philosophy that you need to 'be a bully to beat a bully', raising a myriad of ethical considerations. Furthermore, the emotional difficulties of children who bully their peers at school are seldom taken into account in the design of interventions to resolve the issue. Yet, if we are to develop effective strategies for addressing the problem, it is essential to understand the processes and prior experiences that lead a child to engage in bullying behaviour. In this chapter, we focus on research about the mental health and emotional needs of children and young people who bully, and consider some of the interventions derived from this knowledge.

Individual characteristics of children who bully

Many studies of children who bully confirm that they have a range of difficulties in their peer relationships, including high conflict with peers, association with similarly aggressive peers and susceptibility to negative peer pressure (Pepler, Jiang, Craig, & Connolly, 2008). This can persist over time. Studies examining the continuity of abusive peer relationships suggest that the roles of bullies and victims remain quite stable from elementary to middle school and high school (Pörhölä, 2016; Salmivalli, Lappalainen, & Lagerspetz, 1998; Schäfer, Korn, Brodbeck, Wolke, & Schulz, 2005; Sourander, Helstela, Helenius, & Piha, 2000). For example, in their eight-year longitudinal study among Finnish students, Sourander et al. (2000) found that bullying at age eight was associated with bullying at age 16, and being bullied at age eight was associated with being bullied at age 16. Those who bully at school are most likely to continue to engage in various kinds of abusive behaviours in their social relationships. Particularly males who bully at school have been shown to have a heightened risk for sexual harassment (DeSouza & Ribeiro, 2005; Pellegrini, 2002) and dating violence (Connolly, Pepler, Craig, & Taradash, 2000; Pepler, Craig, Connolly, & Henderson, 2002).

There is strong evidence too suggesting that children who bully have a higher than average incidence of mental health difficulties (Cowie, 2010; Perren, Dooley, Shaw, & Cross, 2010; Sourander et al., 2010; Winsper, Lereya, Zanarini, & Wolke, 2012). Kumpulainen, Rasanen, and Henttonen (1999) found that bullies, in particular those who were bully-victims at primary school, had more psychiatric symptoms at the age of 15 years. The probability of being deviant at the age of 15 years was higher among children involved in bullying at the age of 8 or 12 years than among non-involved children. Similarly, Kaltiala-Heino, Rimpalä, Rantanen, and Rimpalä (2000), in a large-scale survey of 14– to 16-year-old Finnish adolescents taking part in the School Health Promotion Study (8787 in 1995, 7643 in 1997), found that anxiety, depression and psychosomatic symptoms were most frequent among bully-victims and equally common among bullies and victims. Winsper et al. (2012), using a birth cohort study, found that bully victim status was predictive of self-injury and suicide ideation. On the surface, children who bully often appear confident, assertive and popular; they also tend to exhibit a lack of empathy for the suffering of their victims (Sutton, Smith, & Swettenham, 1999). This has been described in the literature as a process of 'moral disengagement' whereby the child who bullies tends not to take any moral responsibility for the suffering that he/she is causing to others (Tognetta, Avilés, & Rosário, 2016). Interviews frequently elicit rationalisations for their aggressive behaviour that minimise the outcomes for victims and provide justification for the actions. For example, bullies will often state that the victim provoked them in some way and so deserved the treatment that they had received. Winsper et al. (2012) found that the peers of the bully/victims identified them as the most rejected and least popular children.

Furthermore, as Terranova, Sheffield Morris, and Boxer (2008) found from their sample of 124 middle school children, those who carry out direct physical bullying (as opposed to psychological or indirect bullying) lack the qualities of self-regulation and also do not fear the consequences of their aggression; deficits in effortful control disrupted the development of pro-social skills and values, so reducing the repertoire of responses available to bullies in this study when they interacted with their peers.

Green and Price (2016) carried out in-depth studies of children who persistently bullied others and found that they were more likely than other children to have experienced significant problems in their personal relationships from an early age. As previous research indicated (e.g. Orpinas & Horne, 2006; Smith, Bowers, Binney, & Cowie, 1993), secure parental and peer relationships act as protective mechanisms that buffer against bullying. The basis for positive relationships with others begins as home (see Luca in chapter 8 and Giovaziolas and Malikiosi-Loizos in chapter 10). If there are difficulties in these early relationships within the family, then crucial opportunities for reinforcing and modelling positive social skills are missing from that child's experience.

Green and Price (2016) present a number of case studies of persistent bullies who appeared to be especially resistant to school preventative interventions. Their in-depth interviews confirmed the earlier studies with regard to family relationships. John and Rebecca, for example, perceived the power-based behaviour that their parents used to enforce discipline as a perfectly normal way of relating to others. The aggressive 'scripts' enacted by these parents inadvertently reinforced their children's bullying behaviour at school. Two case studies provide illustration. John, for example, as a young adult reflecting back on his childhood, appeared to view any attention as better than none; his aggressive behaviour towards vulnerable peers masked his need to be followed in order to escape an inner sense of loneliness. John lacked the modelling within his family of sensitive, empathic awareness of others' feelings so he was actually unaware of the suffering that he was causing to others. Since bullying appeared to meet his social goals of acceptance by peers, it was very difficult for him to change. Similarly, Rebecca, a persistent bully aged eight years at the time of the study, experienced relationship difficulties within the family from an early age. Her mother had very strict rules and often used physical punishment to keep discipline; since the parents had divorced, she only saw her father (to whom she said that she felt closer) fortnightly. She had great difficulty in forming friendships at school. She often fell out with her peers who, as a consequence, left her on her own. Within her family, she fought frequently with her sister whom she described as both 'a friend and an enemy'.

Other researchers have identified bullies as having a narcissistic preoccupation with the self and over-sensitivity to any form of actual or perceived criticism. Nail et al. (2014) propose that some children bully their peers as a means of defending themselves against deep-seated feelings of vulnerability. From this perspective, bullying behaviour is a means of fending off latent feelings of self-doubt and vulnerability by dominating and intimidating weaker peers. This *defensive egotism*, as Nail et al. (2014) define it, correlates significantly with bullying, as they found in their study of 92 sixth-graders who had recently made the transition from elementary to secondary school. In this study, children who scored highly in defensive egotism, in particular the boys, tended to bully other boys with low peer-reported self-esteem. By choosing such weak targets, the bullies had a high likelihood of success and an opportunity to relieve their own feelings of vulnerability.

The social context of bullying

Salmivalli et al. (1998) observed that peers are frequently bystanders during episodes of bullying and the nature of their response has a powerful influence on whether the bullying continues or is challenged. Salmivalli's research has been seminal here since she and her colleagues identified a range of participant roles in bullying to include: bullies, victims, assistants to the bully, reinforcers of the bully, defenders of the victim and outsiders (Salmivalli, 2010, 2014); this research indicates the powerful role that bystanders can play as audience to the 'drama' of a bullying episode. These findings are supported by Garandeau et al. (2014) who found that the behaviour of bystanders was crucial in the continuation of bullying behaviours.

As we saw in the previous section, bullies can be identified as individuals with aggressive personalities and a strong need to achieve their own goals with regard to social acceptance and status within the peer group (Pellegrini, 2002) and to alleviate their own vulnerabilities (Nail et al., 2014) regardless of any discomfort or distress caused to others. This means, however, as Salmivalli (2010) points out, that the bully is also very dependent on the group for this affirmation. More often, the group reinforces the bully's power and status by rating him or her as 'cool' and 'popular', even if there are elements of fear involved in these constructions. One possible explanation is that the group applauds the bully's ability to challenge adult values and norms of behaviour. Furthermore, children who bully usually surround themselves with cliques of peers who share their attitudes towards people perceived as different or vulnerable (for example, through xenophobia, homophobia, sexism, negative views of disability) and these young people continually reinforce the aggressive behaviour so that it is increasingly viewed by the bully as socially acceptable. The members of the cliques will typically include participant roles such as assistant to the bully, reinforcer of the bully, the outsider who is unconcerned by the victim's distress (Salmivalli, 2010) and the bystander who is amused by the drama of seeing a peer humiliated or denigrated (Kernaghan & Elwood, 2013).

Green and Price (2016) propose a cycle of bullying with supportive factors in the social environment that interact with the bully's personal characteristics as follows:

- The child engages in bullying behaviour to gain status and identity;
- The school community perceives this child as a bully;
- The child continues, as expected, to act as a bully;
- Being a bully becomes internalised as part of the child's self-concept;
- The child affirms this negative self-view by associating with similarly aggressive peers.

Interventions that target the child who bullies

Interventions in a variety of forms have been developed over the years, ranging from those that focus on punishment and sanctions, those that target the bully in a group context and those that work therapeutically with individuals. The most successful interventions take account of the complex individual and social reasons that underlie bullying behaviour and provide alternative ways of relating to others. Additionally, good interventions not only support the victim but also develop safe strategies for adults and peers to sustain the self-esteem of the bully in ways that are not aggressive.

Small-group work with bullies

Given the complexity of the personal circumstances and mental health difficulties of children who bully, it is not surprising that the impact of different forms of disciplinary, therapeutic and remedial approaches is hard to unravel and therefore its effectiveness is difficult to measure. However, there is evidence that small group work with very aggressive children can be effective in changing their behaviour and enhancing their capacity to relate positively with their peers. Nurture-based practice, grounded in attachment theory (Bennathan & Boxall, 2014), is an increasingly influential approach to the inclusion of children with social, emotional and behavioural difficulties and is very relevant to the issue of the child who bullies. From this perspective, children who are placed in nurture groups (NGs) have experienced dysfunctional or disruptive parenting in their early years. While NGs have many of the features of family life, such as soft furnishings, kitchen and dining facilities, they are not designed to replace family life but rather to complement it. The trained NG staff work collaboratively with the parents and, in fact, the experience of the NG appears to have a positive influence on the ways in which parents interact with their children. NGs focus primarily on internalising models of effective relationships and forming attachments to loving and caring adults, so allowing the children to achieve a sense of security and safety at school. Evaluations of the impact of NGs (e.g. Bennathan & Boxall, 2014; Cooper & Whitebread, 2007; Scott Loinaz, 2015; Seth-Smith, Netali, Fonagy, & Jaffey, 2010) reveal statistically substantial improvements in terms of children's social and emotional development, social engagement and behaviours showing secure attachment.

The Method of Shared Concern, developed by Pikas (2002) aims to create a set of ground rules that will enable children who engage in bullying behaviour and those whom they bully to co-exist within the same school community. While the impact of this innovative method remains anecdotal, a very similar method, the Support Group Method, has been evaluated (Robinson & Maines, 2007; Sharp, Cowie, & Smith, 1996; Winsper et al., 2012; Young, 1998; Young et al., 2015). This intervention creates a forum consisting of bullies, bystanders and defenders that focusses on the feelings of all participants, including those of the bully. There are particular outcomes in the process. The first is that the method creates a context in which the bully is given the opportunity to reflect on the victim's feelings by imagining what it must have been like to be a victim. The bully is encouraged to express concern for the victim within the safety of the group and, if possible, to come to some form of realisation that the bullying actions were wrong. The second key outcome is that, since the facilitator places the emphasis on the expression of feelings, the process of change is a collective one involving not only the perpetrators but also the bystanders, onlookers and potential defenders. A consistent finding, as evaluations have shown, is that participants feel better about themselves through the experience of helping others. This even includes bullies! For example, Young et al. found that 57% of the bullies who participated in the Support Group Method in their study reported significantly higher levels of happiness as a result. It is possible that the Support Group Method could replace the personal satisfaction associated with being a bully with more positive peer interaction as a source of happiness. Van der Ploeg, Steglich, and Veenstra (2016), in their study of the effects of the Support Group Method in the Dutch KiVa project, found that the effects, while positive initially, did not last throughout the school year; however, they did find that victims who experienced a support group had more defenders at the end of the school year than those without.

Therapeutic work with individual bullies

As the research indicates, children engage in bullying for a range of different reasons, so the interventions need to be adapted to the particular needs of the individual and take account of that young person's peer group, their family values and behaviour patterns, as well as the characteristics of their community. Hazler (1996) describes the Promoting Issues in Common (PIC) Method, which works to change the bully-victim relationship by enabling bullies to understand the fears and anxieties that they have in common with those they bully. The rationale behind PIC is that everyone benefits when people seek to understand, work with and care for others. By reinforcing bullies' good behaviour when it occurs – 'catching them being good' – through a traditional behaviour modification approach, the rewarding of low-level pro-social behaviour is likely to promote its recurrence, provided that the reward is offered in a consistent manner. But at a deeper level it is also necessary to work therapeutically to change the cognitions that many bullies hold and which, too often, are reinforced by the supporters in their immediate peer group.

Figure 9.1 below shows the interrelationship between factors which may lead a child or young person to bully, possible effects of bullying on the individual and interventions and approaches to change the bullying behaviour.

Tapson (2014) used Story Stems and focus groups to elicit the perspectives of young people aged 11–18 years who had been identified as bullies by their schools and who had been referred to therapeutic centres where they had each received professional counselling. She noted in her reflective journal that the work with these young people is endlessly challenging since they often appeared to resist all efforts to help them. She noted how inconsiderate the young people were to the staff at the centre to which they had been referred. To give an idea of the tensions among the young people, Tapson (2014, p. 91) describes an event that occurred as she carried out her research:

> "One (Andy) had squared his shoulders, clenching and unclenching his fists, and the other (Jason) leant slightly backward in his chair. The other

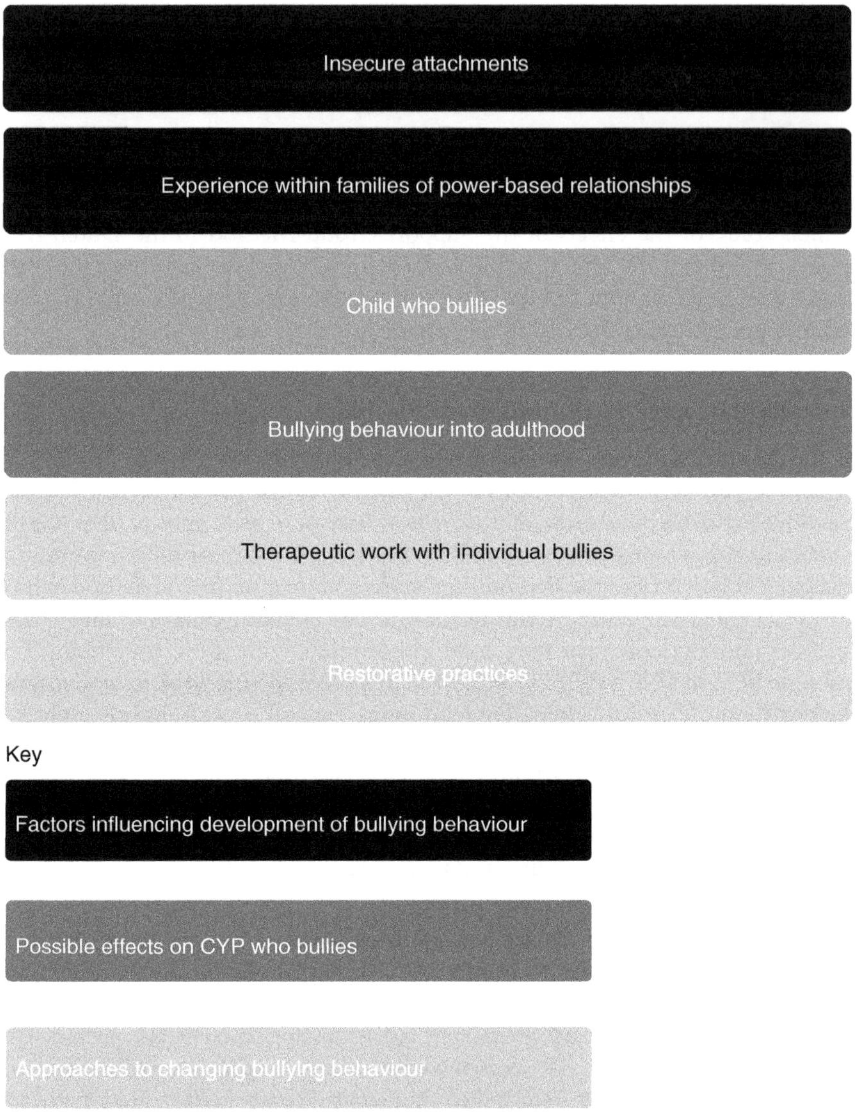

Figure 9.1 The interrelationship between factors leading to bullying, the impact on bullies and approaches to changing bullying behaviour

staff appeared oblivious to this interaction and responded only to the verbal retorts being exchanged between the two boys but, as a newcomer and non-participant observer, I felt powerless to intervene. Suddenly, the tables separating the two boys were overturned by Andy who fell upon Jason, beating him savagely, knocking out two teeth and breaking his nose . . . I

> noticed that the two boys were both heaving with rage and panting. Andy had experienced a violent childhood and was often physically chastised by his parents". As he engaged in the violent attack of Jason, Tapson observed that he was "overwhelmed by an impotent anger that was greater than the sum of his being."

The exposure of the staff to the anger and aggression of their young clients put them at risk of exhaustion and disillusionment in their capacity to put into practice their person-centred, non-judgemental values. The counsellors in this study confided that they had experienced repressed feelings of anger towards these young people and that they very much needed guidance on how to maintain their boundaries and how to manage their own emotions.

Conclusion

There are important implications for intervention work with these challenging young people to change the quality of their peer relationships and to give them contexts in which to explore their own emotions and identities. Abusive bullying relationships are damaging for both target and perpetrator. On the surface, the bullies appear to win through the abuse of their power over others. This clearly provides rewards for continuing to engage in this kind of behaviour but in the longer term the outcomes are not good for the bully either. As Pörhölä (2016) argues, these individuals fail to achieve integration into their peer community and, as a result, fail to develop positive peer interaction skills since their apparent popularity is based on fear rather than genuine liking. In new situations, for example when they go to university, such young people, with a history of having bullied their schoolmates, may also experience being disliked by most peers, and therefore see the new peer community at university as a threat. In this situation they may end up gathering around them a group of similarly aggressive peers who encourage them to continue their abusive ways of relating to others. As a result, the participant role of bully may transfer from one social context to another since such individuals continue to feel the need to gain social power over their peer group and will as a consequence continue to target people who are in some way vulnerable. As Pörhölä (2016) argues, these young people have previously gained social power by bullying others, so the risk of them repeating the same strategy is high.

Implications for practice

Although nurturing and restorative approaches have been demonstrated to be effective, they are very expensive and demanding on those who are involved. There is a strong evidence base for working therapeutically with individuals and in small groups to change both the behaviour and cognition of those who bully, as the behaviour of children who bully can be changed by placing emphasis on the emotional aspects of their experience.

The various approaches require different skills and expertise. There are supportive strategies that can be adopted by educators, such as creating nurturing communities in the classroom where relationships are valued and people are encouraged to care for one another, which will help to address the emotional needs of all the children in that class. This would be enhanced by an in-depth appreciation of the link between children's relationship difficulties and their origins in the family and the community.

Working directly with persistent bullies helps them to understand why they bully and what can be done to support them in changing their behaviour. The needs of the victims cannot be ignored, but the use of approaches that work directly with those who bully in order to address their emotional needs will strengthen any whole-school strategy, as it will be dealing with the cause as well as the effect. Perhaps the use of the pejorative term 'bully' needs to be rethought. Without condoning the ways in which children who bully deal with their social and emotional difficulties, we argue that those who bully others can be seen themselves as victims of their circumstances, and so they deserve our understanding and guidance.

The literature consistently reveals that children who bully are more likely than other children to have mental health difficulties and so, as parents, teachers or healthcare professionals, we are duty-bound to offer them support and insight into their personal issues. Certainly in extreme cases, these children and young people need person-centred interventions that enable them to explore and understand their own vulnerabilities and that address the dynamics of their families, difficult as such therapeutic work may be (Cowie & Colliety, 2010). As Green and Price (2016) and Tapson (2014) argue, on the basis of intense therapeutic work with extremely aggressive children and young people. it is essential to overcome feelings, however understandable, such as outrage, anger, revulsion and vengefulness, if we are to help reduce the phenomenon of bullying; based on their experiences, professionals need to seek appropriate supervision or emotional support when the children who bully reject or rebuff their well-meaning offers of help. Finally, in view of the continuities of bullying over time, it is essential to work towards preventing these young people from perpetuating their cruel, anti-social behaviour from childhood through adolescence into adulthood. We are all members of communities where, as participants and observers we can challenge bullying behaviour whenever we encounter it.

References

Bennathan, M., & Boxall, M. (2014). *Effective intervention in primary schools.* London: Routledge.

Connolly, J., Pepler, D., Craig, W., & Taradash, A. (2000). Dating experiences of bullies in early adolescence. *Child Maltreatment, 5*, 299–310.

Cooper, P., & Whitebread, D. (2007). The effectiveness of nurture groups on student progress. *Emotional and Behavioural Difficulties, 12*(3), 171–190.

Cowie, H. (2010). Cyberbullying and its impact on young people's emotional health and well-being. *The Psychiatrist, 37*, 167–170. doi:10.1192/pb.bp.112.040840.

Cowie, H., & Colliety, P. (2010). Cyberbullying: Sanctions or sensitivity? *Pastoral Care in Education, 28*(4), 261–268.

DeSouza, E. R., & Ribeiro, J. (2005). Bullying and sexual harassment among Brazilian high school students. *Journal of Interpersonal Violence, 20*(9), 1018–1038.

Garandeau, C., Lee, I., & Salmivalli, C. (2014). Differential effects of the KiVa anti-bullying programme on popular & unpopular bullies. *Journal of Applied Developmental Psychology, 35*, 44–50.

Green, D., & Price, D. (2016). *Multiple perspectives on persistent bullying: Capturing and listening to young people's voices*. London: Routledge.

Hazler, R. J. (1996). *Breaking the cycle of violence: Interventions for bullying and victimization*. Washington, DC: Accelerated Development/Taylor & Francis.

Kaltiala-Heino, R., Rimpalä, M., Rantanen, P., & Rimpalä, A. (2000). Bullying at school – An indicator of adolescents at risk for mental health disorders. *Journal of Adolescence, 23*, 661–674.

Kernaghan, D., & Elwood, J. (2013). All the (cyber) world's a stage: Framing cyberbullying as a performance. *Cyberpsychology: Journal of Psychosocial Research on Cyberspace*, 7(1), 1–5.

Kumpulainen, K., Rasanen, E., & Henttonen, I. (1999). Children involved in bullying: Psychological disturbance and the persistence of the involvement. *Child Abuse and Neglect, 23*, 1253–1262.

Nail, P. R., Simon, J. B., Bihm, E. A., & Beasley, W. H. (2014). Defensive egotism and bullying: Gender differences yield qualified support for the compensation model of aggression. *Journal of School Violence*. http://dx.doi.org/ 10.1080/15388220.2014.938270 downloaded 14th August, 2016.

Orpinas, P., & Horne, A. M. (2006). *Bullying prevention: Creating a positive school climate and developing social competence*. Washington, DC: American Psychological Association.

Pellegrini, A. D. (2002). Bullying, victimization, and sexual harassment during the transition to middle school. *Educational Psychologist, 37*(3), 151–164.

Pepler, D., Craig, W., Connolly, J., & Henderson, K. (2002). Bullying, sexual harassment, dating violence, and substance use among adolescents. In C. Wekerle & A. M. Wall (Eds.), *The violence and addiction equation: Theoretical and clinical issues in substance abuse and relationship violence* (pp. 153–168). Philadelphia: Brunner/ Mazel.

Pepler, D., Jiang, D., Craig, W., & Connolly, J. (Mar–Apr 2008). Developmental trajectories of bullying and associated factors. *Child Development, 79*(2), 325–338. doi:10.1111/ j.1467-8624.2007.01128.x.

Perren, S., Dooley, J., Shaw, T., & Cross, D. (2010). Bullying in school and cyberspace: Associations with depressive symptoms in Swiss and Australian adolescents. *Child and Adolescent Psychiatry and Mental Health, 4*, 28–38.

Pikas, A. (2002). New developments in the shared concern method. *School Psychology International, 23*(3), 307–326.

Pörhölä, M. (2016). Do the roles of bully and victim remain stable from school to university? Theoretical considerations. In H. Cowie & C.-A. Myers (Eds.), *Bullying among university students* (pp. 35–47). London: Routledge.

Robinson, G., & Maines, B. (2007). *Bullying*. London: Sage.

Salmivalli, C. (2010). Bullying and the peer group: A review. *Aggression and Violent Behaviour, 15*, 112–120.

Salmivalli, C. (2014). Participant roles in bullying: How can peer bystanders be utilized in interventions? *Theory Into Practice, 53*, 286–292.

Salmivalli, C., Lappalainen, M., & Lagerspetz, K. M. J. (1998). Stability and change of behaviour in connection with bullying in schools: A two-year follow-up. *Aggressive Behaviour, 24*, 205–218.

Schäfer, M., Korn, S., Brodbeck, F. C., Wolke, D., & Schulz, H. (2005). Bullying roles in changing contexts: The stability of victim and bully roles from primary to secondary school. *International Journal of Behavioural Development*, *29*, 323–335.

Scott Loinaz, E. (2015). Comparing nurture group provision with one-to-one counselling. *The International Journal of Nurture in Education*, *1*(1), 25–32.

Seth-Smith, F., Netali, L., Fonagy, P., & Jaffey, D. (2010). Do nurture groups improve the social, emotional and behavioural functioning of at risk children? *Educational and Child Psychology*, *27*, 21–34.

Sharp, S., Cowie, H., & Smith, P. K. (1996). How to respond to bullying behaviour. In S. Sharp & P. K. Smith (Eds.), *Tackling bullying in your school* (pp. 79–101). London: Routledge.

Smith, P. K., Bowers, L., Binney, V., & Cowie, H. (1993). Relationships of children involved in bully/victim problems at school. In S. Duck (Ed.), *Learning about relationship processes* (pp. 184–212). London: Sage.

Sourander, A., Brunstein, K. A. B., Ikomen, M., Lindroos, J., Luntamo, T., Koskelainen, M., Ristkari, T., & Helenius, H. (2010). Psychosocial risk factors associated with cyberbullying among adolescents. *Archives of General Psychiatry*, *67*, 720–728.

Sourander, A., Helstela, I., Helenius, H., & Piha, J. (2000). Persistence of bullying from childhood to adolescence: A longitudinal 8-year follow-up study. *Child Abuse and Neglect*, *24*, 873–881.

Stroud, S. R. (2016). 'Be a bully to beat a bully': Twitter ethics, online identity and the culture of quick revenge. In A. Davisson & P. Booth (Eds.), *Controversies in digital ethics* (pp. 264–278). London: Bloomsbury Press.

Sutton, J., Smith, P. K., & Swettenham, J. (1999). Bullying and theory of mind: A critique of the 'social skills deficit' view of anti-social behaviour. *Social Development*, *8*, 117–127.

Tapson, C. (2014). *An interpretative phenomenological study of young people who bully and their counsellors*. Unpublished PhD thesis, University of Surrey.

Terranova, A. M., Sheffield Morris, A., & Boxer, P. (2008). Fear reactivity and effortful control in overt and relational bullying: A six-month longitudinal study. *Aggressive Behaviour*, *34*(1), 104–115.

Tognetta, L. R. P., Avilés, J. M., & Rosário, P. J. S. (2016). Bullying, a moral issue: Representations of self and moral disconnects, *Revista de Educación*, *373* (July–September), 9–32.

Van der Ploeg, R., Steglich, C., & Veenstra, R. (2016). The support group approach in the Dutch KiVa anti-bullying programme: Effects on victimisation, defending and wellbeing at school. *Educational Research*, 58(3), 221–236 http://dx.doi.org/10.1080/00131881.2016.1184949 downloaded August 2016.

Winsper, C., Lereya, T., Zanarini, M., & Wolke, D. (2012). Involvement in bullying and suicide-related behaviour at 11 years: A prospective birth cohort study. *Journal of the American Academy of Child & Adolescent Psychiatry*, *51*(3), 271–282.

Young, K., Kashdan, T., McKnight, P., Blalock, D., Yuen, M., & Richberg, J. (2015). Happy and unhappy bullies: Evidence for theoretically meaningful subgroups. *Personality and Individual Differences*, *75*, 224–228.

Young, S. (1998). The support group approach to bullying in schools. *Educational Psychology in Practice*, *14*, 32–39.

Chapter 10

The moderating role of father acceptance in the relationship between victimisation and depressive symptoms

Theodoros Giovazolias and Maria Malikiosi-Loizos

Introduction

Research literature supports the evidence that perceived parental acceptance or rejection has a strong influence on the child's emotional, cognitive and behavioural functioning. It seems that parental rejection is strongly related to the child's maladaptive behaviour. Parental behaviour perceived as neglecting, cold or aggressive correlates highly with children's anxiety, depression, conduct disorders and delinquency. Research findings also indicate the differential influence of the father and mother on the child's well-being.

The present research tries to shed light on the father's role in the relationship between children's experiences and victimisation and the development of depressive symptoms. Two hundred and forty pupils of 5th and 6th grade (M^{age} = 11.38) completed questionnaires about maternal and paternal acceptance-rejection, depressive symptoms and victimisation. The conditional effects were examined using the PROCESS programme. The results showed that experiences of victimisation predicted the development of depressive symptoms in our sample. In addition, it was found that paternal but not maternal) acceptance moderated the relationship between these two variables. These findings highlight the importance of father's role both in the psychological well-being of children as well as in the complex phenomenon of peer rejection.

Bullying in Greek schools

Bullying/victimisation is a continuously growing phenomenon worldwide and can take several forms: from the traditional forms of bullying including verbal, physical, sexual and racist bullying to cyberbullying which seems to be increasing in recent years. A plethora of research studies is dedicated to the incidents, forms and effects of bullying on the individual (Arsenault et al., 2006). The damaging outcomes of bullying as well as protective strategies against it, have been extensively studied (Cowie & Jennifer, 2008; Cowie, 2012). Special attention has concentrated on victimisation in schools and the negative consequences it has on the students involved Cowie and Jennifer (2007). Comparative cross-national studies show almost 16% of youngsters to have been victims of bullying (Craig et al., 2009).

The phenomenon of bullying has developed into a serious problem in Greece as well, considering that the country occupies the third place among 40 countries studied (Craig et al., 2009). Other studies that have been conducted in Greek schools show similarly that about 6% of pupils identified as bullies and almost 15% as victims (Sapouna, 2008). More recent data reported about 8% being bullies and victims, while approximately 16% were victims (Giovazolias, Kourkoutas, Mitsopoulou, & Georgiadi, 2010). In another cross-national study, Greece was reported to have an increase of almost 29% in a 10-year period (Molcho et al., 2009). Similar results have been reported in a recent study regarding Greek university students (Giovazolias & Malikiosi-Loizos, 2016).

Emotional difficulties attached to bullies and victims

Aggressive and anti-social behaviour is often accompanied by psychosocial maladjustment and depressive symptoms (Hawker & Boulton, 2000). Peer victimisation is particularly linked with depressive symptoms (Olweus, 1993; Hawker & Boulton, 2000; Espelage & Swearer, 2003; Fekkes, Pijpers, & Verloove-Vanhorick, 2004). Much research has accumulated documenting depressive symptoms in youngsters involved in bullying episodes (Kaltiala-Heino, Fröjd, & Marttunen, 2010; Papadaki and Giovazolias, 2015).

In a meta-analytic review covering data from 20 years' studies, Hawker and Boulton (2000) reported victimisation as more strongly related to depression than other forms of maladjustment. Researchers investigating this type of behaviour have tried to explain not only the individual aspects but also the social context, in which bullying takes place. The social context may include the culture, nationality, the neighbourhood, family etc. Bullying others but also being bullied has been found to be related to emotional and behavioural difficulties stemming to a large extent from the family climate and parental bonding (Conners-Burrow, Johnson, Whiteside-Mansell, McKelvey, & Gargus, 2009).

Parental role

Supportive families and parental warmth are considered important in fostering children's social and emotional well-being (Bowes, Maughan, Caspi, Moffitt, & Arseneault, 2010) and have proved to buffer them from the impact of stressful events (Masten & Shaffer, 2006). Studies have come to the conclusion that the family and family relations are partially responsible for the onset of psychological maladjustment and aggressive behaviour in their children (Lereya, Samara, & Wolke, 2013). Punitive or uninterested parents may cause psychological difficulties such as depression and anxiety in their children (Bayer, Sanson, & Hemphill, 2006; Richaud de Minzi, 2006). Perceived parental rejection seems to predict fairly accurately children's aggressive behaviour and delinquency (Khaleque & Rohner, 2002).

A meta-analysis of 45 studies examining the association between parenting and childhood depression showed that parental rejection accounted for 8% of the variance in child depression (McLeod, Weisz, & Wood, 2007). Another meta-analysis of 43 worldwide studies showed that approximately 26% of the variability in children's psychological adjustment was accounted for by perceived parental rejection (Khaleque & Rohner, 2002).

The parent-child relationship has been studied using several slightly different but interrelated dimensions. Parental involvement, support, engagement, responsibility, acceptance or rejection are among the most often encountered measurable variables when studying the influence of parental bonding in child's cognitive, emotional and social development. The present study concentrates on the dimension of perceived parental acceptance or rejection as developed and studied by Rohner (2004). According to Interpersonal Acceptance-Rejection Theory (IPARTheory, formerly known as PARtheory, Rohner, 2014) the way people organize their perceptions of parental acceptance or rejection centres around four classes of behaviour: warmth/affection or coldness/lack of affection, hostility or aggression, indifference or neglect and undifferentiated rejection (Khaleque & Rohner, 2002). The warmth dimension has to do with the affectionate bond created between parents and children and is expressed through comfort, concern, care, nurturance or simply love, whereas rejecting parental behaviour refers to feelings of resentment and anger and other hurtful behaviours and can be experienced as cold and unaffectionate, hostile and aggressive, indifferent or undifferentiated.

Several studies have tried to investigate the differential effect of father and mother acceptance or rejection on their offspring's well-being (Carrasco & Rohner, 2013). Although initially studies concentrated on the importance of mother-child relationship and bonding (Cooksey & Fondell, 1996), more recent studies conclude that father involvement in child rearing and the bond between father and child is of equal if not of greater importance for the child's behaviour and development (Ang, 2006; Giovazolias, 2014).

Research has tried to shed light on the particular role fathers play in their offspring's behavioural and psychological well-being. Statistical analyses which estimate the unique contribution of each parent on the child's behaviour show that father's accepting or rejecting behaviour is the only significant predictor of certain specific behaviours, after controlling for the mother's behaviour (Rohner & Veneziano, 2001). Contrary to the general impression, it seems that today's fathers are directly involved in childrearing, engaged not only in leisure and play activities but also in nurturing and caregiving. Partly due to the rise of employed mothers but also due to changes in societal attitudes toward fatherhood, it seems that men participate more actively in the family life (Cabrera, Tamis-LeMonda, Bradley, Hofferth, & Lamb, 2000).

Studies have concentrated on the important contribution of fathers to the social, emotional and cognitive development of their children (Marsiglio, Amato, Day, & Lamb, 2000). An impressive amount of research has attempted to shed light on the impact of father–child bonding on children's development. For instance, it has been found that the father's involvement in play and other activities promotes children's cognitive development and academic achievement (Alfaro, Umana-Taylor, & Bamaca, 2006). Secure father-child bonding is also related to the child's resilience and tolerance for stress (Mischel, Shoda, & Peake, 1988). Children with caring fathers are characterised by social competence (Barber, Stoltz, & Olsen, 2005), have more friends and positive peer relations (Hooven, Gottman, & Katz, 1995) and engage in fewer delinquent behaviours (Bronte-Tinkew, Moore, & Carrano, 2006). On the other hand, father rejecting behaviour is associated with the child's aggressive behaviour (Olweus, 1993) and depressive symptoms (Richaud de Minzi, 2006).

In studying the differential effect of mother and father acceptance/rejection on children's well-being, research evidence shows the unique contribution of father love on children's social, emotional and cognitive functioning (Rohner & Veneziano, 2001). Perceived paternal rejection seems to be more related to the child's aggressive behaviour than perceived mother rejection (Khaleque & Rohner, 2002).In their study, Flouri and Buchanan (2002) attested that father involvement in family life may act as a buffer against their child's victimisation and to bullying avoidance behaviours. In studying the mediating role of depression in the relationship between maternal rejection and bullying, Papadaki and Giovazolias (2015) report the moderating effect of father emotional support in this relationship.

The present study examines the relationship between victimisation and depressive symptoms in school-aged children. We also examine the moderating effect of paternal and maternal acceptance in the relationship between victimisation and depressive symptoms.

Methodology

Sample

The sample of this study consisted of 240 5th and 6th grade elementary school children (46.2% boys), from four schools of Rethymno, Crete in Greece, aged between 10 and 12 years (M = 11.38, SD = 0.71). All participants came from intact families with both parents living at home. The parents' educational status was quite high, with 1.7% of fathers and 1.3% of mothers having less than a high school education, 49.6% of fathers and 51.7% of mothers having secondary education, and 48.8% of fathers and 47.1% of mothers having a college/university degree.

Measures

Parental Acceptance-Rejection. Perceived parental acceptance and rejection was measured with the Parental Acceptance-Rejection Questionnaire – child version (PARQ, Rohner, 2005). Participants responded to two versions of the child PARQ, assessing children's perceptions of maternal (PARQ_Mother) and paternal (PARQ_Father) acceptance-rejection, respectively. Both versions of the PARQ are translated and adapted into Greek (Tsaousis, Giovazolias, & Mascha, 2012), combining the continuum of parental acceptance-rejection. These are 24-items self-report questionnaires, including identical items for the mother and for the father (e.g. "My mother/my father sees me as a big nuisance", and "My mother/my father seems to dislike me"). For better clarity in the presentation of results we scored the scales in the direction of acceptance, so that higher score indicates more perceived acceptance. Both scales had high reliability with $\alpha = .89$ (mother version) and $\alpha = .90$ (father version), respectively.

Depression

Depressive symptoms were assessed using the Center for Epidemiological Studies Depression Scale (CES-D, Radloff, 1977). The CES-D consists of 20 self-report items, measuring symptoms of depression as defined by the American Psychiatric Association' Diagnostic and Statistical Manual (APA, 1994). Sample items include: "I thought my life had been a failure", "I had crying spells". Children had to answer whether the questions fitted the way they had felt or they had behaved in the previous week. The higher the score, the more depressive symptomatology children displayed. The reliability of this scale was high with $\alpha = .91$.

Victimisation

The Peer Experiences Questionnaire (PEQ, Vernberg, Jacobs, & Hershberger, 1999), translated and adapted to Greek sample, (Giovazolias et al., 2010), was used to measure experiences of victimisation in our sample. We used only the 9-item Victimization of Self (VS) subscale (e.g. "A student ignored me on purpose to hurt my feelings"). The higher the score, the more victimisation children reported. The VS scale had high reliability ($\alpha = .85$).

Procedure

The administration of the questionnaires took place in the participants' classrooms, during ordinary class sessions and lasted approximately 40 minutes. Issues of anonymity and confidentiality were particularly highlighted, along with the voluntary participation in the study. Permission to conduct the research was granted by the Greek Ministry of Education. There was no payment or other incentive to complete the questionnaires. The data were collected during the 2015 spring semester. Eventually, they were encoded, transferred and analysed with SPSS 21, at the University of Crete.

Plan of analysis

The collected data were analysed using descriptive statistics, independent-samples *t* test, correlations and hierarchical multiple regressions. The proposed moderation models were tested using PROCESS, a versatile modelling tool for observed variable mediation and moderation. This approach, based on bootstrapping, is considered an advancement over previous methods of assessing mediation/moderation effects because of the increased reliability of findings (Hayes, 2013). The analyses were based on 5000 bootstrapped samples, using bias-corrected 95% confidence intervals. Finally, in order to plot the moderating role of father acceptance/rejection, we used Soper's Interaction software v. 1.4. (Soper, 2006).

Results

Gender differences in the variables under consideration were studied using non-parametric tests for independent samples (*t*-test). The strength and direction of the relationships between variables were tested using Spearman's rho coefficient. The use of non-parametric tests was decided on the basis of the data being non-normally distributed as it was shown by the use of the Kolmogorov-Smirnov statistic.

The mean score for both perceived maternal acceptance (PMA) ($M = 84.35$, $SD = 9.42$) and perceived paternal acceptance (PPA) ($M = 84.23$, $SD = 9.83$), indicated that overall participants perceived their parents as quite loving and warm. In addition, there were no differences in the perceived mother and father acceptance-rejection between boys and girls. Similarly, independent samples *t*-tests showed that there are no gender differences in the reported levels of victimisation of self (VS) and depressive symptoms (DS).

Spearman's rho correlations among all predictor and criterion variables in the total sample showed that there was a positive correlation between VS and DS ($rho = .532, p < .001$).

Further, PPA was negatively correlated with VS ($rho = -.395, p < .001$) as well as DS ($rho = -.541, p < .001$). PMA was also correlated negatively with VS and DS ($rho = -.421, p < .001$) and ($rho = -.548, p < .001$), respectively.

In order to examine gender as a moderating factor in the relationship between parental rejection and social anxiety, we used the PROCESS tool described earlier. In order to plot the impact of predictor on outcome for men and women separately we used simple slope analysis (Frazier, Tix, & Barron, 2004).

We first examined the moderating effect of paternal acceptance in the relationship between victimisation and depressive symptoms. In the first step it

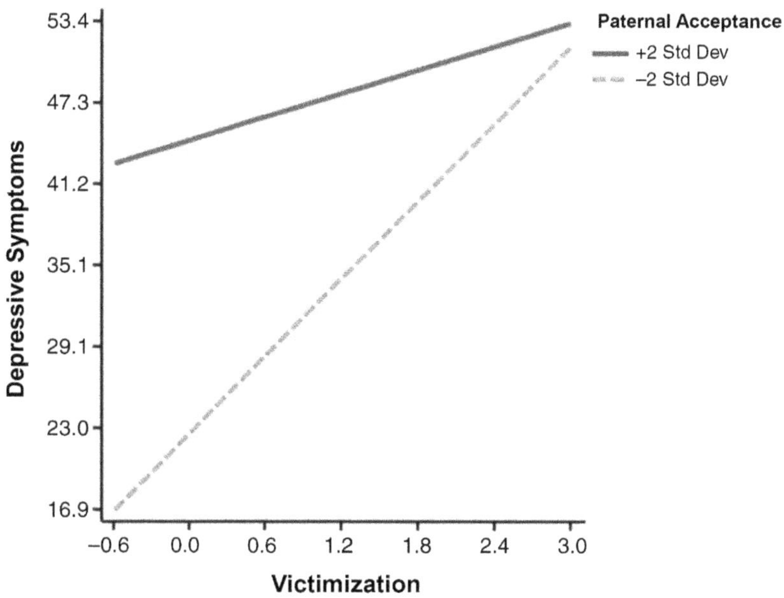

Figure 10.1 Graphical representation of the simple moderation effect of paternal acceptance in the relationship between victimisation and depressive symptoms scores (the red line depicts the condition of high paternal acceptance and the dashed line the condition of low paternal acceptance)

was found that victimisation predicts depressive symptomatology (B = .532, t = 9.681, BCa *CI* [6.480, 9.791]). It was also found that the interaction between victimisation and paternal rejection (the moderator) has a statistically significant effect on depressive symptoms (B = .172, t = 3.259, BCa *CI* [–.276, –.068]). The model explains 43.7% of the total variance in depressive symptoms scores. From simple slope analysis (Figure 10.1), we notice that victimisation has a greater impact on the levels of depressive symptoms in the condition of low paternal acceptance (B = 9.754, t = 6.637, BCa *CI* [6.859, 12.650]) than in the condition of high paternal acceptance (B = 2.987, t = 2535, BCa *CI* [.666, 5.308]).

We then tested the moderating effect of maternal acceptance in the relationship between victimisation and depressive symptoms but found no moderating effect (B = .082, t = 1.382, BCa *CI* [–.199, .035]).

Discussion

The results of this study showed that experiences of victimisation are strongly correlated with the development of depressive symptoms in school-aged children. This finding confirms previous finding that have long underlined the consequences of victimisation by peers in the mental health of victims, especially in relation to internalising difficulties. For example, it has been found that victimisation relates to internalising problems such as anxiety, depression, feelings of loneliness and low self-esteem (Hawker & Boulton, 2000). Further, the exposure to bullying behaviours has been associated with different emotional states, such as anger, guilt, confusion and the intense sadness experienced by the victim (James, Sofroniou, & Lawlor, 2003; Luis, 2004).

A key finding of this study was the moderating effect of paternal (and not maternal) acceptance in the relationship between victimisation and symptoms of depression; that is, in the condition of higher perceived paternal acceptance, children's victimisation had a lower effect in the development of depressive symptoms than in children who perceived their fathers to be more rejecting. However, this buffering effect was not supported for the case of maternal acceptance. Taken together, these results highlight the importance of paternal role on children's psychological adjustment, as has been noted also in other studies (Desjardins & Leadbeater, 2011). In addition, it provides further support to evidence which suggest that paternal accepting behaviour is negatively related to internalising behaviours (Day & Padilla-Walker, 2009). Especially with regards to the experiences of victimisation, these results confirm previous findings that have also found that paternal acceptance functions as a form of social support, protecting victimised children from the effects of their negative experiences (Flouri & Buchanan, 2002; Papadaki & Giovazolias, 2015). The contribution of our findings lies also in expanding the literature that suggests that fathers contribute to the development of a child in many ways, often in a more influential manner and/or distinct manner when compared to mothers (Rohner & Veneziano, 2001). As noted earlier, it has been noted that paternal acceptance-rejection is a stronger indicator than maternal acceptance-rejection for certain behaviours in children (Day & Padilla-Walker, 2009), such as protection against the occurrence of bullying behaviours in children (Flouri & Buchanan, 2003; Ok & Aslan, 2010). A possible explanation for this might be that fathers may express support, warmth and affection to their children in a different way from mothers, but they may have an equally important impact on youths' psychological state. For example, it has been shown that fathers express their support or warmth through guidance and training of social skills, academic abilities, as well as management practices of emotions, and these qualities seem to help children become more independent (Desjardins & Leadbeater, 2011). The findings of this study seem to also contradict previous studies that emphasise only the protective role of the mother in the Greek family (Georgiou, 2008).

However, the results of this study should be considered in relation to certain limitations. More specifically, the size of the sample was fairly small and limited to elementary school children, therefore reducing the generalisability of the results to the general population. Similarly, as this study was cross-sectional in nature, it was not possible to determine the direction of the relationship between the development of depressive symptoms in children and their experiences of victimisation.

In concluding, our results add further evidence that highlights the need for the development of intervention anti-bullying programmes which would include in their approaches the active role of the father. Our findings suggest that the father should not be considered as less important to the child's development compared to the mother. This practice would reflect the gradual change of society's beliefs concerning parental roles, contemporary research data concerning the influence of the father to the development of the child as well as men's desire to actively be involved in their children upbringing (Gage & Kirk, 2002).

References

Alfaro, E. C., Umana-Taylor, A. J., & Bamaca, M. Y. (2006). The influence of academic support on Latino adolescents' academic motivation. *Family Relations*, *55*(3), 279–291.

Ang, R. P. (2006). Fathers do matter: Evidence from an Asian school-based aggressive sample. *The American Journal of Family Therapy*, *34*, 79–93.

APA – American Psychiatric Association (1994). *Diagnostic and statistical manual of mental disorders* (4th ed.). Washington, DC: American Psychiatric Association.

Arsenault, L., Walsh, E., Trzesniewski, K., Newcombe, R., Caspi, A., & Moffitt, T. (2006). Bullying victimization uniquely contributes to adjustment problems in young children: A nationally representative cohort study. *Pediatrics*, *118*, 130–138.

Barber, B. K., Stoltz, H. E., & Olsen, J. A. (2005). Parental support, psychological control, and behavioural control: Assessing relevance across time, culture, and method. *Monographs of the Society for Research in Child Development*, *70*(4), 1–151.

Bayer, J. K., Sanson, A. V., & Hemphill, S. A. (2006). Parent influences on early childhood internalizing difficulties. *Journal of Applied Developmental Psychology*, *27*, 542–559.

Bowes, L., Maughan, B., Caspi, A., Moffitt, T. E., & Arseneault, L. (2010). Families promote emotional and behavioural resilience to bullying: Evidence of an environmental effect. *The Journal of Child Psychology and Psychiatry*, *51*(7), 809–817.

Bronte-Tinkew, J., Moore, K. A., & Carrano, J. (2006). The father-child relationship, parenting styles, and adolescent risk behaviours in intact families. *Journal of Family Issues*, *27*(6), 850–881.

Cabrera, N. J., Tamis-LeMonda, C. S., Bradley, R. H., Hofferth, S., & Lamb, M. E. (2000). Fatherhood in the twenty-first century. *Child Development, 71*, 127–136.

Carrasco, M. A., & Rohner, R. P. (2013). Parental acceptance and children's psychological adjustment in the context of power and prestige. *Journal of Child and Families Studies, 22*, 1130–1137.

Conners-Burrow, N. A., Johnson, D. L., Whiteside-Mansell, L., McKelvey, L., & Gargus, R. A. (2009). Adults matter: Protecting children from the negative impacts of bullying. *Psychology in the Schools*, *46*, 593–603.

Cooksey, E. C., & Fondell, M. M. (1996). Spending time with the kids: Effects of family structure on fathers' and children's lives. *Journal of Marriage and the Family*, *58*, 693–707.

Cowie, H. (2012). *From birth to sixteen: Children's health, social, emotional and linguistic development.* London: Routledge.

Cowie, H., & Jennifer, D. (2007). *Managing school violence: A whole school approach to good practice*. London: Paul Chapman.

Cowie, H., & Jennifer, D. (2008). *New perspectives on bullying*. Maidenhead: Open University Press.

Craig, W., Harel-Fish, Y., Fogel-Grinvald, H., Dostaler, S., Hetland, J., Simons-Morton, B., et al. (2009). A cross-national profile of bullying and victimization among adolescents in 40 countries. *International Journal of Public Health, 54*, 216–224.

Day, R. D., & Padilla-Walker, L. M. (2009). Mother and father connectedness and involvement during early adolescence. *Journal of Family Psychology, 23*(6), 900–904.

Desjardins, T. L., & Leadbeater, B. J. (2011). Relational victimization and depressive symptoms in adolescence: Moderating effects of mother, father, and peer emotional support. *Journal of Youth and Adolescence, 40*, 531–544.

Espelage, D. L., & Swearer, S. M. (2003). Research on school bullying and victimization: What have we learned and where do we go from here? *School Psychology Review, 32*, 365–383.

Fekkes, M., Pijpers, F. I., & Verloove-Vanhorick, S. P. (2004). Bullying behaviour and associations with psychosomatic complaints and depression in victims. *The Journal of Pediatrics, 144*(1), 17–22.

Flouri, E., & Buchanan, A. (2002). Life satisfaction in teenage boys: The moderating role of father involvement and bullying. *Aggressive Behaviour, 28*, 126–133.

Flouri, E., & Buchanan, A. (2003). The role of mother involvement and father involvement in adolescent bullying behaviour. *Journal of Interpersonal Violence, 18*(6), 634–644.

Frazier, P. A., Tix, A. P., & Barron, K. E. (2004). Testing moderator and mediator effects in counselling psychology research. *Journal of Counselling Psychology, 51*, 115–134.

Gage, J. D., & Kirk, R. (2002). First-time fathers: Perceptions of preparedness for fatherhood. *Canadian Journal of Nursing Research, 34*(4), 15–24.

Georgiou, S. N. (2008). Bullying and victimization at school: The role of mothers. *British Journal of Educational Psychology, 78*, 109–125.

Giovazolias, T. (2014). The moderating role of parental power/prestige on the relationship between parental rejection and psychological maladjustment in a Greek student sample. *Cross-Cultural Research, 48*(3), 240–249.

Giovazolias, T., Kourkoutas, E., Mitsopoulou, E., & Georgiadi, M. (2010). The relationship between perceived school climate and the prevalence of bullying behaviour in Greek schools: Implications for preventive inclusive strategies. *Procedia – Social and Behavioural Sciences, 5*, 2208–2215.

Giovazolias, T., & Malikiosi-Loizos, M. (2016). Bullying at Greek universities: An empirical study. In H. Cowie & C. A. Myers (Eds.), *Bullying among university students: Cross-national perspectives* (pp. 110–126). London: Taylor & Francis.

Hawker, D. S. J., & Boulton, M. J. (2000). Twenty years' research on peer victimization and psychosocial maladjustment: A meta-analytic review of cross-sectional studies. *Journal of Child Psychology and Psychiatry, 41*(4), 441–455.

Hayes, A. F. (2013). *Introduction to mediation, moderation, and conditional process analysis: A regression-based approach*. New York: Guilford Press.

Hooven, C., Gottman, J. M., & Katz, L. F. (1995). Parental meta-emotion structure predicts family and child outcomes. *Cognition and Emotion, 9*(2–3), 229–264.

James, D. J., Sofroniou, N., & Lawlor, M. (2003). The response of Irish adolescents to bullying. *Irish Journal of Psychology, 24*, 22–34.

Kaltiala-Heino, R., Fröjd, S., & Marttunen, M. (2010). Involvement in bullying and depression in a 2-year follow-up in middle adolescence. *European Child & Adolescent Psychiatry, 19*, 45–55.

Khaleque, A., & Rohner, P. R. (2002). Perceived parental acceptance-rejection and psychological adjustment: A meta-analysis of cross cultural and intracultural studies. *Journal of Marriage and the Family, 64*, 54–64.

Lereya, S., Samara, M., & Wolke, D. (2013). Parenting behaviour and the risk of becoming a victim and a bully/victim: A meta-analysis study. *Child Abuse & Neglect, 37*(12), 1091–1108.

Luis, N. B. (2004). Bullying: Concealed by behavioural and somatic symptoms. *Journal of Developmental and Behavioural Pediatrics, 25*(5), 348–349.

Marsiglio, W., Amato, P., Day, R. D., & Lamb, M. E. (2000). Scholarship on fatherhood in the 1990s and beyond. *Journal of Marriage and Family, 62*, 1173–1191.

Masten, A. S., & Shaffer, A. (2006). How families matter in child development: Reflections from research on risk and resilience. In A. Clarke-Stewart & J. Dunn (Eds.), *Families count: Effects on child and adolescent development* (pp. 5–25). New York: Cambridge University Press.

McLeod, B. D., Weisz, J. R., & Wood, J. J. (2007). Examining the association between parenting and childhood depression: A meta-analysis. *Clinical Psychology Review, 27*, 986–1003.

Mischel, W., Shoda, Y., & Peake, P. K. (1988). The nature of adolescent competencies predicted by preschool delay of gratification. *Journal of Personality and Social Psychology, 54*, 687–696.

Molcho, M., Craig, W., Due, P., Pickett, W., Harel-Fisch, Y., Overpeck, M., & the HBSC Bullying Writing Group. (2009). Cross-national time trends in bullying behaviour 1994–2006: Findings from Europe and North America. *International Journal of Public Health, 54*, 225–234.

Ok, S., & Aslan, S. (2010). The school bullying and perceived parental style in adolescents. *Procedia Social and Behavioural Sciences Journal, 5*, 536–540.

Olweus, D. (1993). *Bullying at School: What we know and what we can do*. Oxford: Blackwell Publishers.

Papadaki, E., & Giovazolias, T. (2015). The protective role of father acceptance in the relationship between maternal rejection and bullying: A moderated mediation model. *Journal of Child and Family Studies, 24*, 330–340.

Radloff, L. S. (1977). A CES-D scale: A self-report depression scale for research in the general population. *Applied Psychological Measurement, 1*(3), 385–401.

Richaud de Minzi, M. C. (2006). Loneliness and depression in middle and late childhood: The relationship to attachment and parental styles. *The Journal of Genetic Psychology, 167*(2), 189–210.

Rohner, R. P. (2004). The parental 'acceptance-rejection syndrome': Universal correlates of perceived rejection. *American Psychologist, 59*, 830–840.

Rohner, R. P. (2005). Parental Acceptance-Rejection Questionnaire (PARQ): Test manual. In R. P. Rohner & A. Khaleque (Eds.), *Handbook for the study of parental acceptance and rejection*, (pp. 43–106). CT: Rohner Research Publications.

Rohner, R. P. (2014). PARTheory gets a new name: Interpersonal acceptance-rejection theory (IPARTheory). *International Society for Interpersonal Acceptance and Rejection Newsletter, 8*(3), 6.

Rohner, P. R., & Veneziano, R. A. (2001). The importance of father love: History and contemporary evidence. *Review of General Psychology, 5*(4), 382–405.

Sapouna, M. (2008). Bullying in Greek primary and secondary schools. *School Psychology International, 29*(2), 199–313.

Soper, O. S. (2006). *Interaction* [computer programme]. Retrieved from www.danielsoper.com/Interaction

Tsaousis, I., Giovazolias, T., & Mascha, K. (2012). Translation and Psychometric Properties of the Child Parental Acceptance-Rejection Questionnaire (PARQ) – Short form in Greek. In K. J. Ripoll Núñez, A. L. Comunian, & C. M. Brown (Eds.), *Expanding horizons: Current research on interpersonal acceptance* (pp. 215–228). FL: Brown Walker Press.

Vernberg, E. M., Jacobs, A. K., & Hershberger, A. L. (1999). Peer victimization and attitudes about violence during early adolescence. *Journal of Clinical Child Psychology*, *3*, 386–395.

Theme 4

The social and cultural contexts which challenge or promote school bullying

While much research traditionally focusses on the *individual* aspects of bullying by exploring the characteristics of perpetrators and victims and their relationships within the family, more recently there has been a shift towards examining the *social contexts* in which bullying takes place. In chapter 11, Holly Powell-Jones considers the influence that the social media have in spreading and perpetuating bullying among young people. Additionally, researchers have turned their attention to the role of bystanders in either challenging or facilitating bullying behaviour on the part of peers. Salmivalli (2010, 2014) highlighted the *social* nature of bullying by identifying a range of participant roles that go beyond the relationship between bully and victim to locate bullying within the wider setting of peer group dynamics as a whole. From this perspective, Rubina Hanif and Sadaf Zaheer, in chapter 14, explore the range of participant roles within the particular culture of the school, arguing that bullying is a social phenomenon since bystanders are usually present during an episode of bullying, whether online or offline. These bystanders often supply the bully with social rewards such as laughing and cheering at the victim's discomfort and humiliation. In this way, whether wittingly or not, the bystanders reinforce the bullying behaviour in their role as spectators of the 'drama'. The perpetrators do not usually act alone but rely on support from their assistants as well as tacit approval by witnesses who fail to take action in support of the victim. In chapter 12, Carmel Cefai also examines cultural aspects of school bullying by discussing how schools can create social contexts that foster resilience among vulnerable children. In chapter 13, Wendy Sims-Schouten and Simon Edwards place the whole concept of resilience within a neoliberal framework and explore the implications for schools in creating a climate that facilitates emotional health and well-being.

Chapter 11

Bullying and social media

Holly Powell-Jones

Introduction

This chapter aims to present an overview of current knowledge on youth cyberbullying, including via social media. This area has attracted a huge amount of attention in recent years from academics, the media, police, the criminal justice system, politicians, parents, teachers, charities and technology companies. The vast range of existing studies – spanning fields of psychology, health, youth studies, education and sociology – has occasionally produced conflicting findings and recommendations. At one end of the spectrum are accusations of 'moral panics' around youth, deviance and new technology, with claims that protectionist approaches are used to justify increased surveillance and restrictions on young people (Cesaroni, Downing, & Alvi, 2012; Kelly, 2000; Waldron, 2014). At the other are warnings over a multitude of new digital risks facing the young generation, the likes of which many adults are unaware of, inexperienced with or ill-equipped to manage (Korenis & Billick, 2014; Mishna, Saini, & Solomon, 2009; Strom, Strom, Walker, Sindel-Arrington, & Beckert, 2011). Before any solutions can be considered, we must first identify and critically analyse the issue itself. This chapter will explore key questions, such as how cyberbullying is defined, the role of technology and social media, how harmful and prevalent the practice is, and suggestions for interventions.

I will also draw on first-hand experience running a legal education project in schools, entitled 'Online and Social Media Law and Ethics'. In 2013, the newly formed Office of the Police and Crime Commissioner for Surrey provided funding for community projects aimed at reducing or preventing crime. This project was designed as part of a bid by local media company Eagle Radio Ltd. to address youth cyber offending. We delivered assemblies and workshops to pupils and staff at secondary schools across the county, educating them about the law in relation to online publishing/broadcasting and digital communication (Powell-Jones, 2015). Over the course of one year, the project reached more than 30 schools and 9,000 pupils, and was recommissioned for a further two years. In addition to direct, regular contact with young people aged 11- to 18-years-old, this project involved formal and informal conversations with hundreds of school staff, teachers and parents, all of whom have contributed to my understanding and approach to this somewhat controversial subject.

Why are social media relevant?

The importance of social and digital media in the lives of young people in Britain today cannot be understated. It is estimated roughly half of all children in the UK have used a social networking site by the age of 10, with 70% of 12–15-year-olds having their own online profile (KnowTheNet, 2014; ONS, 2015). Four out of five young social media users log on at least once every day, and the amount of time spent online has trebled over the last decade to an average of 27 hours per week in the UK (Ofcom, 2015). In some areas, personal smartphone ownership among under-18s has risen by almost a fifth over the past two years to 97% (Powell-Jones, 2016). Platforms such as Facebook, WhatsApp, Snapchat, YouTube and Instagram are increasingly popular with young people and access via mobile devices is fast becoming the norm (Lilley & Ball, 2013; Lilley, Ball, & Vernon, 2014; ONS, 2015). For many teenagers, digital forms of communication have not only become integrated into social life, but form an integral part of it, with young people having to make a conscious effort to 'opt out' rather than 'opt in' (Boyd, 2014). Online interaction and social media have necessarily become a key concern for stakeholders invested in children and young people (Livingstone & Bulger, 2012).

In light of this, young people's behaviour and experiences must be framed within the context of new technologies, with particular focus on the 'affordances' they offer for social interaction (Livingstone, 2009). For example, ask.fm and YikYak provide anonymity for users; Facebook Live allows real-time video broadcasting to an online audience; Snapchat content can be set to 'vanish' once it's been received, and WhatsApp provides automatic encryption for private messaging. Some argue these affordances play a part in actively encouraging and facilitating risky online behaviour (Ofcom, 2015; Shariff, 2015, p. 77). With new forms of communication come potential new norms for social interaction among young people. Despite this, continuing 'digital divides' mean there is rarely a level playing field for this interaction. Children's online experiences vary according to their confidence, skills, abilities, access to resources and support, as well as the size and nature of existing social networks (Buckingham, 2008). In some cases, technological advances and increased Internet-access can leave children more vulnerable to risk (Livingstone, Kirwil, Ponte, & Staksrud, 2014). For this reason, it is important to avoid the temptation to overestimate children's digital capabilities or to overly generalise their experiences (Koutropoulos, 2011).

What kinds of social media are young people using?

Social media platforms, and the ways that they are being used, are constantly evolving. Data from various surveys indicate that Facebook remains the dominant Social Networking Site (SNS) for young people (Lilley et al., 2014; Ofcom, 2015; Purdy & York, 2016). Yet, the Global Social Media Impact Study claims many teens are abandoning Facebook, favouring private messaging apps such as WhatsApp and Snapchat instead (2013). Academics and young people themselves claim this is partly due to the 'familial gaze' of parents (who also have Facebook accounts), which they want to avoid when communicating with peers (Robards & Vromen, 2015). Boyd's vast ethnographic study of teenagers in the US also seems to support the notion that young people want to engage and experiment with social networking away from the prying eyes of judgemental adults (Marwick & Boyd, 2014a; Marwick & Boyd, 2014b).

Data from nearly 8,000 students participating in the Surrey OPCC project reveals a similar pattern. Facebook was the most popular SNS in 2013–14, with 81% of pupils reporting having a profile, but this fell to 66% the following year and just 48% in 2015–16. Meanwhile, Instagram, Snapchat and WhatsApp all appear to be gaining popularity among students (Powell-Jones, 2015). The data also shows private messaging apps appear to be more popular among younger students, with older students preferring sites that enable publishing and broadcasting to a public online audience. Student participation in online gaming and online dating also has potential repercussions both in terms of the nature of online bullying and the platforms used to enact it (Borrajo, Gámez-Guadix, & Calvete, 2015; Chang et al., 2014; Dittrick, Beran, Mishna, Hetherington, & Shariff, 2013; Gordon-Messer, Bauermeister, Grodzinski, & Zimmerman, 2013; Zweig, Dank, Yahner, & Lachman, 2013). On average, 58% of students say they take part in online gaming, although this rises to 76% among younger students (Powell-Jones, 2016). Although a very small percentage of pupils admitted to online dating, -0.4% of students under 15, and 3% of 15- to 18-year-olds – the issue raises huge child protection concerns (Powell-Jones, 2016). Many dating platforms have changed their policy to only allow over 18s, although the NSPCC has criticised a lack of robust age-verification processes to support these changes (McGoogan, 2016).

Defining 'cyberbullying'

Cyberbullying is often framed as a 'new' threat to children, particularly within media coverage (Harrison, 2013; Pertusini, 2011). It is commonly defined by scholars as bullying enacted via electronic means, for example via mobile phones, online websites, social media or digital messaging apps. Many empirical studies use Olweus's paradigm of traditional bullying, exploring issues of intentionality, repetition and power imbalances between perpetrators and targets (Holt, Burruss, & Bossier, 2010; Pelfrey et al., 2013). Cyberbullying research, however, is often conflated with cyber aggression, and many of the following behaviours are included in studies with children:

- Posting text or images that hurt or embarrass someone
- Being cruel or mean via electronic means
- Posting false information about someone/spreading rumours
- Teasing
- Nasty or upsetting comments
- 'Trolling' or 'flaming'

(Lilley et al., 2014; Shariff, 2015; Purdy & York, 2016; Talwar, Gomez-Garibello, & Shariff, 2014)

There is also a huge debate among researchers as to whether risky digital practices such as 'sexting' between young people should be considered as abusive behaviour or a harmless form of flirting (Gabriel, 2014; Korenis & Billick, 2014; Lee & Crofts, 2015; Phippen, 2012; Ringrose, Gill, Livingstone, & Harvey, 2012; Shariff, 2015). The broad and potentially ambiguous term 'cyberbullying' can create confusion about what ought to be causing concern when it comes to children's online interaction (Cassidy, Faucher, & Jackson, 2013). This is often the case among researchers, teachers and parents, so it is unsurprising that similar confusion exists among students (Shariff, 2015). There is, as yet, no clear, unequivocal definition of cyberbullying; something that researchers have, for the most part, now come to accept (Deschamps & McNutt, 2016). A positive side-effect of this, however, is that it forces us to challenge pre-existing assumptions and adopt more of a youth-perspective when investigating the subject. When it comes to what is 'harmful' vs. 'harmless' online, positioning young people as the experts of their own experiences and doing research *with* them (not 'on' them) is arguably a strength of existing and future research (see Cowie and Myers in chapter 1).

How prevalent is cyberbullying?

One of the major challenges when assessing rates of cyberbullying is that, much like traditional bullying, the issue is thought to go unreported – or, at the very least, hugely under-reported (Hinduja et al., 2008; Li, 2010; Purdy & York, 2016). In one of the largest ever studies into children and online risks, where over 10,000 children were asked 'What bothers you about the Internet?', cyberbullying was a significant concern, with around one in five children mentioning it (Hasebrink, Livingstone, Haddon, & Ólafsson, 2009). Despite the high rate of concern, just 6% of children claim to have actually been bullied online (Livingstone, Haddon, Görzig, & Ólafsson, 2011). Studies indicate rates of cyberbullying to be anything between 3% (Purdy & York, 2016) and one in three (Lilley et al., 2014), but it is likely that issues with defining 'cyberbullying' could be hindering attempts to quantify prevalence of the phenomenon.

Research does suggest that cyberbullying is less prevalent than traditional 'offline' bullying. In 2014, the NSPCC provided 7,296 youth counselling sessions specifically related to online bullying (2015). However, that constitutes less than a third of the overall 25,700 sessions related to bullying more generally in the same year (Bentley et al., 2016). The Annual Bullying Survey of 3,000 young people in the UK found that less than one in four victims of bullying said this included online abuse, and that the frequency of experiences for cyberbullying was far lower than verbal or physical bullying (Ditch the Label, 2015). Similar studies have found that out of 23% of children who were victims of any kind of bullying, just 5% reported *only* being bullied online (Waasdorp et al., 2015). Olweus claims it is a relatively "low-prevalence phenomenon", involving children who are already involved in traditional bullying, and argues social media have *not* created vast numbers of 'new' victims and bullies (2012, p. 528). Even if this is the case, that does not mean the issue should not merit concern, as the impact on young victims can be profound.

How harmful is cyberbullying?

Many existing studies warn of severe potential consequences for children who are victimised online, including serious mental health problems like mood disorders, adjustment reactions, anxiety disorders, depression, substance abuse and even suicide (Korenis & Billick, 2014; Völlink, Dehue, & McGuckin, 2016). The media have also raised the profile of teenage suicides with potential links to cyberbullying in recent years. In 2013, the deaths of 15-year-old Joshua Unsworth, 14-year-old Hannah Smith and 17-year-old Daniel Perry were *all* reported to be connected to abuse via ask.fm, with their parents placing some blame on the social networking site itself (BBC News, 2013; Bryne, 2013; Tozer, 2013). The issue has had similar coverage in North America, with the suicides of teenagers Rehtaeh Parsons, Amanda Todd and Peyton James all connected to online abuse. Despite some adults' continuing assumption that the digital environment is 'not real' and victims can simply 'switch off' their aggressors, studies show strong links between online bullying and real harm. It is claimed some aspects of social media can actually compound and intensify feelings of powerlessness and victimisation, such as the potential for 'collective perpetration', mass audiences/witnesses, anonymity of perpetrators, constant access to the victim(s) and the permanence of online content (Dittrick et al., 2013; Ševčíková, Šmahel, & Otavová, 2012; Parris, Varjas, Meyers, & Cutts, 2012).

However, some researchers are adamant that the harm caused by cyberbullying is equal to – or even less than – traditional bullying (Bauman, 2013; Hase, Goldber, Smith, Stuck, & Campain, 2015). Young people have themselves argued that the performative nature of social interaction in front of an online audience can lead to hyped-up 'drama', and what may appear to adult outsiders as harmful can be harmless (Marwick & Boyd, 2014b). Some studies find that student victims are easily able to ascribe negative attributes to cyberbullies, rather than themselves, and that negative effects caused by nasty comments online are rarely long-lasting (Lilley et al., 2014; Parris et al., 2012). Other research reveals young people have no moral concerns whatsoever about some types of cyber aggression, believing that the Internet has a different set of moral codes from the offline social world (Li, 2010; Selwyn, 2008). Some researchers argue it is vital to investigate youth norms in their own context, and avoid an automatic 'framework of harm' when it come adolescents' behaviour online (Boyd, 2014; Gabriel, 2014). This argument can perhaps be supported by studies revealing that adults and adolescents tend to differ in their assessment of what is 'risky', 'deviant' and 'harmful' online (McAfee, 2015; Ofcom, 2015).

Yet, young people are rarely clear cut in their moral evaluations of cyberbullying, with younger children in particular appearing unsure of the difference between harmful and harmless actions online (Pyżalski, 2012; Shariff, 2015; Talwar et al., 2014). Unsurprisingly, adolescents who admit to cyber-intimidation of others are likely to judge scenarios of online aggression less severely than their peers. Peer-to-peer aggression (as opposed to targeting strangers), intention to harm and power imbalances tend to attract more severe condemnation of cyberbullying behaviours among young people (Talwar et al., 2014; Whittaker & Kowalski, 2015). In some situations, students may actively defend cyberbullies, arguing for their 'right to freedom of speech', 'what happens online should stay online', or that victims should simply 'deal with it' (Cowie & Myers, 2014; Li, 2010). This shows that the seriousness of cyberbullying is constantly being questioned by young people themselves. Some academics, while acknowledging the potential for harm, also argue that cyberbullying practices are fairly 'normal' for teenagers and something that they may simply grow out of (Cesaroni et al., 2012; Sakellariou, Carroll, & Houghton, 2012; Smith, 2014). It could be the case that this issue is more of a concern for adults than it is for young people, but it nonetheless remains a popular subject of academic study. Perhaps the most relevant debate now is whether cyberbullying ought to be examined as a unique phenomenon, or as part of a wider 'umbrella' of different bullying behaviours (Olweus, 2012; Thomas, Connor, & Scott, 2015; Waasdorp, 2015).

What are the risk factors?

New technology and online environments are often discussed as being 'conducive' to bullying. Research into how cyberbullying occurs shows that text messaging, Facebook and social media are common 'venues' for victimization, and that the more time a child spends online, the more their risk of abuse increases (Livingstone, 2009; Purdy & York, 2016; Py alski, 2012; Rice et al., 2015; Whittaker & Kowalski, 2015). Narratives constructed by young people show a strong association between online anonymity and risky behaviour, such as cyberbullying (Keipi & Oksanen, 2014). Online anonymity is often associated with a 'disinhibition effect', reduction in social control, moral disengagement, desensitisation and a sense of freedom from repercussions (Kyriacou & Zuin, 2016; Görzig & Ólafsson, 2013; Mason, 2008; Suler, 2004). Online spaces are often perceived by adults and children alike to be without rules or regulation, or at the very least without consistent, regular enforcement of them by any authority (Arntfield, 2015). Parents and teachers, in particular, raise concerns over a perceived lack of accountability and supervision of children online. Virtual environments have even been compared to the island in Golding's 'Lord of the Flies', where, without corrective adult intervention, children are likely to become uncivilised and ultimately destructive (Shariff, 2013; Strom et al., 2011).

Risk factors for cyberbullying are predominantly social, rather than technological. Much like traditional bullying, cyber aggression is linked to high rates of loneliness, low self-worth, low levels of popularity and perpetrators having been victimised themselves (Navarro, Yubero, & Larrañaga, 2015; Schoffstall & Cohen, 2011). Gender is thought to make a difference, although there is disagreement as to whether boys or girls are more likely to participate in cyber aggression (Erdur-Baker, 2010; Görzig & Ólafsson, 2013; Rice et al., 2015; Yang & Salmivalli, 2013). There is a significant correlation between children experiencing or engaging in bullying both online *and* offline, providing support for claims that cyberbullying could be just a new manifestation of an existing social problem (Olweus, 2012; Selwyn, 2008; Thomas et al., 2015). Numerous studies indicate that cyberbullying predominantly occurs within existing social contexts. Victims report that online abuse does not originate from 'anonymous strangers', but, more often than not, from friends or fellow students (Ditch the Label, 2015; Mishna et al., 2009; Purdy & York, 2016; Waasdorp et al., 2015). This emphasises the need for schools to be a vital site for cyberbullying intervention and prevention programmes.

Far from being 'different' from our offline social worlds, it may be the case that online environments and interactions mimic them. Young people are more likely to be cyberbullied because of physical appearance, physical or mental disabilities, special needs, academic performance, sexual orientation, race, ethnicity or nationality (Cassidy et al., 2013; Cesaroni et al., 2012; Rice et al., 2015; Shariff, 2015). This suggests that the Internet may merely be a site for reproducing and amplifying existing social inequalities and prejudices. Cyber hate speech ought to be a significant concern with regard to young people, as research shows that homophobic, racist, xenophobic, Islamophobic and misogynistic sentiments are increasingly prevalent on social media (Antijoule, 2013; Copsey, Dack, Littler, & Feldman, 2013; Miller et al., 2016; Nagle, 2013; Wendling, 2015). Children who use social media will likely be exposed to this sooner or later in their digital lives, and the concern is that it may be perceived as 'normal' online. Young people exhibiting cyberbullying behaviour based on 'difference' demonstrates that the problem goes beyond that of the technology itself.

How can we reduce cyberbullying? Reflections from the OPCC surrey project

Many parents feel that monitoring and regulating children's social media activity is the simplest way to reduce the risk of them being victimised (or bullying others) online. Although this has found to be effective in some instances, it can be tricky to implement (Khurana et al., 2012). Adolescents' technological skills often outstrip that of their parents, with spyware, parental controls, blocks, filters and other technological solutions easily circumnavigated (McAfee, 2012/15). The restriction and/or surveillance of young people's online activity have also been criticised as potentially breaching their rights (Boyd, 2014; Livingstone, 2009; Livingstone & Bulger, 2012). It is primarily viewed as the responsibility of schools to address cyberbullying risks to children, with esafety becoming compulsory in 2009 and a key part of Ofsted inspections in 2012. Despite this, inconsistencies remain in how the subject is addressed in the UK, with calls for increased standardisation of methods and resources (Hasebrink et al., 2009). School cyberbullying initiatives are thought to increase reporting rates, but there is little conclusive evidence for their effectiveness in altering students' behaviour online (Mishna, Cook, Saini, Wu, & MacFadden, 2011; Schilder, Brusselaers, & Bogaerts, 2016).

Findings from the 2015–16 OPCC report show that much of the problem may lie in incorrect perceptions of what constitutes 'serious' or criminal conduct online. When offered a series of scenarios to respond to involving online risk, less than a quarter of students recognised that sending threats, abuse or malicious messages via Twitter could potentially lead to a criminal arrest (Powell-Jones, 2016). While recognition of the seriousness of hate speech was more prominent among under 18s, on average of 41% of students indicated that they did not think a racist tweet could potentially result in a prison sentence (Powell-Jones, 2016). These results, although insufficient to shed light on the issue of why or when students are likely to have these perceptions, flag a specific need for further research in this area. Explorations of deviant or criminal behaviour, including online and on social media, must consider to what extent an offender perceives their actions to be breaching a legal, moral or social boundary in the first place (Becker, 1967; Sykes & Matza, 1957).

Existing legal, criminal and human rights legislation surrounding digital interaction are rarely discussed in an education context, and school staff sometimes admit to being confused about the law (Koutropoulos, 2011; Purdy & York, 2016; Shariff, 2009). Students are equally unsure about what kinds of online behaviour constitute criminal offences, or whether issues such as age, intention or ignorance of the law might reduce the risk of penalties (Powell-Jones, 2015). While some researchers argue that there are insufficient mechanisms for bringing cyberbullies to justice, others express concern over punitive measures, such as criminalisation (Arntfield, 2014; Cesaroni et al., 2012; Shariff, 2013, 2015). Either way, discussion of the law in relation to cyber-misuse should be considered a vital part of education on the matter. Boyd has criticised how the media continue to describe "serious criminal acts of aggression by teens as bullying, rather than using terms like stalking, harassment and abuse" (2008, p. 132), and this was a key consideration when designing and implementing the 'Online and Social Media Law and Ethics' OPCC project in Surrey schools (Table 11.1).

Figures from the Ministry of Justice show that the number of people convicted of communications offences has soared over the past 10 years (Channel 4 News, 2015). Not only that, but the maximum sentence for these offences was increased to two years – up from six months – in April 2015 (CPS.gov.uk). These legal and criminal changes clearly constitute a shift in society: either in terms of the prevalence of these offences, the punitive measures being taken against them or potentially both. Many students, parents and school staff are shocked to learn that under-18s can face criminal action for cyber abuse, and to discover that the age of criminal responsibility in England and Wales is 10. Seventy prosecutions for communications offences in 2014 were against juveniles, and a Freedom of Information request revealed that thousands more children were the subject of police investigations (Channel 4 News, 2015; Pisa, 2014). This is despite the fact that guidelines for the Crown Prosecution Service advise that prosecuting children for social media offences is "rarely likely to be in the public interest" (Saunders, 2014, p. 10).

Schools and parents often wish to deal with instances of cyberbullying without involving the police or courts, even when there are potentially criminal offences being committed. However, those studying youth cyberbullying in an academic context can arguably justify a criminological approach to exploring the issue (Arntfield, 2014/15; Cesaroni et al., 2012). The potential consequences

Table 11.1 Examples of criminal legislation in England and Wales relevant to discussion of cyberbullying in schools

- **The Malicious Communications Act 1988/The Communications Act 2003** (Penalises messages that are grossly offensive, obscene, indecent, menacing or false. Penalises electronic communication that conveys a threat and where there is intent to cause distress or anxiety to a recipient)
- **The Protection from Harassment Act 1997** (Penalises causing deliberate alarm or distress to a target, putting someone in fear of violence, or forcing unwanted communication and contact, including through social media)
- **Offences Against the Person Act 1861** (Penalises credible threats of violence to the person, with a threat to kill)
- **The Public Order Act 1986/2006 amendment/2008 amendment** (Penalises displaying, publishing or distributing threatening, abusive or insulting material intended to stir up racial hatred, i.e. on the grounds of colour, race, ethnic origin and nationality. Similar penalties introduced for threats on the grounds of religion or sexual orientation)
- **The Children's Act 1978/The Criminal Justice Act 1988/the Sexual Offences Act 2003/the Amendment to the Criminal Justice and Courts Bill 2015** (Penalises the distribution, or possession with a view to distributing, indecent photographs or video of under 18 years old)

Adapted from CPS.gov.uk (Saunders, 2014; Powell-Jones, 2015) and penalties for young people who bully via social media can stretch far beyond the confines of peers, home or school. While this may be a source of anxiety for parents and teachers, it can equally provide some reassurance and sense of empowerment to victims, and should not be ignored. Although not a replacement for developing empathic moral frameworks, discussion of existing laws and penalties for social media abuse can enable discussions with young people to move beyond subjective ideas about what is 'nice' or 'nasty' online behaviour. Inclusion of news stories and real life case studies showing the consequences of social media abuse for the perpetrator, as well as the victim, can have more impact on students than simply negative moral judgement from teachers or parents (Powell-Jones, 2015).

Ultimately, it will be down to young people themselves to first respond to situations online, as we know that reporting rates for cyberbullying remain low (Purdy & York, 2016). Positive peer influence and schemes that involve and include young people are far more likely to be effective at reducing cyberbullying than adult monitoring or disapproval. But monitoring, support and intervention from peers are unlikely to be successful if students remain unable to 'define the line' between serious and harmless conduct online (Kyriacou & Zuin, 2016; Shariff, 2015). Our role as adults is to facilitate the necessary educational discussions to open up this 'closed door subject' (Purdy & York, 2016): empowering young people with adequate knowledge of the legal and ethical considerations of social media use, and perhaps allowing them to educate us about the changing role that new media and technology play in their everyday social lives.

References

Antijoule, N. (2013). *The hate crime report: Homophobia, biphobia, and transphobia.* London: Galop.

Arntfield, M. (2014). Cybercrime & cyberdeviance. In R. Linden (Ed.), *Criminology: A Canadian perspective* (8th ed., pp. 500–516). Toronto, ON: Nelson Education.

Arntfield, M. (2015). Toward a cybervictimology: Cyberbullying, routine activities theory, and the anti-sociality of social media. *Canadian Journal of Communication, 40*(3), 371–388.

Bauman, S. (2013). Cyberbullying: What does the research tell us? *Theory Into Practice, 52*(4), 249–256.

BBC News. (2013). Hannah Smith death: Father says daughter was a victim of cyberbullies. *BBC News*, 6 August 2013 [Online]. Retrieved from www.bbc.co.uk/news/uk-england-leicestershire-23584769 (accessed 14 July 2016).

Becker, H. (1967). *Outsiders: Studies in the sociology of deviance.* New York: Macmillan.

Bentley, H., O'Hagan, O., Raff, A., & Bhatti, I. (2016). *How safe are our children? The most comprehensive overview of child protection in the UK 2016.* London: NSPCC.

Borrajo, E., Gámez-Guadix, M., & Calvete, E. (2015). Justification beliefs of violence, myths about love and cyber dating abuse. *Psicothema, 27*(4), 327–333.

Boyd, D. (2008). The role of networked publics in teenage social life. In D. Buckingham (Ed.), *Youth, Identity, and Digital Media.* The John, D., & Catherine, T. MacArthur Foundation Series on Digital Media and Learning. Cambridge, MA: The MIT Press.

Boyd, D. (2014). *The social lives of networked teens.* London: Yale University Press.

Bryne, P. (2013). Daniel Perry suicide: Teenage blackmail victim received death threats on ask.fm. *Mirror.co.uk*, 16 August 2013, Updated 16 August [Online]. Retrieved from www.mirror.co.uk/news/uk-news/daniel-perry-suicide-teenage-blackmail-2172896 (accessed 14 July 2016).

Buckingham, D. (2008). *Beyond technology: Children's learning in the age of digital culture.* Cambridge: Polity Press.

Cassidy, W., Faucher, C., & Jackson, M. (2013). Cyberbullying among youth: A comprehensive review of current international research and its implications and application to policy and practice. *School Psychology International, 34*, 1–38.

Cesaroni, C., Downing, S., & Alvi, S. (2012). Bullying enters the 21st century? Turning a critical eye to cyber-bullying research. *Youth Justice, 12*(3), 199–211.

Chang, F.-C., Chiu, C.-H., Miao, N.-F., Chen, P.-H., Lee, C.-M., Huang, T.-F., & Pan, Y.-C. (2014). Online gaming and risks predict cyberbullying perpetration and victimization in adolescents. *International Journal of Public Health, 60*(2), 257–266.

Channel 4 News. (2015). Internet 'troll' convictions soar: Is social media to blame? *Channel 4 News*, 24 May 2015 [Online]. Retrieved from www.channel4.com/news/internet-trollconvictions-ministry-of-justice

Copsey, N., Dack, J., Littler, M., & Feldman, M. (2013). *Anti-Muslim hate crime and the far right.* Teeside University: Tell MAMA.

Cowie, H., & Myers, C.-A. (2014). Bullying amongst university students in the UK. *International Journal of Emotional Education, 6*(1), 66–75.

CPS.gov.uk. *The Crown Prosecution Service: Communications offences* [Online]. Retrieved from www.cps.gov.uk/legal/a_to_c/communications_offences/

Deschamps, R., & McNutt, K. (2016). Cyberbullying: What's the problem? *Canadian Public Administration, 59*(1), 45–71.

Ditch the Label. (2015). *Annual Bullying Survey 2015*, April 2015 [Online]. Retrieved from www.ditchthelabel.org/annual-bullying-survey-2015/ (accessed 11 July 2016).

Dittrick, C., Beran, T., Mishna, F., Hetherington, R., & Shariff, S. (2013). Do children who bully their peers also play violent video games? A Canadian national study. *Journal of School Violence, 12*(4), 297–318.

Erdur-Baker, Ö. (2010). Cyberbullying and its correlation to traditional bullying, gender and frequent and risky usage of internet mediated communication tools. *New Media & Society, 12*(1), 109–125.

Gabriel, F. (2014). Sexting, selfies and self-harm: Young people, social media and the performance of self-development. *Media International Australia, 151*, 104–112.

Gordon-Messer, D., Bauermeister, J. A., Grodzinski, A., & Zimmerman, M. (2013). Sexting among young adults. *The Journal of Adolescent Health, 52*(3), 301–306.

Görzig, A., & Ólafsson, K. (2013). What makes a bully a cyberbully? Unravelling the characteristics of cyberbullies across twenty-five European countries. *Journal of Children and Media*, 7(1), 9–27.

The Guardian. (2014). Number of children who are victims of cyberbullying doubles in a year. *Press Association*, 14 November 2014 [Online]. Retrieved from www.theguardian.com/society/2014/nov/14/35pc-children-teenagers-victims-cyberbullying-fears-grooming-tinder-snapchat (accessed 11 July 2016).

Harrison, A. (2013). Cyber-bullying: Horror in the home. *BBC News*, 17 August 2013 [Online]. Retrieved from www.bbc.co.uk/news/education-23727673 (accessed 14 March 2016).

Hase, C., Goldber, S., Smith, D., Stuck, A., & Campain, J. (2015). Impacts of traditional bullying and cyberbullying on the mental health of middle school and high school students. *Psychology in Schools*, *52*(6), 607–617.

Hasebrink, U., Livingstone, S., Haddon, L., & Ólafsson, K. (2009). *Comparing children's online opportunities and risks across Europe: Cross-national comparisons for EU Kids Online*. LSE, London: EU Kids Online.

Hinduja, S., & Patchin, J. W. (2008). Cyberbullying: An exploratory analysis of factors related to offending and victimization. *Deviant Behaviour*, *29*(2), 129–156.

Holt, T. J., Burruss, G. W., & Bossier, A. M. (2010). Social learning and cyber-deviance: Examining the importance of a full social learning model in the virtual world. *Journal of Crime & Justice*, *33*(3), 31–60.

Keipi, T., & Oksanen, A. (2014). Self-exploration, anonymity and risks in the online setting: Analysis of narratives by 14–18-year olds. *Journal of Youth Studies*, *17*(8), 1097–1113.

Kelly, P. (2000). The dangerousness of youth-at-risk: The possibilities of surveillance and intervention in uncertain times. *Journal of Adolescence*, *23*(4), 463–473.

Khurana, A., Bleakley, A., Jordan, A B., & Romer, D. (2014). The protective effects of parental monitoring and internet restriction on adolescents' risk of online harassment. *Journal of Youth and Adolescence*, *44*(5), 1039–1047.

KnowTheNet.org. (2014). Under-age Social networking – dangers. *Survey conducted by Opinium*, 11 February 2014 [Online]. Retrieved from http://ourinsight.opinium.co.uk/survey-results/ *under-age-social-networking-dangers* (accessed 13 March 2016).

Korenis, P., & Billick, S. B. (2014). Forensic implications: Adolescent sexting and cyberbullying. *The Psychiatric Quarterly*, *85*(1), 97–101.

Koutropoulos, A. (2011). Digital natives ten years after. *MERLOT Journal of Online Learning and Teaching*, 7(4), 525–538.

Kyriacou, C., & Zuin, A. (2016). Cyberbullying and moral disengagement: An analysis based on a social pedagogy of pastoral care in schools. *Pastoral Care in Education*, *34*(1), 34–42.

Lee, M., & Crofts, T. (2015). Gender, pressure, coercion and pleasure: Untangling motivations for sexting between young people. *British Journal of Criminology*, *55*, 454–473.

Li, Q. (2010). Cyberbullying in high schools: A study of students' behaviours and beliefs about this new phenomenon. *Journal of Aggression, Maltreatment & Trauma*, *19*(4), 372–392.

Lilley, C., & Ball, R. (2013). *Younger children and social networking sites: A blind spot*. London: NSPCC.

Lilley, C., Ball, R., & Vernon, H. (2014). *The experiences of 11–16 year olds on social networking sites*. London: NSPCC.

Livingstone, S. (2009). *Children and the internet: Great expectations, challenging realities*. Cambridge: Polity Press.

Livingstone, S., & Bulger, M. (2012). A global research agenda for children's rights in the digital age. *Journal of Children and Media*, *8*(4), 317–335.

Livingstone, S., Haddon, L., Görzig, A., & Ólafsson, K. (2011). *Risks and safety on the Internet: The perspective of European children*. London: EU Kids Online.

Livingstone, S., Kirwil, L., Ponte, C., & Staksrud, E. (2014). In their own words: What bothers children online? *European Journal of Communication*, *29*(3), 271–288.

Marwick, A. E., & Boyd, D. (2014a). Networked privacy: How teenagers negotiate context in social media. *New Media & Society*, *16*(7), 1051–1067.

Marwick, A. E., & Boyd, D. (2014b). 'It's just drama': Teen perspectives on conflict and aggression in a networked era. *Journal of Youth Studies*, *17*(9), 1187–1204.

Mason, K. L. (2008). Cyber-bullying: A preliminary assessment for school personnel. *Psychology in the Schools*, *45*(4), 323–348.
McAfee. (2012). *The digital divide: How the online behaviour of teens is getting past parents*, 25 June 2012 [Online]. Retrieved from blogs.mcafee.com/consumer/thedigitaldividestudy (accessed 12 November 2014).
McAfee. (2015). *Latest teens, tweens and technology research shows parents need a pat on the back but there is still work to be done*, 21 June 2015 [Online]. Retrieved from https://blogs.mcafee.com/consumer/latest-teens-tweens-and-technology-research-shows-parents-need-apat-on-the-back-but-there-is-still-work-to-be-done/ (accessed 13 March 2016).
McGoogan, C. (2016). Tinder is banning under 18s – previous limit was 13. *The Telegraph*, 9 June 2016 [Online]. Retrieved from www.telegraph.co.uk/technology/2016/06/09/tinder-to-banunder-18s-from-dating-app/ (accessed 3August 2016).
Miller, C., Arcostanzo, F., Smith, J., Krasodomski-Jones, A., Wiedlitzka, S., Jamali, R., & Dale, J. (2016). *Hate speech after Brexit*. Centre for Analysis of Social Media, Demos, 11 July 2016 [Online]. Retrieved from www.demos.co.uk/project/hate-speech-after-brexit/ (accessed 11 July 2016).
Mishna, F., Cook, C., Saini, M., Wu, M.-J., & MacFadden, R. (2011). Interventions to prevent and reduce cyber abuse of youth: A systematic review. *Research on Social Work Practice*, *21*, 5–14.
Mishna, F., Saini, S., & Solomon, S. (2009). Ongoing and online: Children and youth's perceptions of cyber bullying. *Children and Youth Services Review*, *31*(12), 1222–1228.
Nagle, A. (2013). Not quite kicking off everywhere: Feminist notes of digital liberation. In C. Fowley, C. English, & S. Thouesny (Eds.), *Internet research, theory and practice: Perspectives from Ireland*. Dublin: Research-publishing.net.
Navarro, R., Yubero, S., & Larrañaga, E. (2015). Psychosocial risk factors for involvement in bullying behaviours: Empirical comparison between cyberbullying and social bullying victims and bullies. *School Mental Health*, 7(4), 235–248.
NSPCC. (2015). *"Always there when I need you": ChildLine review: what's affected children in April 2014–March 2015*. London: NSPCC.
Ofcom. (2015). *Children and parents: Media use and attitudes report 2015*. Published 20th November 2015. London: Ofcom.
Olweus, D. (2012). Cyberbullying: An overrated phenomenon? *European Journal of Developmental Psychology*, *9*(5), 520–538.
ONS digital. (2015). *Internet use in the UK: What are the facts?*, 22 May 2015 [Online]. Retrieved from http://visual.ons.gov.uk/internet-use/ (accessed 22 May 2015).
Parris, L., Varjas, K., Meyers, J., & Cutts, H. (2012). High school students' perceptions of coping with cyberbullying. *Youth & Society*, *44*(2), 284–306.
Pelfrey, W. V. Jr., & Weber, N. L. (2013). Keyboard gangsters: Analysis of incidence and correlates of cyberbullying in a large urban student population. *Deviant Behaviour*, *34*(1), 68–84.
Pertusini, A. (2011). Cyberbullying is a new threat for children. *Telegraph.co.uk*, 23 June 2011 [Online]. Retrieved from www.telegraph.co.uk/education/educationadvice/8593880/Cyberbullying-is-a-new-threat-for-children.html (accessed 3 March 2016).
Phippen, A. (2012). *Sexting: An exploration of practices, attitudes and influences*. Plymouth: NSPCC.
Pisa, N. (2014). Twitter trolls jailed for sending abusive messages. *Sky News*, 24 January 2014 [Online]. Retrieved from http://news.sky.com/story/1200521/twitter-trolls-jailed-for-sending-abusivetweets (accessed 22 November 2015).

Powell-Jones, H. (2015). *Online and social media law and ethics – Final report 2014/15.* Eagle Radio Ltd. and the Office of the Police and Crime Commissioner, Surrey.

Powell-Jones, H. (2016). *Online and social media law and ethics – Final report 2015/16.* Eagle Radio Ltd. and the Office of the Police and Crime Commissioner, Surrey.

Purdy, N., & York, L. (2016). A critical investigation of the nature and extent of cyberbullying in two post-primary schools in Northern Ireland. *Pastoral Care in Education, 34*(1), 13–23.

Pyżalski, J. (2012). From cyberbullying to electronic aggression: Typology of the phenomenon. *Emotional & Behavioural Difficulties, 17*(3/4), 305–317.

Rice, E., Petering, R., Rhoades, H., Winetrobe, H., Goldbach, J., Plant, A., Montoya, J., & Kordic, T. (2015). Cyberbullying perpetration and victimization among middle-school students. *American Journal of Public Health, 105*(3), 66–72.

Ringrose, J., Gill, R., Livingstone, S., & Harvey, L. (2012). *A qualitative study of children, young people and 'sexting': A report prepared for the NSPCC.* Institute of Education, Kings College London, London School of Economics and the Open University.

Robards, B., & Vromen, A. (2015). Logging out? Why young people love to hate Facebook. *The Conversation*, 6 February 2015 [Online]. Retrieved from https://theconversation.com/logging-out-whyyoung-people-love-to-hate-facebook-36358 (accessed 13 March 2016).

Sakellariou, T., Carroll, A., & Houghton, S. (2012). Rates of cyber victimization and bullying among male Australian primary and high school students. *School Psychology International, 33*, 533–549.

Salmivalli, C. (2010). Bullying and the peer group: A review. *Aggression and Violent Behaviour, 15*, 112–120.

Salmivalli, C. (2014). Participant roles in bullying: How can peer bystanders be utilized in interventions? *Theory Into Practice, 53*, 286–292.

Saunders, A. (2014). *Guidelines on prosecuting cases involving communications sent via social media*, 17 October 2014 [Online]. Retrieved from www.parliament.uk/documents/lordscommittees/communications/socialmediaoffences/DPPLetter171014.pdf (accessed 4 June 2015).

Schilder, J. D., Brusselaers, M. B. J., & Bogaerts, S. (2016). The effectiveness of an intervention to promote awareness and reduce online risk behaviour in early adolescence. *Journal of Youth and Adolescence, 45*(2), 286–300.

Schoffstall, C. L., & Cohen, R. (2011). Cyber aggression: The relation between online offenders and offline social competence. *Social Development, 20*(3), 587–604.

Selwyn, N. (2008). A safe haven for misbehaving? An investigation of online misbehaviour among university students. *Social Science Computer Review, 26*(4), 446–465.

Ševčíková, A., Šmahel, D., & Otavová, M. (2012). The perception of cyberbullying in adolescent victims. *Emotional and Behavioural Difficulties, 17*(3–4), 319–328.

Shariff, S. (2009). Confronting cyber-bullying: What schools need to know to control misconduct and avoid legal consequences. Cambridge: Cambridge University Press.

Shariff, S. (2013). Chapter 9: Defining the line on cyber-bullying: How youth encounter and distribute demeaning information. In J. Behesthi & A. Large (Eds.), *the information behaviour of a new generation: Children and teens in the 21st century*. Washington, DC: Scarecrow Press.

Shariff, S. (2015). *Sexting and cyber-bullying: Defining the line for digitally empowered kids.* New York: Cambridge University Press.

Smith, P. K. (2014). *Understanding school bullying, its nature and preventative strategies.* London: Sage.

Strom, P., Strom, R., Walker, J., Sindel-Arrington, T., & Beckert, T. (2011). Adolescent bullies on Cyber Island. *NASSP Bulletin, 95*(3), 195–211.

Suler, J. (2004). The online disinhibition effect. *Cyberpsychology and Behaviour*, 7(3), 321–326.

Sykes, G. M., & Matza, D. (1957). Techniques of neutralization. *American Sociological Review*, *22*(6), 664–670.

Talwar, V., Gomez-Garibello, C., & Shariff, S. (2014). Adolescents' moral evaluations and ratings of cyberbullying: The effect of veracity and intentionality behind the event. *Computers in Human Behaviour*, *36*, 122–128.

Thomas, H. J., Connor, J., & Scott, J. (2015). Integrating traditional bullying and cyberbullying: Challenges of definition and measurement in adolescents – A review. *Educational Psychology Review*, *27*(1), 35–152.

Tozer, J. (2013). Schoolboy, 15, bullied to death by trolls on the internet: Friends say vile posts drive him to despair. *Mail Online*, 7 April 2013. Updated 8 April 2013 [Online]. Retrieved from www.dailymail.co.uk/news/article-2305332/Joshua-Unsworth-15-bullied-death-trolls-internet.html (accessed 14 July 2016).

Völlink, T., Dehue, F., & McGuckin, C. (Eds.). (2016). *Cyberbullying: From theory to intervention*. London: Routledge.

Waasdorp, T. E., & Bradshaw, C. P. (2015). The overlap between cyberbullying and traditional bullying. *The Journal of Adolescent Health*, *56*(5), 483–488.

Waldron, L. M. (2014). Cyberbullying: The social construction of a moral panic. In L. Robinson, S. Cotten, & J. Schulz (Eds.), *Communication and information technologies annual* (Studies in Media and Communications, Vol. 8, pp. 197–230). Emerald Group Publishing Limited.

Wendling, M. (2015). 2015: The year that angry won the internet. *BBC News*, 30 December 2015 [Online]. Retrieved from www.bbc.co.uk/news/blogs-trending-35111707 (accessed 14 July 2016).

Whittaker, E., & Kowalski, R. M. (2015). Cyberbullying via social media. *Journal of School Violence*, *14*(1), 11–29.

Yang, A., & Salmivalli, C. (2013). Different forms of bullying and victimization: Bully-victims versus bullies and victims. *European Journal of Developmental Psychology*, *10*(6), 723–738.

Zweig, J. M., Dank, M., Yahner, J., & Lachman, P. (2013). The rate of cyber dating abuse among teens and how it relates to other forms of teen dating violence. *Journal of Youth and Adolescence*, *42*(7), 1063–1077.

Chapter 12

Fostering resilience in vulnerable children

Carmel Cefai

Introduction: bullying amongst vulnerable children

Children and young people with special educational needs and disabilities (SEND) are one group of children who may be particularly vulnerable to bullying (McLaughlin, Byers, & Vaughn, 2010; Rose, Espelage, Aragon, & Elliott, 2011). Blake, Lund, Zhou, Kwok, and Benz (2012) found higher prevalence rates of victimisation amongst students with disability, when compared to mainstream students, in US primary, middle and high schools, ranging from 25% to 34%. Students with social skills and communication problems are particularly susceptible to be victims of bullying (Rose et al., 2011). In a review of studies on victimisation in Europe and North America, McLaughlin et al. (2010) reported that children with SEND faced increased risk of victimisation in both mainstream and special settings, ranging from 80% for students with learning disabilities, 70% for students with autism to 40% for students with speech and language difficulties; some studies indicated that students with mild or hidden disabilities may be even more at risk. Chatzitheochari, Parsons, and Platt (2014) found that primary school students with SEND are twice as likely as other peers to experience chronic bullying.

Bullying against children from ethnic minorities, different cultural backgrounds or migrant families, is another area which has been largely neglected in research on school bullying (Eslea & Mukhtar, 2010). In a study in a number of European countries, Elamé (2013) reported that in some of the countries, Roma and migrant children do not feel at ease with their peers at school, with an overall average of 58% of such children being bullied. In a recent study with over 7000 children aged 7 to 13 in Scandinavian countries, Bjereld, Daneback, and Petzold (2015) reported that the prevalence of bullying was significantly higher amongst immigrant children when compared to native children in Sweden, Norway and in the Nordic countries as a whole.

Another form of widespread (though often unreported) discriminatory bullying is homophobic or LGBT bullying. A recent report on LGBT students in the UK suggests that about a quarter of such students will miss school because of homophobic bullying, while about one-third will experience problems with schoolwork (Stonewall, 2015). GLEN (2015) suggests rampant homophobic bullying in the US, with 74% of LGBT students being verbally harassed because of their sexual orientation and 55% because of their gender expression; 36% were physically harassed because of their sexual orientation and 28% because of their gender expression; and 17% were physically assaulted because of their sexual orientation and 11% because of their gender expression. Stonewall (2012) reported similar findings with students in the UK. Some 55% of LGBT students experienced direct bullying while more than 96% heard homophobic language at the school, while only half reported that their schools consider homophobic bullying as wrong. Another 32% of those who experienced bullying changed their future educational plans because of it, 60% said it had a direct negative impact on their school work, while 41% have attempted or thought about suicide or self-harmed.

Protecting vulnerable children from bullying and disadvantage: a resilience perspective

The resilience perspective is concerned with the protection of vulnerable children from bullying, abuse, disadvantage, discrimination and other barriers in their development by focussing on their strengths and assets. It seeks to identify those factors which provide protection for such children and facilitate their healthy development, academic success and social and emotional competence. Resilience is not about some children having innate qualities (traits) which make them invulnerable in the face of risk and adversity (Rutter, 2015). Rather than an extraordinary process for some, it is 'ordinary magic', that is, "ordinary responses focusing on strengths" (Masten, 2001, p. 228) and facilitated by supportive systems (Ungar, 2012). Resilience is about successful adaptation, both internal and external, both academic and socio-emotional, despite adversity (Masten, 2011). It is not just coping with adversity, but about continuing to grow and develop healthily despite adversity (Rutter, 2015). Rather than just bouncing back to pre-trauma level (surviving), resilience is about moving forward (thriving), the capacity to keeping riding and surfing the waves (Cefai et al., 2015). It is a process of growth.

Resilience may be construed as a dynamic transactional process between the individual and the context, underlining how particular individual qualities and contextual processes interact to facilitate the healthy development and growth of children and young people facing or experiencing risk in their lives. Bonanno (2012) posits that resilience depends on the interaction between the nature of the event (such as the severity or chronicity of the event), the person's qualities (such as personality, coping style and qualities such as self-efficacy, planning and goal setting, problem solving, optimism, sense of control and agency) and the context/s (such as the availability and quality of social support and healthy relationships). Within such a perspective, resilience is something which can be nurtured and developed from a young age by helping children to develop resilience-enhancing qualities while providing protective social contexts at home, at school, in the peer group and in the community (Ungar, 2012). Rutter

(2015) argues that resilience is not a characteristic that can be taught or measured since it is an interactive process that can only be identified as a response to adversity. He agrees, however, that children may be provided with experiential learning experiences which provide them with the competencies that make them better prepared to face adversity in their life and to function in a resilient way. Having the tools to deal effectively with manageable challenges and stresses strengthens also the child's resolve and ability to overcome adversity and keep thriving, a process Rutter calls 'steeling' (Rutter, 2015). Providing vulnerable children with resilience tools while providing protective and supportive contexts, will thus maximise the likelihood of positive and healthy growth in cognitive, emotional, social and other facets of development (cf Masten, 2011; Ungar, 2012). As Ungar (2008) put it:

> resilience is both the capacity of the individual to navigate their way to health-sustaining resources, including opportunities to experience feelings of well-being, and a condition of the individual's family, community and culture to provide these health resources and experiences in culturally meaningful ways.
>
> (p. 225)

The next section describes a skills-based resilience programme for early years and primary schools which seeks to promote young children's resilience by providing them with the psychological resources to deal effectively with adversity and barriers in their development, while encouraging the adults in children's lives such as school staff and parents to provide healthy relationships and create supportive, assets-based contexts.

RESCUR surfing the waves: A resilience curriculum for schools

RESCUR Surfing the Waves is a resilience curriculum for early and primary schools developed by six universities in Europe (Image 12.1). It has been developed to help vulnerable children in Europe such as those coming from ethnic, migrant and low socio-economic communities and children with special educational needs and disability, who may be at risk of bullying, prejudice, discrimination, social exclusion, absenteeism, early school leaving and school failure. Its objective is to empower such children by providing them with the requisite competencies to overcome adversity and barriers in their development and continue to grow and thrive despite disadvantage.

Themes

RESCUR Surfing the Waves consists of six major themes spiralling from the early years to the end of the primary school years at higher levels of complexity.

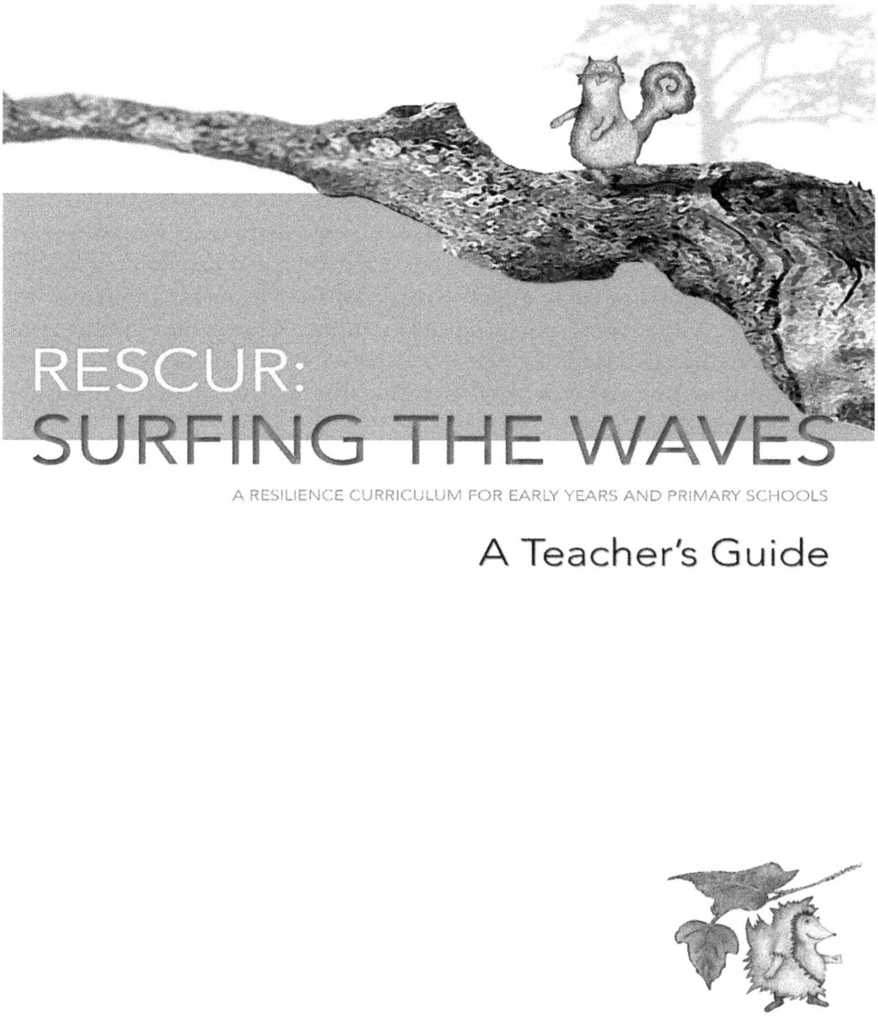

Image 12.1 RESCUR Teachers' Guide
Reproduced with kind permission of Antonija Balic Simrac

The themes have been identified through a review of the literature in the area, and reflect both internal and external resources, such as self-awareness, problem solving, positive attitudes, optimism, adaptability, perseverance, self-efficacy, agency, self-determination, high academic expectations, empathy and collaboration, as well as external resources such as caring and supportive relationships and meaningful participation at home, at school and in their peer group (Benard, 2004; Dimakos & Papakonstantinopoulou, 2012; Hutchinson &

Dorsett, 2012; Elamé, 2013; Bowles et al., 2015; Rutter, 2015). Each theme consists of two subthemes, while the sixth theme includes six subthemes. The first two themes are focussed on developing communication skills and healthy relationships. *Developing communication skills* focusses on expressing and standing up for oneself (first subtheme), and listening to and understanding others (second subtheme). The first subtheme presents three topics on expressing feelings and needs, standing up for oneself and assertive conflict resolution, while the second subtheme focusses on effective listening, understanding others, and communicating ideas effectively. The first subtheme of theme 2 *Establishing and maintaining healthy relationships* focusses on establishing and maintaining healthy relationships, exploring such topics as making friends, seeking and providing support and developing nurturing relationships. The second subtheme on enhancing cooperative skills, empathy and moral reasoning, helps children to develop collaboration and team-building, empathy and engaging in ethical and responsible behaviour.

Developing a growth mindset, the third theme, is essential not only for children to manage challenges successfully, but also to turn them into opportunities for growth and development (Seligman, Parks, & Steen, 2004). The first subtheme on positive and optimistic thinking seeks to develop the competence of engaging in optimistic thinking, reflecting and challenging unhelpful thoughts, and overcoming challenges with a positive attitude. The second subtheme is aimed at developing the skill of becoming aware of, identifying and regulating positive emotions, focussing on the three 'Hs', namely hope, happiness and humour (Image 12.2). *Developing self-determination* is an essential skill in overcoming adversity and keeping on the pathway of growth and healthy development. The first subtheme focusses on the development of problem-solving skills, including risk assessment, resource evaluation and establishing realistic plans. The second subtheme focusses on empowerment and autonomy, including a sense of purpose and meaning in life, agency and self-efficacy, and self-advocacy. *Building on strengths*, the fifth theme, covers two main areas, namely building a positive self-concept and self-esteem, and using strengths in academic and social engagement.

The sixth theme, *Turning challenges into opportunities*, seeks to enable vulnerable children to develop the competence of turning challenges and adversity into opportunities for growth. In the first subtheme, children learn how to face adversity and challenges with courage and persistence. Dealing effectively with rejection by teachers, peers and family members is the second subtheme, while the third subtheme seeks to enable children to understand and deal with loss in their lives. The other subthemes include dealing with family-related stressors, such as family conflict, unrealistic parental expectations and divorce, dealing with bullying and conflict at school, and understanding and dealing effectively with changes and transitions at school, home and the community.

Image 12.2 Theme 3 poster

Reproduced with kind permission of Antonija Balic Simrac

Principles and strategies

RESCUR Surfing the Waves has been developed on the basis of an overarching framework built from the existing evidence on what works in resilience education. Programmes which are not embedded into the formal curriculum and which are delivered as added, bolt-on activities by outside experts, are unlikely to have long-term effects on student behaviour (Greenberg et al., 2003; Durlak, Weissberg, Dymnicki, & Taylor, 2011). *RESCUR Surfing the Waves* has thus been developed as a universal intervention programme targeting all children in the classroom, with experiential, skills-based activities, delivered regularly by the classroom teacher as part of the curriculum. It includes a set curriculum consisting of three manuals of activities according to age group (early years, early primary and late primary), resources, a teachers' guide and a parents' guide. It takes a spiral approach, building the key competencies from the early years to the infant and the junior years in the primary school, with increasing complexity at each developmental level, building on what learners have already learned, and equipping them with skills needed for different stages in their development.

For resilience and socio-emotional programmes to be effective, they need follow the SAFE approach, that is, to take a sequenced step-by-step approach, make use of experiential and participative learning, focus on skills development and have explicit learning goals (CASEL, 2005; Durlak et al., 2011; Rutter, 2015). RESCUR activities follow a sequenced structure, with explicit learning outcomes, mindfulness activity, storytelling and discussion of the story, practical, interactive activities such as role play and drawing and a take-home activity. Skills development is facilitated through experiential and collaborative learning, with learners highly engaged in the learning process, and through the practice and application of the skill learnt in the other academic subjects and take-home activities. The teachers are strongly encouraged to infuse the resilience competencies being taught into the other academic subjects so as to facilitate the generalisation and internalisation of the competencies being learned (Elias & Synder, 2008).

RESCUR Surfing the Waves makes use of storytelling as the main medium of instruction. During storytelling, learners have the opportunity to explore their thoughts and feelings on the topic so as to gain insights into their own and others' behaviour (Hankin, Omer, Elias, & Raviv, 2012). Sherlock the squirrel and Zelda the hedgehog are the two character stories in the early years and early primary stories, while fables and real life stories feature in the late primary school stories. Sherlock is bespectacled and purple, representing difference and diversity, while Zelda's broken spikes signify disability (Image 12.3). The use of puppets is strongly recommended in Sherlock's and Zelda's stories (Image 12.4).

Although a universal programme, *RESCUR Surfing the Waves* takes an inclusive approach, with activities reflecting the diversity of learners, particularly children coming from disadvantaged backgrounds. This avoids the risk of labelling and stigmatisation when targeting specifically the difficulties of children from disadvantaged background. The curriculum makes use of developmentally and culturally appropriate resilience competencies with application to real-life situations, particularly within a European context. Each theme includes activities reflecting the challenges and difficulties faced by vulnerable children, such as bullying, prejudice, discrimination, lack of friends, language barriers, difficulty in accessing learning and exclusion. Besides being encouraged to reflect on their own challenges, learners are also requested to explore how other children can help the character in difficulty, thus promoting such values as empathy, understanding and solidarity.

The activities are presented at varying levels of difficulty – basic, intermediate and advanced – to enable the teacher to adapt the activities according to the developmental level of the learners and to be culturally responsive to their varying needs. Adaptations, however, need to take place without compromising the integrity of the curriculum (Greenberg, 2010), and the Teachers' Guide which includes also an implementation index, underlines the need for teachers to maintain fidelity and consistency of delivery (cf. Durlak et al., 2011).

Image 12.3 Sherlock and Zelda, the two curriculum mascots

Reproduced with kind permission of Antonija Balic Simrac

Image 12.4 Puppets of Sherlock and Zelda

Reproduced with kind permission of Antonija Balic Simrac

In line with the inclusive and developmental approach of the curriculum, assessment is developmental and formative, with teachers' and learners' checklists at the end of each theme. The teacher completes the checklist on each learner at the end of each theme to assess whether the learning goals have been adequately developed. The learners' checklist (primary school level only) assesses whether the learner is able to perform and to practice that skill. Both checklists include also a qualitative component focussed on strengths, needs and targets for improvement. With the early years, the teacher may devise more visual, practical activities to help the learners engage in self-reflection, such as drawings, role play, stories and other illuminative, child-friendly techniques.

Parents are considered an invaluable resource in the implementation of *RESCUR Surfing the Waves*, and their collaboration and participation is one of the main criteria for programme effectiveness (Downey & Williams, 2010). Each activity includes a take-home activity sheet, where the children and their parents work together on tasks related to the skills covered at school. This also serves to reinforce and generalise the skill to different contexts. The Learner Portfolio includes these worksheets and other learners' work, and serves as a home-school conduit for resilience building. RESCUR includes also a Parents' Guide (Image 12.5) which is given to the parents by the school once it starts the programme implementation. The guide introduces the parents to the programme and its respective themes, topics and activities, and provides practical strategies on what they can do to help their children develop and apply the resilience skills tackled at school.

Besides the direct 'taught' approach, *RESCUR Surfing the Waves* includes also a 'caught' component, where the resilience skills may also be grasped through the classroom and the whole-school contexts. Jennings and Greenberg (2009) argue that the teaching of competences by the classroom teacher also impacts the teachers' overall practice and leads to a paradigm shift in the teaching and learning processes, with resilience becoming embedded within the classroom climate. The daily classroom relationships, pedagogy, activities, resources and management become the arena where learners have the opportunity to observe, practice and apply resilient behaviour in academic and social activities. The Teachers' Guide includes a chapter how the teachers may organise the classroom as a caring community built on warm and caring relationships, collaboration, inclusion, meaningful engagement and participation in decision making (cf. Cefai, 2008).

RESCUR Surfing the Waves promotes resilience education as a whole-school approach, positioning the whole-school community in partnership with parents and the local community engaged in resilience building, reinforcing and completing the work done in the classrooms (cf. Weare & Nind, 2011; Cefai & Cavioni, 2014). The Teachers' Guide includes a chapter describing how the whole-school community may work collaboratively together to create a whole-school climate and ethos conducive to resilient behaviour. The teachers' own resilience and well-being is another key factor in resilience building in school. School staff need to take active steps to maintain their own resilience and

Image 12.5 The Parents' Guide

Reproduced with kind permission of Antonija Balic Simrac

well-being in order to be more effective in their efforts to promote students' resilience (Beltman, Mansfield, & Price, 2011; Mansfield, Beltman, Price, & McConney, 2012), and the Teachers' Guide includes also a chapter on how teachers may maintain their own health and well-being.

Conclusion

RESCUR Surfing the Waves has been piloted in about 80 schools and over 200 classrooms in six European countries, with each country implementing and evaluating one theme or part of a theme. The overall feedback from 199 teachers and 1935 students was very positive, describing the curriculum as being highly engaging, meaningful and relevant. The experiential activities, the stories and the two characters, Sherlock and Zelda, the mindfulness exercises, the ready-made teacher friendly and student friendly resources and work sheets, and the take-home activities, were all mentioned as some of the most useful and interesting components of the curriculum. Teachers and students found the curriculum also relevant and useful for students' everyday life, with teachers indicating that there was a positive change in students' behaviour related to the implemented theme, particularly with the older students. The great majority of the teachers said that the students greatly enjoyed and participated actively in the activities, and that many parents also found the programme useful for their children. The teachers also appreciated the focus on the social and emotional aspects of learning and the opportunity to engage with the learners in this area. Similarly, the students also appreciated the opportunity to work and learn together in 'new and enjoyable ways' on 'unusual' topics. They liked learning about themselves and their behaviour as well learning about others. They mentioned particularly the two mascots and the stories as the things they liked and from which they learned the most. Both teachers and students suggested that the programme becomes part of the general curriculum in the future. The teachers mentioned that the implementation was rather brief and needed more time to have a lasting effect on student's behaviour.

While the results of the pilot evaluation are quite promising, the programme still needs to be evaluated through a randomised- controlled study to measure its effectiveness in building and enhancing the academic and social and emotional resilience of young children experiencing social and economic disadvantage. It needs to be put to the test to see whether it can bring about a positive change in the behaviour of vulnerable children not only in the short term in the classroom (internal validity), but also whether such change can be maintained across time in different contexts and aspects of children's life (external validity). The identification of what works, when and for whom, will also enable classroom teachers to understand more deeply how the programme works and find a balance between fidelity as suggested in the Teachers' Guide and necessary adaptations in fitting the activities to the local context and the needs of the students. In this way, it is more productive and useful to speak of 'quality adaptation' than of 'implementation failure' when fidelity is not adhered to rigidly (Lendrum, Humphrey, & Greenberg, 2016). Programme fidelity rarely goes over 80%, and positive outcomes may be achieved even with 60% fidelity (Durlak & Dupre, 2008). More important is that any adaptations are made with respect to the programme's principles and implementation guidelines and to fit with the local context and the students' needs.

Acknowledgements

The author would like to thank the other partners and authors of *RESCUR Surfing the Waves: A Resilience Curriculum for Early Years and Primary Schools*, namely Renata Miljević-Riđički, Dejana Bouillet, Tea Pavin Ivanec and Mirjana Milanović (University of Zagreb, Croatia), Anastassios Matsopoulos and Mariza Gavogiannaki (University of Crete, Greece), Maria Assunta Zanetti and Valeria Cavioni (University of Pavia, Italy), Paul Bartolo and Katya Galea (University of Malta, Malta), Celeste Simões, Paula Lebre and Anabela Caetano Santos (University of Lisbon, Portugal), and Birgitta Kimber and Charli Eriksson (Orebro University, Sweden).

References

Beltman, S., Mansfield, C. F., & Price, A. (2011). Thriving not just surviving: A review of research on teacher resilience. *Educational Research Review*, *6*(3), 185–207.

Benard, B. (2004). *Resiliency: What we have learned*. San Francisco, CA: WestEd.

Bjereld, Y., Daneback, K., & Petzold, M. (2015). Differences in prevalence of bullying victimization between native and immigrant children in the Nordic countries: A parent-reported serial cross-sectional study. *Child Care Health Development*, *41*(4), 593–599.

Blake, J. J., Lund, E. M., Zhou, Q., Kwok, O., & Benz, M. R. (2012). National prevalence rates of bully victimization among students with disabilities in the United States. *School Psychology Quarterly*, *27*, 210–222.

Bonanno, G. A. (2012). Uses and abuses of the resilience construct: Loss, trauma, and health – Related adversities. *Social Science & Medicine*, *74*(5), 753–756.

Bowles, L. et al. (2015). Peer victimisation during adolescence and its impact on depression in early adulthood: Prospective cohort study in the United Kingdom. *British Medical Journal*, *350*, h2469.

Cefai, C. (2008). *Promoting resilience in the classroom*. London, UK: Jessica Kingsley Publications.

Cefai, C., & Cavioni, V. (2014). *Social and emotional education in primary school: Integrating Theory and research into practice*. New York, NY: Springer.

Cefai, C., Miljević-Riđički, R., Bouillet, D., Pavin Ivanec, T., Matsopoulous, A., Gavogiannaki, M. et al. (2015). *RESCUR Surfing the Waves. A resilience curriculum for early years and primary schools. A teachers' guide*. Malta: Centre for Resilience and Socio-Emotional Health, University of Malta.

Chatzitheochari, S., Parsons, S., & Platt, L. (2014). *Bullying experiences among disabled children and young people in England: Evidence from two longitudinal studies* London: Institute of Education.

Collaborative for Academic, Social, and Emotional Learning. (2005). *Safe and sound: An educational leader's guide to evidence-based social and emotional SEL programmes*. Retrieved from CASEL: www.casel.org/projects_products/safeandsound.php (accessed 30 December 2015).

Dimakos, I., & Papakonstantinopoulou, A. (2012). Providing psychological and counselling services to Roma students: A preliminary report for a three-year longitudinal project. In P. Cunningham & N. Fretwell (Eds.), *Creating communities: Local, national and global* (pp. 94–103). London, UK: CiCe.

Downey, C., & Williams, C. (2010). Family SEAL – A home-school collaborative programme focusing on the development of children's social and emotional skills. *Advances in School Mental Health Promotion*, *3*(1), 30–41.

Durlak, J. A., & Dupre, E. P. (2008). Implementation matters: A review of research on the influence of implementation on programme outcomes and the factors affecting implementation. *American Journal of Community Psychology, 41*, 327–350.

Durlak, J. A., Weissberg, R. P., Dymnicki, A. B., & Taylor, R. D. (2011). The impact of enhancing students' social and emotional learning: A meta-analysis of school-based universal interventions. *Child Development, 82*(1), 474–501.

Elamé, E. (2013). *Discriminatory bullying: A new intercultural dialogue.* Berlin: Springer Verlag.

Elias, M., & Synder, D. (2008). *Developing safe and civil schools: A coordinated approach to social-emotional and character development.* Retrieved from www.njasp.org/notes/confarc/DSACS_handouts_12_09.doc (accessed 15 April 2016).

Eslea, M., & Mukhtar, K. (2000). Bullying and racism among Asian schoolchildren in Britain. *Educational Research, 42*, 207–217.

Gay and Lesbian Equality Network (GLEN) (2015). LGBT Self-Harm and Suicidality: An Overview of National and International Research Findings. Dublin: GLEN NB 2015

Greenberg, M. T. (2010). School-based prevention: Current status and future challenges. *Effective Education, 2*(1), 27–52.

Greenberg, M. T., Weissberg, R. P., O'Brien, M. U., Zins, J. E., Fredericks, L., Resnik, H., & Elias, M. J. (2003). Enhancing school-based prevention and youth development through coordinated social, emotional, and academic learning. *American Psychologist, 58*(6–7), 466–474.

Hankin, V., Omer, D., Elias, M. J., & Raviv, A. (2012). *Stories to help build emotional intelligence and resilience in young children.* Champaign, IL: Research Press Co.

Hutchinson, M., & Dorsett, P. (2012). What does the literature say about resilience in refugee people? Implications for practice. *Journal of Social Inclusion, 3*(2), 55–78.

Jennings, P. A., & Greenberg, M. T. (2009). Review of educational research. *The Prosocial Classroom: Teacher Social and Emotional Competence in Relation to Child and Classroom Outcomes, 79*(1), 491–525.

Lendrum, A., Humphrey, N., & Greenberg, M. (2016). Implementing for success in school-based mental health promotion: The role of quality in resolving the tension between fidelity and adaptation. In R. S. Schute & P. T. Slee (Eds.), *Mental health and wellbeing through schools: The way forward* (pp. 53–63). London: Routledge.

Mansfield, C. F., Beltman, S., Price, A., & McConney, A. (2012). 'Don't sweat the small stuff': Understanding teacher resilience at the chalkface. *Teaching and Teacher Education, 28*, 357–367.

Masten, A. S. (2001). Ordinary Magic: Lessons from research on resilience in human development. *Education Canada, 49*(3), 28–32.

Masten, A. S. (2011). Resilience in children threatened by extreme adversity: Frameworks for research, practice, and translational synergy. *Development and Psychopathology, 23*(2), 493–506.

McLaughlin, C., Byers, R., & Vaughn, R. P. (2010). *Responding to bullying among children with special educational needs and/or disabilities.* London, EUK: Anti-Bullying Alliance.

Rose, C. A., Espelage, D. L., Aragon, S. R., & Elliott, J. (2011). Bullying and victimization among students in special education and general education curricula. *Exceptionality Education International, 21*(2), 2–14.

Rutter, M. (2015). Resilience: Concepts, findings, and clinical implications. In A. Thapar, D. S. Pine, J. F. Leckman, S. Scott, M. J. Snowling, & E. A. Taylor (Eds.), *Rutter's child and adolescent psychiatry* (pp. 341–351). Oxford, UK: Wiley-Blackwell.

Seligman, M. E., Parks, A. C., & Steen, T. (2004). A balanced psychology and a full life. *Philosophical Transactions of the Royal Society of London: Series B, 359*, 1379–1381.

Stonewall. (2012). *The school report: The experiences of gay young people in Britain's schools in 2012*. London: Stonewall.

Stonewall. (2015). *Education Equality Index 2015*. London: Stonewall

Ungar, M. (2008). Resilience across cultures. *British Journal of Social Work, 38*(2), 218–235.

Ungar, M. (2012). Researching and theorizing resilience across cultures and contexts. *Preventive Medicine, 55*(5), 387–389.

Weare, K., & Nind, M. (2011). Mental health promotion and problem prevention in schools: What does the evidence say? *Health Promotion International, 26*(S1), i29–i69.

Chapter 13

Bullying and resilience within a neoliberal framework

Implications for mental health and well-being

Wendy Sims-Schouten and Simon Edwards

Introduction

According to *The Good Childhood Report* (Pople, Gwyther, Main, & Bradshaw, 2015), the most common response to the question about what prevents a good life in childhood, is bullying. There is evidence that children's experiences of bullying are significant predictors of well-being, not only in childhood, but also into adult life and mental health and well-being therein (Copeland, Wolke, Angold, & Costello, 2013; Wolke, 2014); resilience is key here. Resilience as a concept has been the property of well-intentioned researchers with a focus on identifying a particular set of outcomes, behaviours and processes that are indicative of mental health and well-being (e.g. Rutter, 2006; Ungar, 2004). (See also Cefai in chapter 12). Rutter (1985) argues that resilience is a dynamic process that varies over time and is dependent on the interaction and accumulation of individual and environmental factors. In this chapter, we take the view that discourses around resilience that inform contemporary approaches towards bullying are shaped by neoliberal notions, which emphasise decontextualised readings of bullying, and locate accountability and responsibility for coping with this with the individual (see also, Joseph, 2013). Neoliberal education policy as Webb, Gulson, and Pitton (2013) claim, complements and extends the production of the self, whilst teaching practice linked to this promotes the development of autonomous and free individuals, who are provided with self-regulated mechanisms with the ultimate goal to become responsible for their own care (2013, p. 3). In this chapter, we show that self-responsibility, self-care and accountability are tricky concepts to apply to victims of bullying. Victims of bullying generally don't have a choice, and the power-imbalance that is integral to this means that 'self-responsibility' cannot be assumed or expected.

This chapter draws on our research around talk and narratives in relation to bullying, resilience and stigma (e.g. childhood obesity and body-bullying) with a specific focus on the voices of young people, parents, early years practitioners and teachers (Sims-Schouten, 2015; Sims-Schouten & Cowie, 2016; Sims-Schouten & Edwards, 2016). Following Walkerdine (2003), psychology has a central place within neoliberalism, propping up the 'autonomous subject', who has to manage a constant self-liberalism, within a changing economy and shifting family forms. This produces particular challenges, and there is a need to uncover the regulative aspects that underpin this. Below, we will present examples of talk in relation to bullying in secondary schools and early childhood, as well as childhood obesity and body-bullying. In our analysis we use a combination of discourse analysis and thematic analysis, recording and examining patterns (or 'themes') within the data (see Attride-Stirling, 2001), as well as focussing on the wider common sense discourses and ideologies that the participants draw on (see Billig, 1997; Potter, 1997). The first section will focus on bullying in secondary schools, followed by childhood obesity and bullying; the final section will cover perceptions of bullying in early childhood.

Neoliberalism, bullying and education

Harvey (2007) and other critics of neoliberalism explain that once neoliberal goals and priorities become embedded in a culture's way of thinking, institutions that don't regard themselves as neoliberal will nevertheless engage in practices that mime and extend neoliberal principles. Educational institutions are an example of this. Bullying has been widely researched, from focussing on emotion attributions of bullies, victims and bully-victims (Perren, Gutzwiller-Helfenfinger, Malti, & Hymel, 2012) and school-adjustment (Betts, Rotenberg, Trueman, & Stiller, 2012), to interventions, such as peer support (Cowie, 2011) and support-based approaches (Bray & Lee, 2007; Ttofi & Farrington, 2011). Yet, as Boulton and Boulton (2012) suggest, bullying continues to be common in schools, with students becoming more and more impervious to anti-bullying lessons and campaigns. Commonplace interpretations of bullying incidents and interventions lie in a collaborative relational context (e.g. Cowie, 2011; Menesini, Nocentini, & Camodeca, 2013), reflecting an understanding of the social nature of the students' interactions and practices. Neoliberal viewpoints are interesting in this light. In a qualitative study on perceptions of bullying, from teachers', parents' and young people's perspective (Sims-Schouten & Edwards, 2016), we found re-occurrences of talk that reflected neoliberal notions of self-determinism, placing responsibility of dealing with bullying incidents on the victims. The research was based on focus group interviews (n = 40, in a total of eight focus groups) with teachers, parents and young people (mean age = 14-years-old). Five key themes in relation to self-responsibility appeared from the data, namely 'working through situations by themselves' – 'man up' – 'self-confidence' – 'don't need help' – 'to stand up for oneself': see below for examples. The first two examples come from focus group interviews with teachers around bullying:

> Sometimes they have to learn how to work through some of these situations by themselves.

> It's like, I'm sorry you feel this way, man up, in the nicest possible way.

In both examples presented above, the young person is constructed as responsible for developing his/her own coping mechanisms in the face of bullying (see the focus on 'by themselves' and 'man up'). The same is evident from the example below, which comes from an interview with parents:

They just need to learn to be self-confident

See below for two examples from interviews with young people around bullying:

> Nah I don't need help with that. I am well capable to deal with this myself!

> You can stand up to them, that is what you should, do sticking up for myself

Both examples suggest that young people need to be 'capable' and 'stick up for themselves'. The sociologist Zygmunt Bauman neatly summarised the paradox of our era as: "Never have we been so free" (Bauman, 2000). Yet, this freedom, it appears, comes at a price. In the talk and narratives of the participants in our study, resilience and 'dealing with bullying' are constructed as a knowledge repertoire, a learned skill, which enables the individual to bridge the gap between the *de jure* (becoming) and the *de facto* (given – whom one wants to become) self, to be independent, which includes a prescribed notion of autonomous individuation and self with its intrinsic acceptance of responsibility for self-care. Emerging from this is a notion of freedom which requires the individual to live by their wits in a constantly shifting and fluid social landscape but often without adequate tools to do so. However, this self-responsible freedom is no longer optional but is one's fate. The individual is deemed responsible for their self-determinism, where freedom is defined as the freedom *to* survive and manage risks (social and interpersonal) independently (to an extent) of adult or peer support. The separation of the young person from external support, both within the classroom and with peers, is managed through gradual stepping back and by-standing through processes of 1) developing or learning self-confidence; 2) encouraging standing up for them-selves or to 'man-up', which are perceived as enabling the individual to gain the freedom *to* survive in the adult world.

As such, two key assumptions are highlighted: 1) That all young people have the capacity and behavioural characteristics to develop resilience, 'man up' and stand up for themselves, and 2) that all young people hold equal positions of social and cultural capital within the classroom and within their socialising relationships. This assumption reflects Webb et al. (2013) where all subjects are equally positioned and where there is no space in discussion for consideration of different or inequitable locations of subjects. However, as Bauman and Donskis (2013, p. 198) claim, this concern for human rights and individual autonomy is actually "a mask to cover its indifference, its consumption of itself and others, its turning away from faces and eyes, its safe isolation."

What emerges from the data in terms of stakeholders is a notion of placing responsibility or blame on the victim, thereby protecting others around the child (e.g. schools) from responsibility for intervention or blame, thus reducing risk of disruption to their role, within that social site and identity within that narrative. At the same time, where intervention is favoured in terms of dealing with the bullies (something to which some of the participants referred), this is located within the context of the stakeholders' relationships with the young person who is the victim. Here, the main focus appears to be on helping the victim become more resilient and self-confident, thereby putting the ball back in their court. Equality, it seems, is desired (indeed demanded); not where equality is made possible through external means though, but through developing the capacity for self-assertion. Inequality in the ability of each individual to stand up for themselves is interpreted as a deficit in an individual's skill repertoire.

However, research has found that children may be more or less resilient at different points in their lives, depending on the interaction and accumulation of individual and environmental factors (Rutter, 2006). In addition to this, children may develop resilience in one area of their lives but not in others; as such, the development of resilience is a dynamic process. It follows that it is questionable whether 'manning-up' and 'learning to be confident' do support resilience, and if Bauman and Donskis are correct, placing this responsibility on the individual only serves to inoculate the external stakeholder from risk of undermining their own carefully managed *de jure* self-identity.

Childhood obesity and bullying within a neoliberal framework

Body-bullying, it could be argued, to some extent results from experiences where bodies have been subject to stigmas inside and outside of school contexts. Childhood obesity and measures to tackle this, including the role of healthy diets and physical exercise, are high on the Government agenda. Tackling obesity is a priority for the current Conservative Government and Public Health England (PHE), which focusses on preventative measures, arguing that 'physical inactivity' is now a national epidemic with the prediction that this generation of young people will live five years less than their parents. Obesity is not just a British phenomenon. In schools across Western societies, curricula and pedagogies are being drastically re-shaped by policies concerned with tackling the so-called childhood 'obesity epidemic' (Lupton, 2014).

There is evidence that relational influences, social structures, material environments and embodiment all play a constitutive role, rather than merely a supplementary role in relation to perceptions and treatment of childhood obesity. In other words, when trying to eradicate the 'obesity crisis' or epidemic, as this has often been referred to, one needs to look at the wider picture. Viewed through a neoliberal lens, it could be argued that parents are encouraged to seek out social opportunities for their children in order to keep them fit and healthy, through a mixture of state and private institutions, engaging with the market as a means to do so (Rich, 2010). Failing to do so leads to stigma and potential bullying of the obese child. This is because childhood obesity is often treated as synonymous to being 'inadequate', 'indulgent' or even 'immoral' (see also Lupton, 2014). Yet, drawing on and utilising facilities in relation to physical activity and healthy eating, and dealing with issues to do with 'fatness', may only be an option to those who have the cultural desire, the social capital and the (economic) means to do so. Thus, the increased focus on childhood obesity and 'fatness' is framed within moral and health ideologies that function to monitor and 'correct' children who do not fit into the thinness ideal. This in and of itself marks 'fat' children as deficient with related consequences. From a neoliberal viewpoint, it could be argued that success, i.e. in maintaining good levels of (mental) health and well-being, depends on individual effort and talents, meaning that responsibility lies with the individual child and their family, and authorities should give people as much freedom as possible to achieve this goal; this may be out of reach to some families. Whilst in the research around bullying in secondary schools, presented earlier on, responsibility was solely place with the victim – in the talk around childhood obesity and body-bullying presented below, both parents and children are constructed as responsible for prevention and intervention; here body-bullying is constructed as the inevitable result of failings (on the part of parents and children) to keep the child's body at an adequate and desirable weight. Below are examples from focus group interviews with parents, teachers and early years practitioners (n = 43, in a total of eight focus groups). The first example comes from an interview with teachers:

> There is a fat boy at my school, and in the lessons some kids say things to him, but he is quite good with his comeback.

In the extract above, an assumption is made that being exposed to bullying (i.e. when others 'say things') is inevitable when someone is 'fat'. Interestingly, the child in question appears to be equipped with the relevant self-help skills and coping mechanisms in order to deal with this. Yet, again the need to be self-responsible and self-caring, appears to be taken for granted here. The next example comes from an interview with parents:

> Sometimes, the bigger kids get bullied; it is usually the parents from a certain background and they give their kids junk food and stuff, and then those kids get targeted at school.

In the example above the parents are constructed as the responsible party, and failing in their task to keep their children fit, healthy and at an adequate weight. The same can be seen in the example below, which comes from a focus group interview with early years practitioners:

> The other day a parent dropped off her little boy at nursery, and he was eating a packet of crisps, because she hadn't had time to give him breakfast.

> And actually, the whole family are quite big, if you know what I mean, and her little boy, he is two, is also on the big side.

Early childhood and bullying will be further discussed in the next section.

Perceptions of bullying in early childhood

When it comes to bullying in early childhood, the research is not only more sparse compared to the volumes of research and literature available around bullying in primary (and especially) secondary schools, there are also ongoing debates as to whether bullying really happens in early childhood (e.g. Alsaker & Nagele, 2008; Monks & Smith, 2013). Here reference is made to the 'pre-morality' (e.g. following Piaget) of young children, as well as the fact that theory of mind, and related comprehension and understandings regarding (right or wrong) behaviour and consequences do not develop until later on (see also Dunn, 2004; Saracho, 2014). These debates and dilemmas were also evident from a study we did around bullying in early childhood. The data comes from six focus groups (n = 36) with parents and early years workers, and is discussed below. As with the talk around childhood obesity and bullying, parents were constructed as responsible. However, unlike the body-bullying talk, young children – both bullies and victims – were treated as lacking in understanding, and as such no responsibility in dealing with this was ascribed to them. This in and of itself is interesting, because it reiterates the need for identifying a responsible party, someone who can be put in charge to deal with the issues.

The first example comes from an interview with parents:

> Some children are easy targets, for example children with disabilities or children from an ethnic minority background, so the parents need to be aware of that and teach children skills to deal with this. But also that children need to be kind to each other.

Here the notion that some children are 'easy targets' is constructed as a given, thereby putting children from ethnic minority backgrounds and children with disabilities on the same line. At the same time the suggestion is made that parents play a crucial role in providing their children, first with the necessary coping skills, and second, to teach them to 'be kind'. The next example comes from an interview with early years practitioners, and again highlights the role of the parents:

> All depends on what the children have seen outside the setting, and basically the parents don't, like discipline them.

Thirty years of neoliberalism, free-market forces and privatisation have taken their toll, as relentless pressure to become autonomous and self-responsible have become normative. In all three studies discussed above, responsibility to 'deal with bullying' and become more resilient is placed on the child and/or their direct family (mostly their mothers). Yet, meritocratic neoliberalism favours certain personality traits and penalises others. It is often those traits that are associated with being in control and powerfulness that victims of bullying lack. As such, neoliberal philosophies are not compatible with vulnerable people, who for one reason or another are (at that particular point in their lives) not equipped with the resources (be it cultural, social or emotional) to become 'self-responsible' and 'self-autonomous'.

Implications and discussion

Neoliberalism is a much-contested term; something that can also be seen in the discussions around bullying presented in this chapter. In contemporary discussions and narratives around bullying and resilience, as with neoliberal ideology, families and individual children become the problem. In their words, the causes and long-term consequences of bullying (such as mental health issues later on in life) are to an extent ignored in favour of making individuals responsible for dealing with the issues in the here and now. As Boulton and Boulton (2012) argue, bullying continues to be common in schools, with students becoming more and more impervious to anti-bullying lessons and campaigns. Within this, it seems a move towards self-responsibility and self-care is stimulated and promoted, with the proliferation of self-help and self-improvement Apps with a focus on well-being and resilience.

Never has there been a bigger focus on the mental health and well-being needs of young children, and how schools and society are failing children on this front. At the same time, the deinstitutionalisation of mental health care has been seen as an all-round good thing. There are, though, some unintended consequences: the effects on family caregivers and the promotion of self-management strategies have devolved responsibility from services to the individual. This, in a way, is a sign of the neoliberal ideology extending into the home. At the same time, there is a sense that we are not equipped to address the central and pivotal transformations in modern social life, e.g. the rise in social media use among young people, the inherent risk of cyber-bullying linked to this and the role of neoliberal ideologies of self-governance. Whilst cyberspace can be a testing ground in which young people can experiment with identities that might be instantiated in the real world, the opposite can also be true and preventative strategies must take seriously the ways in which the late modern world is unfolding and has limited the behavioural options available to all of us and the potential consequences of our choices (Alvi, Downing, & Cesaroni, 2015).

Our society constantly proclaims that anyone can make it if they just try hard enough, all the while reinforcing (economical, material, emotional, social and cultural) privilege and putting increasing pressure on children and their families. We are forever told that we are freer to choose the course of our lives than ever before, but the freedom to choose outside the success narrative is limited. Furthermore, those who fail are deemed to be losers or scroungers, taking advantage of our social security system. Nevertheless, research points to the potentially huge mental health and well-being implications of (cyber) bullying (e.g. see Copeland et al., 2013); self-responsibility, self-autonomy and manning up are not going to cut it here. Additionally, there is still huge stigma attached to mental health problems (Ford, Hamilton, Goodman, & Melter, 2005), as well as controversy around conceptualisations of mental health and well-being (Lofgren, Hewitt, & das Nair, 2015). This again is reinforced by the ideal of unrestricted choice, self-government and self-management, which are the pre-eminent neoliberal political messages of our time, promising freedom. Yet, along with the idea of the perfectible individual, this freedom that we are presented with could well be the greatest untruth of this day and age, putting large sections of the population at a disadvantage. Indeed, as Chomsky (2014) asserts, neoliberalism is ironically neither new nor liberal.

If we want to support children properly in building resilience and 'dealing' with issues around bullying, then a number of mechanisms need to be in place, namely the reduction of the risk (i.e. bullying) itself including the negative chain reactions, establishment and maintenance of self-esteem and self-efficacy, and the opening up of opportunities and a move away from neoliberal conceptions of self-responsibility (see also, Rutter, 1987, 1999). This also includes taking into account that some children are particularly vulnerable to being bullied, including looked-after children, children with special educational needs and children with social, emotional and behavioural difficulties (Cowie, 2012; Sims-Schouten & Cowie, 2016). The UK Department for Education (Department for Education), which is responsible for child protection and education in England, identifies a whole-school approach to mental health and well-being as a protective factor for child and adolescent mental health; multi-agency teamwork is key here, which includes the voice of pupils, parents and staff (DfE, 2014; Weare, 2015). In addition to this, peer support within a school can create opportunities for children and young people to be proactive in challenging bullying when they observe it (Cowie, 2011).

References

Alsaker, F. D., & Nagele, C. (2008). Bullying in kindergarten and prevention. In W. Craig & D. Pepler (Eds.), *An international perspective on understanding and addressing bullying* (Vol. 1, pp. 230–252). Kingston, Canada: PREVNet.

Alvi, S., Downing, S., & Cesaroni, C. (2015). The self and the 'selfie': Cyber-bullying theory and the structure of late modernity In S. R. Maxwell & S. L. Blai (Eds.), *Violence and crime in the family: Patterns, causes, and consequences* (Contemporary perspectives in family research, Vol. 9, pp. 383–406). Bingley (UK): Emerald.

Attride-Stirling, J. (2001). Thematic networks: An analytic tool for qualitative research. *Qualitative Research, 1*(3), 385–405, doi:10.1177/146879410100100307.

Bauman, Z. (2000). *Liquid modernity*. Cambridge: Polity Press.

Bauman, Z., & Donskis, L. (2013). *Moral blindness: The loss of sensitivity in liquid modernity*. Cambridge: Polity Press.

Betts, L., Rotenberg, K. J., Trueman, M., & Stiller, J. (2012). Examining the components of children's peer linking as antecedents of school adjustment. *British Journal of Developmental Psychology, 30*(2), 303–325. doi:10.1111/j.2044-835X.2011.02041.x

Billig, M. (1997). Rhetorical and discursive analysis: How families talk about the royal family. In N. Hayes (Ed.), *Doing qualitative analysis in psychology?* (pp. 39–54). Hove: Psychology Press.

Boulton, M. J., & Boulton, R. J. (2012). Resistant to the message: Are pupils unresponsive to teachers' anti-bullying initiatives and if so why? *Educational Studies, 38*, 485–489. doi:10.1080/03055698.2011.643112.

Bray, L., & Lee, C. (2007). Moving away from a culture of blame to that of support-based approaches in schools. *Pastoral Care in Education, 25*(4), 4–11. doi:10.1111/j.1468-0122.2007.00419.x.

Chomsky, N. (2014). *Chomsky "neo-liberalism" is neither new nor liberal (2014)*. YouTube. www.youtube.com/watch?v=fGouSUmDKHI

Copeland, W., Wolke, D., Angold, A., & Costello, E. (2013). Adult psychiatric outcomes of bullying and being bullied by peers in childhood and adolescence. *JAMA Psychiatry, 70*(4), 419–426. doi:10.1001/jamapsychiatry.2013.504.

Cowie, H. (2011). Peer support as an intervention to counteract school bullying: Listen to the children. *Children & Society, 25*, 287–292. doi:10.1111/j.1099-0860.2011.00375.x.

Cowie, H. (2012). Taking on bullying from within. *Every Child Journal, 2*(6), 16–21. www.teachingtimes.com

Department for Education. (2014). *Keeping children safe in education: Statutory guidance for schools and colleges*. London: Department for Education.

Dunn, J. (2004). Young children's understanding of other people: Evidence from observations within the family. In M. Woodhead, D. Faulkner, & K. Littleton (Eds.), *Cultural worlds of early childhood* (pp. 101–116). Oxon: Routledge.

Ford, T., Hamilton, H., Goodman, R., & Melter, H. (2005). Service contacts among the children participating in the British child and adolescent mental health surveys. *Child and Adolescent Mental Health, 10*(2), 2–9.

Harvey, D. (2007). *A brief history of neoliberalism*. Oxford: OUP.

Joseph, J. (2013). Resilience as embedded neoliberalism: A governmentality approach. *Resilience: International Policies, Practices and Discourses, 1*(1), 38–52. doi:10.1080/21693293.2013.765741.

Lofgren, A., Hewitt, V., & das Nair, R. (2015). Doing fence sitting: A discursive analysis of clinical psychologists' constructions of mental health. *Qualitative Health Research, 25*(4), 470–485.

Lupton, D. (2014). 'How do you measure up?' Assumptions about 'obesity' and health-related behaviours in 'obesity' prevention campaigns. *Fat Studies, 3*(1), 32–44.

Menesini, N., Nocentini, A., & Camodeca, M. (2013). Morality, values, traditional bullying, and cyberbullying in adolescence. *British Journal of Developmental Psychology, 31*(1), 1–14. doi:10.1111/j.2044-835X.2011.02066.x.

Monks, C. P., & Smith, P. K. (2013). The origins of bullying in young children. In A. Ovejero Bernal, S. Yubero Jimenez, & P. K. Smith (Eds.), *School bullying and violence: International perspectives*. Madrid: Biblioteca Nueva.

Perren, S., Gutzwiller-Helfenfinger, E., Malti, T., & Hymel, S. (2012). Moral reasoning and emotion attributions of adolescent bullies, victims, and bully-victims. *British Journal of Developmental Psychology, 30*(4), 511–530. doi:10.1111/j.2044-835X.2011.02059.x.

Pople, L., Gwyther, R., Main, G., & Bradshaw, J. (2015). *The Good Childhood Report*. London: The Children's Society. Retrieved from www.childrenssociety.org.uk/sites/default/files/TheGoodChildhoodReport2015.pdf

Potter, J. (1997). Discourse analysis as a way of analysing naturally occurring talk. In D. Silverman (Ed.), *Qualitative research: Theory, method and practice* (pp. 144–160). London: Sage.

Rich, E. (2010). Obesity assemblages and surveillance in schools. *International Journal of Qualitative Studies in Education, 23*(7), 803–821.

Rutter, M. (1985). Resilience in the face of adversity: Protective factors and resistance to psychiatric disorder. *British Journal of Psychiatry, 147*, 598–611. doi:10.1192/bjp.147.6.598.

Rutter, M. (1987). Psychosocial resilience and protective mechanisms. *American Journal of Orthopsychiatry, 57*(3), 316–331. http://dx.doi.org/10.1111/j.1939-0025.1987.tb03541.x.

Rutter, M. (1999). Resilience concepts and findings: Implications for family therapy. *Journal of Family Therapy, 21*, 119–144. doi:10.1111/1467-6427.00108.

Rutter, M. (2006). The promotion of resilience in the face of adversity. In A. Clarke-Stewart & J. Dunn (Eds.), *Families count: Effects on child and adolescent development* (The Jacobs Foundation Series on Adolescence, pp. 26–52). Cambridge: Cambridge University Press.

Saracho, O. N. (2014). Theory of mind: Children's understanding of mental states. *Early Child Development and Care, 184*(6), 949–961.

Sims-Schouten, W. (2015). Bullying in early childhood and the construction of young children as premoral agents: Implications for practice. *Pastoral Care in Education: An International Journal of Personal, Social and Emotional Development, 33*(4), 234–245. doi:10.1080/02643944.2015.1094121.

Sims-Schouten, W., & Cowie, H. (2016). Ideologies and narratives in relation to 'fat' children as bullies, 'easy targets' and victims. *Children & Society*, 1–15. doi:10.1111/chso.12147.

Sims-Schouten, W., & Edwards, S. (2016). 'Man up!' Bullying and resilience within a neoliberal framework. *Journal of Youth Studies* 10, 744–760. doi:10.1080/13676261.2016.1171831.

Ttofi, M. M., & Farrington, D. P. (2011). Effectiveness of school-based programmes to reduce bullying: A systematic and meta-analytic review. *Journal of Experimental Criminology*, 7, 27–56. doi:101007/s11292-010-9109-1.

Ungar, M. (2004). A constructionist discourse on resilience: Multiple contexts, multiple realities among at-risk children and youth. *Youth and Society, 35*(3), 341–365. doi:10.1177/0044118X03257030.

Walkerdine, V. (2003). Psychology, postmodernity and neo-liberalism./Psychologic, postmoderne und neoliberalismus. *Journal für Psychologie, 11*(2), 126–148.

Weare, K. (2015). *What works in promoting social and emotional wellbeing and responding to mental health problems in schools? Advice for schools and framework document*. London: National Children's Bureau.

Webb, P., Gulson, K., & Pitton, V. (2013). The neo-liberal education policies of epimeleia heautou: Caring for the self in school markets. *Discourse: Studies in the Cultural Politics of Education, 35*(1), 31–44. doi:10.1080/01596306.2012.739465.

Wolke, D. (2014). *The long-term cost of bullying*. Economic and Social Research Council. Retrieved from www.esrc.ac.uk/files/news-events-and-publications/evidence-briefings/the-long-term-cost-ofbullying-pdf/

Chapter 14

School culture as a determinant of bullying

Exploring the participant roles

Rubina Hanif and Sadaf Zaheer

Introduction

School bullying has become a serious and widespread problem in Pakistani schools and is especially considered to be an issue of high concern for teachers, parents and policy makers. According to the renowned definition of Dan Olweus (1994), bullying refers to a deliberate abusive behaviour against another person that can cause physical, verbal and/or psychological harm. It is typically repeated over time and includes an imbalance or inequality of power between the bully-victim dyad. The studies conducted in the last two decades suggest that bullying is a group process and there are many participant roles played by peers in school settings. Individuals other than the bully and victim often play significant roles in the social dynamics of bullying. Salmivalli, Lagerspetz, Björkqvist, Österman, and Kaukiainen (1996) identified 'participant roles' played by students who reinforce or assist the bully (the 'reinforcer' and the 'assistant'), come to the aid of the victim (the 'defender'), or avoid or ignore the bullying (the 'outsider'). They recommend that interventions designed to reduce bullying address the roles these students play in perpetuating a social climate in the school that reinforces bullying. These participant roles provide a context to the bullying behaviour to occur and recur (Salmivalli et al., 1996).

In a survey conducted in Pakistan, 52% of medical students in the final year reported that while studying at medical school they were the victims of some form of bullying (Ahmer et al., 2008). In another study conducted in the Sindh province of Pakistan, 74% of the participants agreed that bullying in schools was common and 76% of the participants agreed that students did not report to their teachers after bullying (Ahmed, Hussain, Ahmed, & Tabassum, 2012). The rate of the students bullied in the adult group was found to be 57.14%, whereas the rate was 77.14% among the adolescent groups. Similarly, in the adult group, the rate of those students who reported to be never bullied by peers was 20%, whereas the rate among adolescents who were never bullied was 17.14% (Tariq & Tayyab, 2011). It depicts that in Pakistani school cultures the reporting of bullying to teachers and administration is not a common practice. It may be due to multiple reasons. In Pakistani schools, the high rate of bullying is due to lack of effective whole-school based anti-bullying prevention and intervention programmes (Zaheer & Hanif, 2015). The negligence to this epidemic of bullying is deeply rooted in the education system of Pakistan, especially in government or public sector schools where there is a large communication gap present between teachers and students and students feel hesitant to talk to teachers freely about their problems. Government schools are normally understaffed with a large number of students in each class so the adult supervision can't be increased in places like playgrounds, cafeterias and hallways. Teachers can't give targeted attention to bullies and victims and if reported, these sort of bullying incidents are more likely to be ignored. Pakistani schools lack a proper supportive mechanism, i.e. there is no school counsellor present to help students overcome the hazardous effects of bullying.

As established in the literature, school culture is an important inter-individual psychosocial factor that plays a vital role in both aggravating and eradicating the bad practice of bullying in schools. There are many characteristics of the school that can foster or inhibit bullying incidence (Baker, 1998; Espelage & Swearer, 2003). Students start to feel that schools are uncooperative and unsafe when formal rules and/or informal norms inadvertently increase the advantage or power of some students over others. Factors of a school culture such as teacher attitudes, school norms and policies, the general school ethos and teacher-student relationships can act as predictors of the students' academic, emotional, social and moral development (Swearer, Espelage, & Napolitano, 2009).

The relationship between school culture and bullying has gained a considerable amount of attention with regard to research (Hong & Espelage, 2012). Youth belonging to low socio-economic status are the most vulnerable group and they are more prone to bullying and other kinds of violent behaviours. They think of themselves as less resourceful to get protected from the hazardous effect of bullying. They consider their school as an unsafe and a negative place; this further increases the risk of bullying (Fitzpatrick, Dulin, & Piko, 2007). But, there are some protective positive school factors like perceived teacher support, classroom diversity and school setting with students of multiple races and ethnicity that can help prevent the incidence of bullying (Felix & You, 2011).

The relationship of school culture with bullying and participant roles

Climate and culture of an organisation are known as two overlapping terms or constructs by researchers (Miner, 1995). The climate, values, norms, rules and rituals of the school are known to be the manifestations of the school culture (McDougall & Beattie, 1998; Schneider & Reichers, 1983). Freiberg and Stein (1999) described school culture as the essence or spirit of school that enables students and teachers to love spending time in the school and feel proud to be associated with it. Higgins and Sadh (1998) defined school culture as the norms, educational opportunities and interpersonal relationships that help shape the behaviour of students. Thus, students time and again experience a curriculum that is unwritten, informal and unconsciously planned (Wren, 1999). This informal curriculum is basically defined in this chapter as *school culture* and it further includes school character, beliefs, traditions and values (Power, Higgins, & Kohlberg, 1989).

School culture can help students to get involved in pro-social activities by promoting the ideas of mutual cooperation and connectedness (Carlo, Fabes, Laible, & Kupanoff, 1999). Positive perception of school culture helps students to stay protected from several behavioural and emotional problems. Healthy interpersonal relationships with peers develop a sense of connectedness to the peer group, teachers and school in general (Baker, 1998). Adolescents tend to internalise the expectations of prosocial peers by showing the same prosocial behaviour in response (Battistich, Schaps, & Wilson, 2004). As we know, bullying is a social phenomenon since bystanders are usually present during an episode of bullying, whether online or offline. These bystanders often provide reinforcement to the bully. The perpetrators do not usually act alone but rely on support from their assistants as well as tacit approval by witnesses who fail to take action in support of the victim. So participants' roles are very important for the encouragement or otherwise of perpetrators.

A research study was conducted to investigate the relationship between school culture and empathy among adolescents, and results indicated a positive relationship between the two (Barr & Higgins-D'Alessandro, 2007). The adjustment of the students in school is highly dependent on its culture (Higgins-D'Alessandro & Sadh, 1998; Markman, 2002). Such studies show that school culture is linked with students' and teachers' interpersonal relationships and students' behaviour in school. The academic motivation of the student increases with the positive perception of school culture (Maehr & Fyans, 1989). School culture is also found to be associated with the disciplinary or conduct problems and academic achievement of the students (Purkey, 1990).

Social context is the most important determinant of bullying behaviour, i.e. the social support adolescents get from both peers and teachers at school may determine whether or not a child bullies others (DeMaray & Malecki, 2003). Children who are detached from their significant others at school, for instance teachers, administration and peers, will not demonstrate a prosocial and cooperative behaviour. The perception of students about their social context is very important in determining bullying, i.e. how bystanders behave towards bully and victim; or how students perceive the school environment such as non-supportive, unfair and unfriendly. Bullying is most likely to occur in such a school environment that is perceived to be non-supportive and less nurturing. Research suggests that those students that attend such schools where there is high conflict level and low social support from teachers and peers show more bullying behaviour (Nansel et al., 2001). The social-ecological model proposes that the impact of the school culture is vital to understand and explain the behaviour of an adolescent as well as in producing positive change in their behaviour (Bronfenbrenner, 1979). Contextual factors of school were found to be highly related to the academic achievement, mental health, social relationships and self-concept of children (Baker et al., 2001; Ringeisen, Henderson, & Hoagwood, 2003). When the perceived school culture is unhealthy and is not addressing the needs of students, social and academic problems occur (Eccles et al., 1993).

For approximately two decades, Kasen and colleagues have studied the influence school culture has on different child-related outcomes (Kasen, Berenson, Cohen, & Johnson, 2004; Kasen, Cohen, & Brook, 1998; Kasen, Johnson, & Cohen, 1990). They concluded that those students who attend a school which is high in student-peer and student-teacher conflict show more attentional, conduct and oppositional problems like bullying and aggression than those who belong to well-organised and structured schools focussing more on learning and cooperation. Results of another study showed that adolescents in schools with high levels of conflict, where adults were ineffective and inefficient in keeping order in school and where students disobeyed their teachers and got involved in vandalism and fighting, exhibited more physical and verbal aggression. Children who belong to schools that focussed on learning demonstrated low levels of aggression (Kasen et al., 2004).

In conclusion, research shows that the prime context where most of the bullying takes place is known to be the school (Olweus, 1978). Moreover, intervention efforts undertaken by investigators to reduce or prevent bullying typically are implemented in the school setting. Research clearly shows that school culture does have an impact on the emotional, behavioural and intellectual development of children; however, up till now, limited literature is available on how school culture influences bullying behaviour. There is a strong need to focus on the qualities of the social and emotional climate of the school and how participant roles may be implicated in the facilitation or deterrence of school bullying.

The present study

A substantial amount of research has been done on bullying and peer victimisation. As the majority of this research has been done in the West, therefore, the present study aimed to investigate these variables in Pakistani adolescents using a cross-sectional questionnaire-based survey design.

Aims and hypotheses

The general aim of this study was to examine the relationship between school culture and bullying and participant roles involved in the process of bullying among Pakistani adolescents. It was hypothesised that:

- positive school culture is negatively related with bullying among adolescents;
- positive school culture is negatively related with bully, reinforcer and assistant participant roles;

- positive school culture is positively related with defender and outsider participant roles.

Sample

The sample of the current study consisted of 423 adolescents of both government and private schools and colleges of Pakistan with ages ranging from 12–18 years. The data were purely collected on the basis of convenience sampling depending upon the availability and accessibility of the participants. The sample comprised of 246 (58%) males and 177 (42%) females including 56 (13%) 12 years of age, 81 (19%) 13 years of age, 89 (21%) 14 years of age, 75 (17%) 15 years of age, 69 (16%) 16 years of age, 43 (10%) 17 years of age and 10 (2%) 18 years of age. In the sample, 14 (3%) students were 6th graders, 153 (36%) students were 7th graders, 68 (16%) students were 8th graders, 39 (9%) students were 9th graders, 90 (21%) students were 10th graders and 59 (14%) students were of 1st year Intermediate level. There were 301 (71%) participants from the separate/segregate education system (single-sex education system comprised of all-girls or all-boys schools where girls and boys don't study together in a single institution or a class) and 122 (29%) were from the combined/co-education system (mixed-sex education system where both boys and girls study together in single institution or a class). In the sample, 250 (59%) adolescents were from nuclear/separate family system and 173 (41%) of the students were from joint family system.

Instruments

The following instruments were attached with the demographic and personal information sheet and informed consent:

Illinois Bully Scale (IBS). Illinois Bully Scale (Espelage & Holt, 2001) is considered to be a reliable and valid scale with three further subscales, i.e. Victimisation, Bullying and Fighting. The 18 items present in Bullying subscale are 1, 2, 8, 9, 14, 15, 16, 17 and 18, the items present in Victimisation subscale are 4, 5, 6, and 7 and the items present in Fighting subscale are 3, 10, 11, 12 and 13. The English version of IBS should not be administered to Pakistani adolescents (8- to 18-years-old) because being a non-native language, Pakistani youth lack proper understanding of English. The Urdu translation of Illinois Bully Scale was used to ensure the students' comprehension and understandability. The Urdu translated version of IBS has high reliability, i.e. α =.88 and the alpha reliability coefficients of subscales (.73–.81) are also satisfactory. The CFA on present data also established construct validation of the instrument.

School Culture Scale. The School Culture Scale (Higgins-D'Alessandro & Sadh, 1997) is a 25-item Likert-type scale consisting of four subscales that measure students' perceptions of their school culture. Items range from 1 (*not true at all*) to 5 (*very true*) and higher scores indicate a more positive school culture. The items present in Student – Peer Relationships subscale are 1, 2, 3 and 4, the items present in Student – Teacher Relationships scale are 5, 6, 7, 8 and 9, the items present in School Norms subscale are 10, 11, 12, 13, 14, 15, 16 and 17 and the items present in the fourth subscale, Educational Opportunities, are 18, 19, 20, 21, 22, 23, 24 and 25. The sample items for first subscale, Student – Peer Relationships are "Students generally treat each other with respect and fairness" and "Students help each other even if they are not friends." The sample items for second subscale, Student – Teacher Relationships are "Teachers generally treat students with respect and fairness" and "Teachers give students a say in decisions about school rules." The sample item for third subscale, School Norms is "Some rules are made by votes by both students and teachers". The sample items for fourth subscale, Educational Opportunities, are "Students learn how to speak up and express opinions" and "Students learn how to take other people's points of view." Higgins-D'Alessandro and Sadh found that the School Culture Scale had adequate psychometric properties, i.e. Cronbach's alphas were .81, .79, .91, and .87 for Student – Peer Relationships, Student – Teacher Relationships, School Norms and Educational Opportunities, respectively. The scale was translated in to Urdu for present research and CFA depicted satisfactory model fit on current data.

Ethical considerations

In order to conform to ethical standards, the principals of the relevant schools were contacted and the objectives and procedures of the research were explained to them. A schedule of the research procedure was also provided to the principal. After getting the consent from the school administration, a letter seeking permission was sent out to the parents of those students who were interested in participating in our study. Prior to administering the questionnaires, all the participants voluntarily completed a consent form and the researcher explained the purpose of the study to the participants and addressed their queries about the procedure. All the participants were assured that they can withdraw at any stage from the study. They were also informed that their responses are for research purposes only and will be kept confidential. As peer-nomination procedure was used to identify and assign adolescents to different participant roles, a significant physical distance was kept between the students so that they could not influence one another while responding to the survey items. This ensured throughout the study that no student was physically or mentally harmed by the procedure. Adequate counselling was available during the study and even follow-up counselling sessions were given to the participants after the completion of the study.

Procedure

The data for the study were collected in two steps. In Step I, the peer nomination procedure was used to identify and assign adolescents to different participant roles. For this purpose, the Participant Role Questionnaire (PRQ)-Peer Nomination (Salmivalli, Kaukiainen, & Voeten, 2005) was used. The names of those students who showed willingness to participate in the study were written on the questionnaire in print prior to the distribution to the children and careful instructions were given to the children to think of those class fellows that normally show the kind of behaviour described in the 15 bullying situation related statements. There were five subscales with three items in each of the subscales. These five subscales include bully, reinforcer, assistant, outsider and defender. None of the participants withdrew during the study though they had the option to do so. They were offered follow-up counselling services if any of them felt distressed or upset. Out of the total 423 participants identified and assigned to different participant roles, 81 (19.15%) were found to be bullies, 78 (18.44%) were found to be the reinforcers of the bully, 25 (5.91%) were found to be the assistants of the bully, 77 (18.20%) were found to be the outsiders and 117 (27.65%) were found to be the active defenders of the victim. Whereas 45 (10.60%) were assigned to no roles as they scored high on two or more subscales or they scored below average score on every subscale. It is clear from these figures that the most prevailing participant role in schools is defender (27.65%) and the least prevailing participant role in schools is assistant (5.91%).

In Step II of the study, the other two questionnaires, the Illinois Bully Scale and the School Culture Scale, were administered to the same sample of 423 adolescents.

Results

The correlation analysis shows the relationship between school culture, bullying and participant roles. The positive school culture had a significant negative relationship with bullying ($r = -.65^{**}$). Similarly, positive school culture had a significant negative relationship with bully ($r = -.21^{**}$) and assistant ($r = -.15^{**}$) participant roles and significant positive relationship with defender ($r = .15^{**}$) and outsider ($r = .10^{*}$) participant roles. There was a non-significant relationship between school culture and the reinforcer participant role. To see the predictive relationship of school culture, linear regression analysis was conducted.

Table 14.1 indicates that a positive school culture negatively predicts bullying and various participant roles, i.e. bully participants, reinforcer participant and assistant participant roles; whereas positively predicting defender participants and outsider participant role. Further, stepwise regression analysis was computed to explore the predicting role of subscales of school culture (i.e. teacher-student relationship, student-peer relationship, school norms and educational opportunities) on bullying and participants' roles.

Table 14.2 shows the predictive role of the subscales of school culture (i.e. teacher-student relationship, student-peer relationship, school norms and educational

Table 14.1 Simple linear regression showing the effect of school culture on bullying (N = 423)

Predictors	β	R^2	ΔR^2	*F(df)*
			Bullying	
Age	–.12*	.03	.03	6.11(1,404)**
Gender	.13**			
School Culture	–.66***	.43	.40	282.8(1,403)***
			Bully Participant Role	
Age	–.23***	.13	.13	29.46(2,409)***
Gender	.29***			
School Culture	–.12*	.14	.01	22.04(3,408)***
			Reinforcer Participant Role	
Age	–.13**	.059	.059	12.91(2,409)***
Gender	.22***			
School Culture	.07	.064	.005	9.31(3,408)***
			Assistant Participant Role	
Age	–.22***	.125	.125	29.19(2,409)***
Gender	.29***			
School Culture	–.06	.129	.004	20.07(3,408)***
			Defender Participant Role	
Age	–.02	.01	.01	2.72(2,409)
Gender	.12*			
School Culture	.12***	.04	.03	6.06(3,408)***
			Outsider Participant Role	
Age	–.08	.02	.02	3.71(2,409)*
Gender	.11*			
School Culture	.15**	.04	.02	5.32(3,408)**

opportunities) on bullying and participants' roles. The stepwise regression analysis showed that teacher-student relationship is the strongest predictor of bullying with the $\beta = -.61$ ($p < .001$) which is explaining the maximum variance of 36% ($\Delta R^2 = .36$) followed by school norms, student peer relationship, and educational opportunities. For the bully participant role, educational opportunities is the only predictor of the bully participant role with the $\beta = -.15$ ($p < .01$) explaining the maximum variance of 2% ($\Delta R^2 = .02$). Then for the reinforcer participant role, student-peer relationship predicts the reinforcer participant role with $\beta = .14$ ($p < .01$), which explains the maximum variance of 2% ($\Delta R^2 = .02$) followed by school norms.

Further analysis showed that the teacher-student relationship is the strongest predictor of defender participant role with $\beta = .22$ ($p < .001$) which is

Table 14.2 Stepwise regression showing the effect of subscales of school culture on bullying and participants roles (N = 423)

	β	R^2	ΔR^2	$F(df)$
			Bullying	
Step I				
(Constants)				
Age	−.12*	.02	.02	6.11(2,404)**
Gender	.13*			
Step II				
Teacher-Student Relationship	−.61***	.38	.36	82.52(3,403)***
Step III				
Teacher-Student Relationship	−.46***	.41	.03	69.87(4,402)***
School Norms	−.24***			
Step IV				
Teacher-Student Relationship	−.28***	.42	.02	60.78(5,401)***
School Norms	−.22***			
Student-Peer Relationship	−.24***			
Step V				
Teacher-Student Relationship	−.22**	.43	.01	52.18(6,400)***
School Norms	−.17**			
Student-Peer Relationship	−.22**			
Educational Opportunities	−.15*			
			Bully Participant Role	
Step I				
(Constants)				
Age	−.22***	.12	.12	28.61(2,411)***
Gender	.29***			
Step II				
Educational Opportunities	−.15**	.14	.02	22.77(3,410)***
Student-Peer Relationship	.09			
Teacher-Student Relationship	.07			
School Norms	−.05			
			Reinforcer Participant Role	
Step I				
(Constant)				
Age	−.13***	.06	.06	12.64(2,411)***
Gender	.21***			
Step II				
Student-Peer Relationship	.14**	.08	.02	11.49(3,410)***
Step III				
Student-Peer Relationship	.26***	.10	.02	11.85(4,409)***
School Norms	−.21**			
Teacher-Student Relationship	.12			
Educational Opportunities	.10			
			Defender Participant Role	
Step I				
(Constant)				
Age	−.03	.01	.01	2.93(2,411)
Gender	.12*			

(Continued)

Table 14.2 (Continued)

	β	R^2	ΔR^2	$F(df)$
Step II				
Teacher-Student Relationship	.22***	.06	.04	8.43(3,410)***
Step III				
Teacher-Student Relationship	.33***	.08	.02	8.23(4,409)***
School Norms	–.18**			
Step IV				
Teacher-Student Relationship	.23**	.09	.01	8.06(5,408)***
School Norms	–.25***			
Educational Opportunities	.20**			
Student-Peer Relationship	–.01			
		Outsider Participant Role		
Step I				
(Constant)				
Age	–.09	.02	.02	3.83(2,411)*
Gender	.11*			
Step II				
Teacher-Student Relationship	.17**	.05	.03	6.48(3,410)***
Step III				
Teacher-Student Relationship	.26***	.06	.01	6.01(4,409)***
School Norms	–.14*			
Step IV				
Teacher-Student Relationship	.17*	.07	.01	5.78(5,408)***
School Norms	–.20**			
Educational Opportunities	.17*			
Student-Peer Relationship	.03			

explaining the maximum variance of 4% ($\Delta R^2 = .04$) followed by school norms and educational opportunities. The stepwise regression analysis showed that teacher-student relationship is the strongest predictor of outsider participant role with $\beta = .17$ ($p < .01$) which is explaining the maximum variance of 3% ($\Delta R^2 = .03$) followed by school norms and educational opportunities. When stepwise regression analysis was conducted to find out the role of school culture (i.e. teacher-student relationship, student-peer relationship, school norms and educational opportunities) in predicting assistant participant role, no variable was entered in the regression equation.

Discussion

As established by the literature, the present study has concluded that positive school culture has a very strong and significant negative relationship with bullying. Similarly, school culture and its subscales, i.e. student-peer relationship, teacher-student relationship, school norms and educational opportunities, also have a negatively significant relationship with bullying. The more the culture of the school is positive with healthy relationships (between students and its peers group and teachers and students), strong anti-bullying policies, norms and practices in school and better educational opportunities provided to the students, the less would be the occurrence of bullying in schools (Baker et al., 2001; Ringeisen et al., 2003). The study has also explored the idea that positive school culture has a significantly positive relationship with the defender participant role and the outsider participant role. The positive school culture had a significantly negative relationship with bully and assistant participant roles. The reinforcer participant role was found to have a non-significant positive relationship with school culture. This shows that the more the culture of the school is perceived to be positive by students, the more would be the prevalence of defender and outsider participant roles in schools.

Furthermore, the relationship of the subscales of school culture, i.e. positive teacher-student relationship, student-peer relationship, school norms and educational opportunities with bullying and participants' roles were explored. The findings showed that the teacher-student relationship subscale of school culture is the strongest predictor of bullying then follows the school norms, student-peer relationship and educational opportunities. The more the students perceive their school culture to be positive (i.e. positive teacher-student relationship, student-peer relationship, school norms and educational opportunities), the less will be the occurrence of bullying in school settings.

The educational opportunities dimension of school culture was found to be the only predictor of the bully participant role and showed a negative significant relationship. Student-peer relationships were the significant positive predictors of the reinforcer participant role, whereas school norms were the significant negative predictor of the reinforcer participant role. The teacher-student relationship and educational opportunities dimensions of school culture showed a significant positive relationship with both the defender and outsider participant roles, whereas school norms dimension showed negative significant relationship with defender and outsider participant roles.

The conceptual model used in this study had great implications for bullying prevention and intervention. It will increase the understanding that contextual factors (i.e. school culture) should be given equal importance as that of individual factors while studying bullying. The results deduced from this study can be efficiently and successfully used to encourage the role of school authorities and school counsellors in devising whole school-based effective anti-bullying preventions and interventions.

The participant role approach used in the present study also has strong implications for devising anti-bullying prevention and intervention plans. The interventions should be targeted to change bystander behaviours, because this will lessen the incentives received by bullies and, subsequently, will lower the motivation level of bullies to start and continue bullying behaviour. Therefore, it may be possible to bring about positive change in the bystander behaviours by organising awareness building workshops and incorporating such text in the curriculum that can help developing defending behaviour in adolescents. By targeting group norms about bullying, we may be able to help students to act in accordance with their anti-bullying attitudes.

References

Ahmed, M., Hussain, I., Ahmed, S., & Tabassum, R. (2012). Impact of bullying on the performance of the students at primary level in Sindh. *Journal of Education and Practice, 3*(3), 17–24.
Ahmer, S., Yousafzai, A. W., Bhutto, N., Alam, S., Sarangzai, A. K., & Iqbal, A. (2008). Bullying of medical students in Pakistan: A cross-sectional questionnaire survey. *PLoS ONE, 3*(12), e3889.
Baker, J. A. (1998). Are we missing the forest for the trees? Considering the social context of school violence. *Journal of School Psychology, 36*(1), 29–44.
Baker, J. A., Derrer, R. D., Davis, S. M., Dinklage-Travis, H. E., Linder, D. S., & Nicholson, M. D. (2001). The flip side of the coin: Understanding the school's contribution to dropout and completion. *School Psychology Quarterly, 16*(4), 406.
Barr, J. J., & Higgins-D'Alessandro, A. (2007). Adolescent empathy and prosocial behaviour in the multidimensional context of school culture. *The Journal of Genetic Psychology, 168*(3), 231–250.
Battistich, V., Schaps, E., & Wilson, N. (2004). Effects of an elementary school intervention on students' 'connectedness' to school and social adjustment during middle school. *Journal of Primary Prevention, 24*(3), 243–262.
Bronfenbrenner, U. (1979). Contexts of child rearing: Problems and prospects. *American Psychologist, 34*(10), 844.
Carlo, G., Fabes, R. A., Laible, D., & Kupanoff, K. (1999). Early adolescence and prosocial/moral behaviour II: The role of social and contextual influences. *The Journal of Early Adolescence, 19*(2), 133–147.
DeMaray, M. K., & Malecki, C. K. (2003). Importance ratings of socially supportive behaviours by children and adolescents. *School Psychology Review, 32*(1), 108–131.
Eccles, J. S., Midgley, C., Wigfield, A., Buchanan, C. M., Reuman, D., Flanagan, C., & Mac Iver, D. (1993). Development during adolescence: The impact of stage-environment fit on young adolescents' experiences in schools and in families. *American Psychologist, 48*(2), 90.
Espelage, D. L., & Holt, M. (2001). Bullying and victimization during early adolescence: Peer influences on psychological correlates. *Journal of Emotional Abuse, 2*, 123–142.
Espelage, D. L., & Swearer, S. M. (2003). Research on school bullying and victimization: What have we learned and where do we go from here? *School Psychology Review, 32*(3), 365–384.
Espelage, D. L., & Swearer, S. M. (2009). Contributions of three social theories to understanding bullying perpetration and victimization among school-aged youth. In M. J. Harris, ed., *Bullying, rejection, and peer victimization: A social cognitive neuroscience perspective* (pp. 151–170).
Felix, E. D., & You, S. (2011). Peer victimization within the ethnic context of high school. *Journal of Community Psychology, 39*(7), 860–875.
Fitzpatrick, K. M., Dulin, A. J., & Piko, B. F. (2007). Not just pushing and shoving: School bullying among African American adolescents. *Journal of School Health*, 77(1), 16–22.
Freiberg, H. J., & Stein, T. A. (1999). *School climate: Measuring, improving and sustaining healthy learning environments* (pp. 11–29). Philadelphia: Falmer Press.
Higgins-D'Alessandro, A., & Sadh, D. (1998). The dimensions and measurement of school culture: Understanding school culture as the basis for school reform. *International Journal of Educational Research*, 27(7), 553–569.
Hong, J. S., & Espelage, D. L. (2012). A review of research on bullying and peer victimization in school: An ecological system analysis. *Aggression and Violent Behaviour*, 17(4), 311–322.

Kasen, S., Berenson, K., Cohen, P., & Johnson, J. G. (2004). The effects of school climate on changes in aggressive and other behaviours related to bullying. In *Bullying in American schools: A social-ecological perspective on prevention and intervention* (pp. 187–210).

Kasen, S., Cohen, P., & Brook, J. S. (1998). Adolescent school experiences and dropout, adolescent pregnancy, and young adult deviant behaviour. *Journal of Adolescent Research, 13*(1), 49–72.

Kasen, S., Johnson, J., & Cohen, P. (1990). The impact of school emotional climate on student psychopathology. *Journal of Abnormal Child Psychology, 18*(2), 165–177.

Maehr, M. L., & Fyans Jr., L. J. (1989). School culture, motivation, and achievement. *Advances in Motivation and Achievement, 6*, 215–247.

Markman, L. B. (2002). *The impact of school culture on adolescents' prosocial motivation*. Unpublished doctoral dissertation, Fordham University.

McDougall, M., & Beattie, R. S. (1998). The missing link? Understanding the relationship between individual and organizational learning. *International Journal of Training and Development, 2*(4), 288–299.

Miner, J. B. (Ed.). (1995). *Administrative and management theory*. Darthmouth: Dartmouth Pub Co.

Nansel, T. R., Overpeck, M., Pilla, R. S., Ruan, W. J., Simons-Morton, B., & Scheidt, P. (2001). Bullying behaviours among US youth: Prevalence and association with psychosocial adjustment. *JAMA, 285*(16), 2094–2100.

Olweus, D. (1978). *Aggression in the schools: Bullies and whipping boys*. Washington, DC: Hemisphere (Wiley).

Olweus, D. (1994). Annotation: Bullying at school: Basic facts and effects of a school based intervention programme. *Journal of Child Psychology and Psychiatry, 35*, 1171–1190.

Power, C., Higgins, A., & Kohlberg, L. (1989). The habit of the common life: Building character through democratic community schools. In *Moral development and character education: A dialogue* (pp. 125–143), Berkeley: McCutcheon.

Purkey, S. C. (1990). A cultural-change approach to school discipline. In *Student discipline strategies: Research and practice* (pp. 63–76), New York: SUNY Press.

Ringeisen, H., Henderson, K., & Hoagwood, K. (2003). Context matters: Schools and the 'research to practice gap' in children's mental health. *School Psychology Review, 32*(3), 221–234.

Salmivalli, C., Kaukiainen, A., & Voeten, M. (2005). Anti-bullying intervention: Implementation and outcome. *British Journal of Educational Psychology, 75*(3), 465–487.

Salmivalli, C., Lagerspetz, K., Björkqvist, K., Österman, K., & Kaukiainen, A. (1996). Bullying as a group process: Participant roles and their relations to social status within the group. *Aggressive Behaviour, 22*(1), 1–15.

Schneider, B., & Reichers, A. E. (1983). On the etiology of climates. *Personnel Psychology, 36*, 19–39.

Swearer, S., Espelage, D.L. and Napolitano, S.A. (2009). *Bullying prevention and intervention: Realistic strategies for schools* (The Guilford practical intervention in the schools series). New York: Guildford Press.

Tariq, Q., & Tayyab, A. (2011). Bullying and its psychological effects on adult and adolescent student. *Journal of Educational Research, 14*, 2.

Wren, D. J. (1999). School culture: Exploring the hidden curriculum. *Adolescence, 34*(135), 593–596.

Zaheer, S., & Hanif, R. (2015). *Bullying among adolescents as a group process: Exploring the role of empathy, school culture and parenting styles*. Unpublished MPhil dissertation, Quaid-i-Azam University, Islamabad, Pakistan.

Theme 5

Effective interventions and policies to counteract school bullying

Under this theme, the authors evaluate systematic attempts to address the problem of school bullying. One effective prevention and intervention strategy to reduce bullying in schools is the provision of anti-bullying policies and procedures. Here Marilyn Campbell (chapter 15) and James O'Higgins Norman and Keith Sullivan (chapter 16) discuss the extent to which a formal whole-school anti-bullying policy is effective in reducing school bullying. In chapter 17, Jose Maria Aviles justifies the value of the Spanish concept of *convivencia* as a strategy for promoting emotional health and well-being in the school as a whole. In chapter 18, Birgitta Kimber explores the impact of Social and Emotional Training (SET) in two very different cultural settings.

Chapter 15

Paper tiger or effective guidelines

The use of policies and procedures to address school bullying

Marilyn Campbell

Introduction

For a school to write an anti-bullying policy seems a common sense first step to reduce all forms of bullying (see chapter 3). While established practice in a school could be transmitted orally, with school communities being increasingly mobile, both with new intakes of students each year as well as staff changes, it would seem sensible to write down guidelines about both prevention and intervention of bullying. We know the negative consequences for everybody involved in bullying, for the student who is victimised, for the student who perpetrates the bullying, for students who are both victims and perpetrators, for the bystanders and for parents and staff at the school.

A policy is a framework which contains the principles or rules that are intended to determine the actions of the organisation. Procedures which enact the policy are expressed in specific operational and behavioural terms and are often considered separately from the policy to enhance flexibility and enable constant revision. However, school anti-bullying policies often contain the principles and procedures in the one document called a policy. In many countries it is mandatory for schools to have an anti-bullying policy. Anti-bullying legal guidelines that schools must observe were canvassed in EU countries by Ananiadou and Smith in 2002. At that time, Finland, France, Ireland, Malta, Sweden and the UK mandated school anti-bullying policies. Since then at least Austria, Belgium and Denmark have added anti-bullying policies on their education websites.

In the US, education is state-based with nearly all states requiring the development of school policies on bullying which conform to the legal requirements of state anti-bullying laws. Similarly, Canadian provinces are charged with the governance of schools and most provinces have developed safe school frameworks which address bullying (Roberge, 2011).

In 2003 Australia was one of the first countries to develop a national policy for the prevention and management of bullying. Called the National Safe Schools Framework, it was endorsed by all State ministers of Education. As a result schools are encouraged to develop safe school policies which are proactive against bullying and regularly to monitor and evaluate their policies (Cross et al., 2011).

Purposes of anti-bullying policies

The first and most important purpose of an anti-bullying policy is for schools to provide a safe learning environment and prevent mental health issues for its students by reducing bullying. Having an anti-bullying policy also raises awareness of bullying, shows the commitment of the school to address bullying and sets an expected code of behaviour.

Many schools also use anti-bullying policies for marketing and recruitment strategies to promote the school to prospective parents and to avoid litigation (Cornell & Limber, 2015). The legal aspect of having an anti-bullying policy is especially true in the US since the US Supreme Court decision (*Davis v Monroe County Board of Education*, 1999) established that schools could be liable for failure to stop student-to-student sexual harassment. This decision led to many lawsuits from victims of bullying and caused a significant shift in the legal obligations of schools for student behaviour (Alley & Limber, 2009). For example, *Scruggs v Meriden Board of Education* (2005) was a highly-publicised case of a 12-year-old boy dying by suicide after years of physical and verbal abuse because of his learning disability. It was successfully argued that the school failed to follow special education procedures, that the staff were not adequately trained and that the school did not have appropriate anti-bullying policies (Cornell & Limber, 2015).

Creating a policy to avoid litigation is, however, a double-edged sword. As shown in a legal decision recently in Australia (*Oyston v St Patricks College*, 2013) the failure adequately to implement the school's anti-bullying policy resulted in a breach of duty of care resulting in damages in respect to the harm the bullying caused. This shows schools that not only do they have to have an anti-bullying policy but they also need to demonstrably implement it.

Other schools apparently see the creation of an anti-bullying policy as a perfunctory exercise to comply with authorities, a pragmatic reaction to their legal and educational obligations (Edmondson & Zeman, 2011).

Evidence for effectiveness of policies

Given the widespread requirements for schools to have an anti-bullying policy, what evidence is there that these policies per se make a difference in reducing bullying? Evidence-based evaluation of existing anti-bullying policies is important to ensure that 1) there are benefits to the school community by a reduction in bullying; 2) the policies have no unintended negative consequences; and 3) they are not just wasting time and resources (American Psychological Association, 2008). However, there is surprisingly scant research into this question and the findings are mixed.

United Kingdom

One of the first studies of the effectiveness of anti-bullying policies in schools was conducted in England in 1998 by Glover, Cartwright, Gough and Johnson in 25 secondary schools. They found that bullying incidents in schools with policies were less than 10% lower than in those without policies. While staff and students reported that there was a difference in 14 of the schools in the action taken on bullying, the objective evidence was inconclusive as there was no less bullying reported by students.

In a seminal study examining 34 primary school's anti-bullying policies in England, Woods and Wolke (2003) found no correlation between the content and quality of the policies and the prevalence of direct bullying behaviour in students. The authors postulated therefore whether there was a gap between the policy and the implementation of the level of daily functioning in the school. In a surprising finding in the schools with the most detailed policies, students reported more social exclusion bullying.

An extensive survey of 26,000 children aged 11–16 years was conducted in South Wales examining the risk and protective factors of being involved in bullying as a perpetrator or a victim (Lambert, Scourfield, Smalley, & Jones, 2008). It was found that there was less perpetration and victimisation reported by students in schools with clear rules concerning bullying. However, this association was not as influential in the regression analysis as factors such as gender and socio-economic status. A smaller study was conducted by Smith et al. (2012) where a sample of 78 schools' (mostly primary) anti-bullying policies were measured for quality by 34 items decided by experts. The quality of the policies was not correlated with the level of student reported perpetration or victimisation.

In Ttofi & Farrington's (2011) meta-analysis of the effectiveness of school anti-bullying programme it was found that bullying perpetration was decreased by 20–23% and victimisation by 17–20%. In separating the effective components of these programmes, whole-school policies were ranked only seventh after parent training/meetings, playground supervision, disciplinary methods, classroom management, teacher training and classroom rules and then only for a reduction in perpetration but not victimisation.

US

In California, Low and Van Ryzin (2014) assessed the organisational climate of schools by school anti-bullying policies and administrative commitment by staff in 33 elementary schools and found that the organisational climate was linked to some decrease in student bullying perpetration one year later. The policy and the administrative commitment were not, however, disaggregated.

In an extensive study in the US, 25 state laws on bullying (often also called policies by the authors) were analysed into 16 components and then grouped into four broad categories of purpose and definition of the policy (4 components), policy development and review (2 components), school district policy (such as responsibility for reporting bullying to education authorities (6 components) and an additional category (such as how policies are communicated (4 components) (Hatzenbuehler, Schwab-Reese, Ranapurwala, Hertz, & Ramirez, 2015). The policy variables at a state level were linked to individual level data from students reporting bullying. It was found that in states with at least one component out of 4 in the purpose and definition category in their anti-bullying policy, there was a 24% reduced odds of students reporting traditional bullying and 20% reduced odds of student reporting cyberbullying compared to states with no definitional components. Generally the more components the lower the student-reported bullying. The most decreased odds were if the policy included the scope of the school jurisdiction for regulating bullying: a description of prohibited behaviours and a requirement for the district to develop and implement local school policies. A limitation of this study is that the level of analysis was at a state and not a school level. As there was no prior data of bullying in the different states, it is hard to draw conclusions as the states with comprehensive policies could have had good school climates with less bullying before the study was conducted.

The perception of American school psychologists on the effectiveness of anti-bullying policies was mixed, with 53 participants rating it as the most effective strategy to prevent bullying and 43 reporting it was the least effective method (Sherer & Nickerson, 2010). Unfortunately there was no breakdown in the rating of whether the psychologist worked in elementary, middle or high school.

Australia

A study in Australia by Souter and McKenzie (2000) has often been quoted as supporting the view that anti-bullying policies promote change. However, their article provides only rudimentary case studies of four primary and three high schools. Each case study showcased a policy being created as well as the implementation of interventions, strategies and anti-bullying programmes. The evaluation involved administration of a pre- and post-survey in each school after a year of the anti-bullying programmes. None of the schools showed a decrease in student bullying. The policy and programmes were not disaggregated and either no change in student bullying was found or higher rates of bullying were reported for some schools. The authors say this is because students were more willing to report victimisation after understanding what bullying was, that is, the sensitisation effect. Therefore, we can conclude that it is not a study showing evidence of less bullying with an anti-bullying policy.

An Australian study (Cross et al., 2011) also found that bullying prevalence was relatively unchanged from 1999 to 2007, despite the promulgation of the National Safe Schools Framework (NSSF) in 2003 and government funding to schools to enhance their anti-bullying policies. Four years after the NSSF, Cross found that in a sample of 453 schools, 90% of staff reported their school had an anti-bullying policy but 25% did not know its content. Seventy percent of staff also reported a lack of training to effectively address student bullying.

Sexual minority students

It is interesting to note a small body of research on the effect of anti-bullying policies in schools on sexual minority students. It has been shown that if the anti-bullying policy makes specific mention of LGBT students, often called inclusive or enumerated policies, then there is a correlation with less suicides of sexual minority students (Hatzenbuehler & Keyes, 2013) and a correlation with more school connectedness for this population (Diaz, Kosciw, & Gretak, 2010) than in schools with anti-bullying policies which do not mention sexual minority youth. Some studies have also shown a reduction in bullying of sexual minority students (Black, Fedewa, & Gonzalez, 2012; Goodenow, Szalacha, & Wesheimer, 2006) However, other studies (Chesir-Teran & Hughes, 2009; Russell, Day, Ioverno & Toomey, 2016) have not shown the association of these polices with less bullying.

Why do anti-bullying policies seem to be just paper tigers?

Bullying is a complex social problem deeply embedded in society; therefore, policies need to respond to this complexity and cannot be simplistic documents. It is also probably too simplistic to see if bullying is reduced if there is a policy or even if the policy covers what experts think it should. There could be many reasons why anti-bullying policies may not be effective.

Creation of anti-bullying policies

One of the first reasons a policy may not be effective is how it is created. We know that the extent of ownership of a policy and practice by the whole-school community, based on a shared value system, with consistency of implementation leads to more effectiveness of the policy (Smith, Ananiadou, & Cowie, 2003). Glover, Cartwright, Gough, and Johnson (1998) found that schools tending to a social control model of leadership issued a ready-made anti-bullying policy to staff while those tending to social cohesion developed the policy with staff and students. None of the schools in the Glover study, however, included parents and many parents of students who had been victimised expected immediate and severe sanctions applied to the student who bullied which was not in the policy.

It would seem that a school which has a sense of being a community of practice is best placed to involve all stakeholders in creating an anti-bullying policy (Richard, Schneider, & Mallet, 2011). Those schools that either copy another school's policy or use institutionalised formatting to devise the policy are probably not going to have success in effective implementation by all. Bringing the school community together to create the policy could, however, create a community of practice.

Content of anti-bullying policies

Obviously it is important to define what is in an anti-bullying policy and perhaps those polices which leave out important content are not as effective in reducing bullying. Some studies of content analysis of school anti-bullying policies have been conducted (Marsh, McGee, Hemphill, & Williams, 2011; Roberge, 2011). However, it is not evidence-based in that a particular content item has been shown to account for a reduction in bullying but rather the content or quality is based on the opinion of experts. Smith et al. (2008) used face validity to construct criteria for what anti-bullying policies should contain and this is often used for analysis. Swearer, Limber, and Alley (2012) have also proposed a six-step model to create an anti-bullying policy.

Definitions

Definitions need clarity and precision of language yet also need to be understood and applied (Cornell & Limber, 2015). In an examination of Australian school anti-bullying policies, while all schools surveyed included a definition of bullying, some did not include an imbalance of power thereby widening the definition to all types of aggression (Butler et al., 2012). Accurate definitions are important, especially in anti-bullying policies to ensure students experience equitable consequences and to protect staff from being accused of being unfair when enacting the policy. For example, if a student who is victimised physically is thought to have been fighting with the tormentor and both students are punished, then the victimised student will have been unjustly dealt with by both his peers and school staff. All forms of bullying need to specified: physical, verbal, social/exclusion and cyberbullying. Cyberbullying incidents in particular have been a controversial inclusion in school policies as most occur outside of school hours and school grounds. In the United Kingdom these incidents are included as a school responsibility (Smith et al., 2012) and in the US where the consequences of cyberbullying are brought back into the school's learning environment, they are considered to be the school's legal responsibility (Hinduja & Patchin, 2011). All students need to be included with stated inclusions of difference such as sexual minority youth.

Prevention and intervention

The policy needs to start with preventative measures. However, unfortunately reactive measures are much more common in schools' policies (Woods & Wolke, 2003). Individual differences need to be taken into account with provision for extenuating circumstances with a graded continuum of possible consequences and actions to be taken. This is especially important for those students who are both victimised but are also perpetrators. The policy needs to be developmentally appropriate. We know that before the age of 15, young people show poor resistance to peer influence (Gardner & Steinberg, 2005), are risk takers (Hooper, Luciana, Conklin, & Yarger, 2004) and have poor impulse control (Luna, Garver, Urban, Lazar, & Sweeney, 2004). These psychosocial immaturity factors often lead to lapses in judgement (APA, 2008) such as bullying. Thus, an anti-bullying policy needs to have an educative focus that is developmentally appropriate and sees bullying as behaviour to be rectified. The policy also needs to be in accordance with national and state legislation and policy guidelines. The policy needs to be legally defensible, that is if challenged in court it can be defended as the school staff know and understand that their policy was within legal parameters (Shariff, 2008). The policy also needs to be written with clear guidelines so it is enforceable.

Reporting

As teachers often do not see all incidents of bullying, student report is vital. In an anti-bullying policy there should be procedures telling students how and to whom to report. Students, especially boys, are reluctant to tell teachers for many reasons such as rejection by peers for telling and making the bullying worse if the student who was bullying is punished and wants revenge (Cortes & Kochenderfer-Ladd, 2014). Provision for anonymity might need to be provided for the student reporting (Oliver & Candappa, 2007). Professional development needs to be available for all staff in the school, as teacher training institutions tend not to teach about the prevention and intervention of bullying (Spears, Campbell, Tangen, Slee, & Cross, 2015).

All these details of the content of an anti-bullying policy show how complicated creating a policy can be.

Dissemination of the policy

Perhaps the anti-bullying policy is created by the whole community with detailed content but is not disseminated and therefore not effective. Anti-bullying policies are either stand alone or part of the school's behaviour management policy. Dissemination can occur by the use of posters in classrooms, talks at assembly, curriculum modules, articles in school newsletters, websites, student diaries/ planners and staff and parent in-service activities (Butler et al., 2012). Smith et al. (2012) found comparing 142 schools' anti-bullying policies in 2002 and 217 in 2012 that communication the policy was the area of policy scoring that had improved the most over the six-year period. However, Rigby and Johnson (2016) found in a sample of 1688 Australian students in Year 5–10 in 25 schools which all had an anti-bullying policy that only 47.8% students reported that they were aware of the policy.

Implementation of the policy

If the policy is not implemented by school staff, then it cannot be effective. How teachers respond to bullying incidents has been shown to determine to a large extent whether any student will report bullying to them (Cortes & Kochenderfer-Ladd, 2014). Only if the teacher is seen as supportive, knowledgeable about bullying and can offer adequate assistance will they be taken into students' confidence. Therefore, teachers' responses to bullying reporting will either begin a positive or negative cycle of reporting in the school. There need to be induction protocols for new staff, casual staff and new students and their families. To ensure objectivity in the interpretation of the policy and that it is consistently applied, vignettes or scenarios can be given to staff based on the policy, which could be administered each year.

Review and evaluation of the policy

The policy needs to be a living document especially for the procedure. The policies also need to be evaluated to see whether they are achieving their objective to decrease bullying by surveys or interviews (Farrington, 2001).

Future research

As can be seen, despite the fact that many countries mandate that schools have an anti-bullying policy, there is as yet scant evidence on the effectiveness of these policies in preventing or reducing bullying. Future research needs to fill this gap by well-designed, longitudinal studies examining not only the content of the policies but also their implementation. Research is also needed on the mediating mechanisms such as the effect on social norms and school climate to determine the reasons anti-bullying policies are effective or not. It has been hypothesised that social norms are influenced by policies and that policies could change the acceptability of bullying (Hatzenbuehler et al., 2015). With anti-bullying policies in force for over 15 years in many countries, this does not seem to be a strong argument. However, public attitudes towards bullying have changed in the last 50 years from the opinion that "bullying is a childhood rite of passage" and "bullying is character building" because of the research on the negative consequences of bullying and the media portrayal of bullying consequences. Perhaps policies need a longer period of time to be established to change social norms in schools.

Conclusion

To create and implement anti-bullying policies effectively and to have positive outcomes is one of the most difficult tasks a school can do. Firstly, for the effective creation and implementation of the policy the school should be a collegial community of practice, showing mutual respect, communicating continually with all stakeholders with a common purpose (Richard et al., 2011). A positive school climate is essential to prevent bullying (Low & Van Ryzin, 2014). A school community that does not have these qualities is less likely to come together sufficiently to develop, articulate and implement an effective anti-bullying policy. There need to be strong cultures and norms as well as formal policies and sanctions in a school to influence students to adopt respectful relationships (Powell, 2012). Secondly, if any of the steps of the anti-bullying policy are not carried out the policy becomes ineffective. If the whole-school community does not own the policy or if the policy lacks definitional or procedural content or it is not disseminated or is not followed and revised, then missing any of the steps renders it a paper tiger. So despite educational authorities ensuring that anti-bullying policies are mandatory for many schools, what at first looks like an easy fix, is in fact extremely complex and difficult in ensuring anti-bullying policies are effective in preventing and reducing bullying in schools.

References

Alley, R., & Limber, S. (2009). Legal issues for school personnel. In S. M. Swearer, D. L. Espelage, & S. A. Napolitano (Eds.), *Bullying prevention and intervention: Realistic strategies for schools* (pp. 53–73) New York: Guilford Press.

American Psychological Association Zero Tolerance Task Force. (2008). Are zero tolerance policies effective in the schools? *American Psychologist, 63*, 852–862.

Ananiadou, K., & Smith, P. K. (2002). Legal requirements and nationally circulated materials against school bullying in European countries. *Criminal Justice, 2*, 471–491.

Black, W., Fedewa, A., & Gonzalez, K. (2012). Effects of 'safe school' programmes and policies on the social climate for sexual-minority youth: A review of the literature. *Journal of LGBT Youth, 9*, 311–339.

Butler, D., Kift, S., Campbell, M. A., Slee, P., & Spears, B. (2011). School policy responses to cyberbullying: An Australian legal perspective. *International Journal of Law and Education, 16*, 7–28.

Chesir-Teran, D., & Hughes, D. (2009). Heterosexism in high school and victimisation among lesbian, gay, bisexual, and questioning students. *Journal of Youth and Adolescence, 38*, 963–975.

Cornell, D., & Limber, S. (2015). Law and policy on the concept of bullying at school. *American Psychologist, 70*, 333–343.

Cortes, K., & Kochenderfer-Ladd, B. (2014). To tell or not to tell: What influences children's decisions to report bullying to their teachers? *School Psychology Quarterly, 29*, 336–348.

Cross, D., Epstein, M., Hearn, L., Slee, P., Shaw, T., and Monks, H., (2011). National safe schools framework: Policy and practice to reduce bullying in Australian schools. *International Journal of Behavioural Development, 35*(5), 1–7.

Diaz, E., Kosciw, J., & Gretak, E. (2010). School connectedness for lesbian, gay, bisexual and transgender youth: In school victimization and institutional support. *Prevention Researcher, 17*(3), 15–17.

Edmondson, L., & Zeman, L. (2011). Do school bully laws align with prevention best practices. *The Health Educator, 43*(2), 3–11.

Farrington, D. (2001). *Evidence-based policy on crime and justice.* Paper presented at the 3rd International Inter-disciplinary Evidence-Based Policies and Indicators Conference, University of Durham, July.

Gardner, M., & Steinberg, L. (2005). Peer influence on risk taking, risk preference, and risky decision making in adolescence and adulthood: An experimental study. *Developmental Psychology, 41*, 625–635.

Glover, D., Cartwright, N., Gough, G., & Johnson, M. (1998). The introduction of anti-bullying policies: Do policies help in the management of change? *School Leadership and Management, 18*(1), 89–105.

Goodenow, C., Szalacha, L., & Wesheimer, K. (2006). School support groups, other school factors, and the safety of sexual minority adolescents. *Psychology in the Schools, 43*, 573–589.

Hatzenbuehler, M., & Keyes, K. (2013). Inclusive anti-bullying policies and reduced risk of suicide attempts in lesbian and gay youth. *Journal of Adolescent Health, 53*, S21–S26.

Hatzenbuehler, M., Schwab-Reese, L., Ranapurwala, S., Hertz, M., & Ramirez, M. (2015). Associations between antibullying policies and bullying in 25 states. *JAMA Pediatrics, 169*(10), 1–8.

Hinduja, S., & Patchin, J. (2011). High tech cruelty. *Educational Leadership, 68*, 48–52.

Hooper, C., Luciana, M., Conklin, H., & Yarger, R. (2004). Adolescents performance on the Iowa Gambling Task: Implications for the development of decision making and ventromedial prefrontal cortex. *Developmental Psychology, 40*, 1148–1158.

Lambert, P., Scourfield, J., Smalley, N., & Jones, R. (2008). The social context of school bullying: Evidence from a survey of children in South Wales. *Research Papers in Education, 23*, 269–291.

Low, S., & Van Ryzin, M. (2014). The moderating effects of school climate on bullying prevention efforts. *School Psychology Quarterly, 29*, 306–319.

Luna, B., Garver, K., Urban, T., Lazar, N., & Sweeney, J. (2004). Maturation of cognitive processes from late childhood to adulthood. *Child Development, 75*, 1357–1372.

Marsh, L., McGee, R., Hemphill, S., & Williams, S. (2011). Content analysis of school anti-bullying policies: A comparison between New Zealand and Victoria, Australia. *Health Promotion Journal of Australia, 22*, 172–177.

Oliver, C., & Candappa, M. (2007). Bullying and the politics of telling. *Oxford Review of Education, 33*, 71–86.

Powell, A. (2012). *More than ready: Bystander action to prevent violence against women in the Victorian community.* Melbourne: Victorian Health Promotion Foundation.

Richard, J., Schneider, B., & Mallett, P. (2011). Revisiting the whole-school approach to bullying: Really looking at the whole school. *School Psychology International, 33*, 263–284.

Rigby, K., & Johnson, R. (2016). *The prevalence and effectiveness of anti-bullying strategies employed in Australian schools.* Adelaide: University of South Australia.

Roberge, G. D. (2011). Countering school bullying: An analysis of policy content in Ontario and Saskatchewan. *International Journal of Education Policy and Leadership, 6*(5), 1–14.

Russell, S. T., Day, J., Ioverno, S., & Toomey, R. B. (2016). Are school policies focused on sexual orientation and gender identity associated with less bullying? Teachers' perspectives. *Journal of School Psychology, 54*, 29–38.

Shariff, S. (2008). *Cyber-bullying; Issues and solutions for the school, the classroom and the home.* London: Routledge.

Sherer, Y., & Nickerson, A. (2010). Anti-bullying practices in American schools: Perspectives of school psychologists. *Psychology in the Schools, 47*, 217–229.

Smith, P. K., Ananiadou, K., & Cowie, H. (2003). Interventions to reduce school bullying. *Canadian Journal of Psychiatry, 48*, 591–599.

Smith, P. K., Kupferberg, A., Mora-Merchan, J., Samara, M., Bosley, S., & Osborn, R. (2012). A content analysis of school anti-bullying policies: A follow-up after six years. *Educational Psychology in Practice, 28*, 47–70.

Souter, A., & McKen zie, A. (2000). The use and effects of anti-bullying and antiHarassment policies in Australian schools. *School Psychology International, 21*(1), 96–105.

Spears, B., Campbell, M. A., Tangen, D., Slee, P. T., & Cross, D. (2015). Bridging the gap of school change: Pre-service teachers' knowledge and understanding of cyberbullying. *Special Edition: Dossiers des Sciences de l'Education, 33*, 109–130.

Swearer, S., Limber, S., & Alley, R. (2012). Developing and implementing effective antibullying policy. In: S. Swearer, D. Espelage, & S. Napolitano (Eds.), *Bullying prevention and intervention* (pp. 39–52). New York: Guilford.

Ttofi, M., & Farrington, D. (2011). Effectiveness of school-based programmes to reduce bullying: A systematic and meta-analytic review. *Journal of Experimental Criminology*, 7, 27–56.

Woods, S., & Wolke, D. (2003). Does the content of anti-bullying policies inform us about the prevalence of direct and relations bullying behaviour in primary schools? *Educational Psychology, 23*(4), 381–401.

Chapter 16

Reducing school bullying

A whole-school approach

James O'Higgins Norman and Keith Sullivan

Introduction

As indicated by Cowie and Myers in chapter 1, in essence earlier researchers understood bullying mostly in terms of *repeated aggressive behaviour* arising from a deliberate intent to cause physical or psychological distress to others. Such a conceptualisation of bullying has sometimes led to a tendency on the part of researchers, policy makers, teachers and parents to overly pathologise those who bully and those who are bullied (Kumpulainen, 2008; Pollastri, Cardemil, & O'Donnell, 2009). Such a focus on bullying *behaviour* alone ignores the reality that a huge amount of bullying occurs within a social setting and can be related to a lack of understanding of diversity and as such may even constitute various forms of discrimination.

Previous research on initiatives to address, for example, homophobic bullying in schools (O'Higgins Norman, Goldrick, & Harrison, 2010), revealed that several schools are now rolling out innovative anti-discrimination initiatives aimed at eliminating bullying. (See also chapter 4). The most successful initiatives focussed on diversity education and were supported by school leadership. While leadership obviously includes school management, it also involves external agencies including government and inspectorates and internally other school leaders such as chaplains, guidance counsellors and year heads in co-operation with parents and students alike.

In summary, it is important that we understand bullying both as a psychological *and* sociological problem. Such a shift in how we understand bullying involves a recognition that while certain individuals are more likely to bully, the context in which they exist can also contribute towards an environment where bullying is more acceptable. Young people are rarely bullied because they are perceived to be the same as everyone else. Rather they are often bullied because they stand out in their environment for being different from their peers. This reality points to the need for schools to promote diversity as a "normal" part of life. The research shows that where young people are provided with an opportunity to reflect on difference as a positive aspect of life levels of bullying and other forms of discrimination decrease (Devine & Vasquez, 1998; Chirot &

Seligman, 2001; Pettigrew & Tropp, 2006; O'Higgins Norman, 2008; O'Moore, 2010; Sullivan, 2010).

Where to start?

Successive international research has shown that in order for an initiative aimed at addressing bullying to be successful, it must be developed as part of a monitored whole-school approach to the problem (Salmivalli, 1999; Smith, Schneider, Smith, & Ananiadou, 2004; O'Higgins Norman et al., 2010; O'Moore, 2010; Sullivan, 2010). However, several elements operating at different and sometimes simultaneous levels have to be considered in any action taken if the school is to truly develop a whole-school approach to the problem of bullying.

It is important that school leaders familiarise themselves with up to date research on bullying and ensure that other key members of staff also have access to the latest research. This will allow school leaders to raise awareness of the issue at staff meetings, on notice boards, with pastoral care teams, staff bulletin, senior management team meetings, or any other way of getting the message across effectively.

The principal (headteacher) will form an anti-bullying committee to help increase awareness and manage change in relation to bullying. It is also probably advisable to ask one member of staff to take specific responsibility for the brief to ensure that it is kept on the agenda. It is important that the committee use a checklist to self-evaluate and decide what action is required to initiate, enhance or change practices that promote acceptance of diversity and reduce bullying within the school. There are seven core elements that can be used as a base for a checklist by school leaders and working groups who are trying to develop a whole-school approach to addressing bullying (see Table 16.1). Each element will be discussed in the following sections.

Leadership and change management

More than one researcher has found that leadership style is critical to successfully resolving bullying within a wider whole-school approach (Minton & O'Moore, 2004; Meyer, 2008; O'Higgins Norman et al., 2010). Furthermore, it is argued

Table 16.1 Seven core elements in a checklist for schools

Leadership and change management
Policy development
Curriculum planning
School ethos
Student voice and bystanders
Student support services
Partnership with parents and local communities

that the individual principal's skills and attitude are central to resolving bullying successfully. In turn, this may depend on the type of leadership model each individual adopts in their practice. As Day, Harris, and Hadfield (2001) concluded from their research, "effective leadership is defined and driven by individual value systems" (p. 32). If a school principal does not recognise bullying as an issue worth addressing then his/her values can impact on the extent to which a school is ready to prevent and address bullying. Brennan and MacRuairc (2011) argue that demonstrating social awareness about what feelings to show in what circumstances is an essential leadership skill for a principal.

The role of the board of management and principal are of great importance in animating a whole-school approach. However, leadership should also be understood to encompass the contribution of relevant government departments, as well as deputy-principals, class tutors, year heads, chaplains, guidance counsellors, subject leaders, parents' councils and even prefects and other students. Fundamentally, it is the responsibility of all those who are identified as leaders within the school community to ensure that practical steps are taken to challenge and respond to bullying. This can be done by principals and other leaders in the school striving to engender in the school values in which bullying is unacceptable (Day et al., 2001). It is also vital that school leaders involve both staff and students in developing and implementing a vision of the school where diversity is accepted and celebrated. The desire to address and change the situation regarding bullying will need to be included within a school development or strategic plan.

The principal has a key role in modelling the type of behaviour that s/he wants staff and students to demonstrate (Fullan, 2005; Kochaneck, 2005; O'Moore, 2010). Nothing will undermine a school approach to bullying more than if the students and staff perceive those in authority to be failing in their responsibilities to develop an environment in which people feel safe, cared for and respected. At the very least this means that senior management must value the entire school community and be sensitive to the personal and professional needs of individuals (Brennan & MacRuairc, 2011). This will involve school leaders being available to emotionally support those affected by bullying issues. There can be some anxiety among school staff about how to prevent and intervene in bullying and so it is important that they have confidence that school leaders will be open and supportive of their needs. Principals will also need to ensure the provision of specific training for members of schools' boards of management, parents and staff, and the results of this training will have to be monitored for its effectiveness in bringing about change within the school.

Finally, the outcomes of a number of successful anti-bullying programmes suggest that school leadership, through the anti-bullying committee, begin the process of bullying prevention with an audit of bullying behaviour (*Olweus Bullying Prevention Programme, 2007; KIVA, 2014)*. This should include students and staff keeping a log of bullying (verbal and physical) as it occurs over a specific period of time. Such an audit will give the working group a clear idea of the extent of the problem within the school and the task of bringing about change within a whole-school framework.

Policy development

Although many countries including the US, UK, and Ireland do not have national laws that specifically deal with bullying as an offence, schools in most countries are now required to have a number of policies in place including one on bullying behaviour and/or harassment (see chapter 3). It is vital to have up-to-date and coherent policies including those on bullying, guidance, relationships and sexuality education, and child protection and to have associated procedures for dealing with bullying. These policies should be developed and reviewed in consultation with all members of the school community, and should emphasise that all types of bullying will not be accepted in the school.

Previous research has shown that schools can over rely on generic policies and templates that fail to acknowledge gender and other variables that influence different experiences and responses to bullying. Bullying has been shown to be both a gendered and sexualised experience (Ging & O'Higgins Norman, 2016; O'Higgins Norman, 2008) and as such school policies need to reflect this. Understanding how girls and boys do friendship, conflict, and conflict resolution off- and online must therefore go beyond gender-blind anti-bullying policies and internet safety programmes, many of which reinforce the notion of female victim culpability and masculine aggression (Dobson & Ringrose, 2016, Ging & O'Higgins Norman, 2016), to take into account the wider social and cultural contexts in which young people operate (Hadley, 2003).

A related but central issue to policy development in schools is that policies need to be evidence based, which means that they should emerge from what has been shown to work in bullying prevention and intervention. There are two levels to this, firstly the policy should be cognisant of research emerging from scholars in this area, but secondly and equally important policies should reflect what has been applied and found to work at a local level. Bradshaw (2015) points out that several questions remain regarding the effectiveness of the various school-based prevention approaches. In fact, recent reviews of bullying prevention approaches produced mixed findings (Farrington & Ttofi, 2009; Ferguson, Miguel, Kilburn, & Sanchez, 2007; Merrell, Gueldner, Ross, & Isava, 2008). As a result, many researchers, policymakers, and practitioners remain unclear as to where the field stands in terms of the evidence-base for bullying prevention. Bradshaw (2015) concludes that a holistic and multidisciplinary approach is needed to advance the field of bullying prevention and to help translate research findings to practice and policy.

School policies should be enabling of good practice and provide teachers with specific guidance on how to engage in prevention and intervention where bullying may occur. In developing policies the school will need to state that any perpetrators of bullying will be dealt with severely and that those who are bullied will receive appropriate support. The school's policy on bullying should also refer to the school's commitment to celebrating the diversity of backgrounds and identities of all in the school community. This commitment will be evident in the school's relationships and sexualities policy and programme. Finally, the anti-bullying policy will need to include an element of monitoring and evaluating incidents of bullying and the mechanisms for these will need to be stated and operated clearly and efficiently as research has shown that a lack of transparency often inhibits young people from reporting bullying to teachers (O'Higgins Norman & Ging, 2013). Teachers must never allow bullying in the form of discriminatory comments or actions to go unchallenged and victims should have confidence in the policies and processes that are employed by schools to address bullying. Why teachers fail to implement and achieve the intentions of policy is difficult to analyse. Looney (2014) warns against a belief that policies are 'implemented' and turn out as intended, and that 'problems' arise because teachers don't follow the instructions they have been given. Such a view ignores the fact that teachers are social actors who operate within a social context and that their ability to implement policies is heavily influenced by their own personal qualities and position within existing social power structures. Future policy development will need to factor in mechanisms to help teachers reflect on their own personal and professional dynamics and how these influence their response to implementing policy.

Curriculum planning for teaching and learning

The purpose of school curriculum has been debated for centuries (Dewey, 1902; Kelly, 2009; Looney & Klenowski, 2008). For some the curriculum is solely concerned with the reproduction of knowledge. From this point of view schools and teachers have a specialist role as gate-keepers of knowledge inducting children and young people according to their abilities into various degrees of elite intellectual spaces. For others the curriculum is about the process of learning and the importance of developing a space in which young people want to learn and develop. In this latter case, the teacher's role is not so much to provide knowledge but to create a process of teaching and learning whereby the young enjoy learning. Looney (2014) points out that there is a third way that mediates between these two opposing worldviews in which curriculum is viewed as both product and process. In terms of planning a curriculum for bullying prevention and intervention it is essential that schools plan and design programmes of learning that are both clear in terms of the product (anti-bullying programme) and the process which is how it is taught in subjects and modelled across the whole-school environment.

There are many opportunities across the curriculum to challenge students to think about their attitudes, to correct misinformation and to raise awareness about the implications of prejudice and discrimination. However, this does not mean that the use of one-off workshops or visiting speakers is enough to tackle bullying in a school. It is more appropriate to discuss issues such as bullying within a broader context, rather than in specific lessons focussing solely on bullying. Such discussions will help students to become more empathetic and to understand that difference is part of life, something to be valued and celebrated and that bullying is a fundamental rejection of human diversity.

While some classes such as Civic, Social and Personal Education (CSPE), Religious Education, and Social Personal and Health Education (including RSE) will provide an obvious platform for teaching and learning about bullying issues, there is a place within most subjects on the curriculum to promote and value diversity and to teach about bullying as something that is wrong. From time to time, and when appropriate, teachers must ensure that they include reference to bullying in their lessons and senior management should ensure that schemes of work reflect this. Furthermore, research has shown that young people can rely on knowledge and understanding about sexual orientation and gender that is deeply stereotyped (O'Higgins Norman, 2008; Ging & O'Higgins Norman, 2016). Consequently, it is important that teachers in all subjects across the curriculum provide positive and non-stereotypical role models of people who identify as LGBT and of people who do not conform to gender stereotypical lifestyles.

School ethos and bullying

At the centre of a whole-school approach to addressing bullying is the creation of a positive school ethos. However, the ethos of a school is in itself an elusive entity, the result of many influencing factors at work in the school community. Fundamentally though, school ethos can be described as the atmosphere that emerges from the interaction of a number of aspects of school life, including teaching and learning, management and leadership, the use of images and symbols, rituals and practices, as well as goals and expectations. School ethos is the dominant pervading atmosphere or character of the school resulting from the habits of behaviour of those who are part of it (Norman, 2003, p. 2; Williams, 2000, p. 74). A positive school ethos is characterised by a respect for the individual regardless of his/her background or identity. Consequently, school ethos can be said to influence every aspect of school life and is a determinant factor in the success of work to address bullying.

Research has shown that some teachers can be nervous about addressing issues such as homophobic bullying in the context of denominational schools (i.e. managed or controlled by religious organisations) (O'Higgins Norman, 2008; Lodge et al., 2008) due to a lack of clarity in relation to how issues of sexual orientation relate to school ethos. Contrasting views on homosexuality between the main religious faiths can often be seen as an obstacle to addressing homophobic bullying in schools. However, regardless of a school's denominational status, most religions and faiths are based on justice and fairness. Therefore, the key issue to address is not so much the range of religious beliefs about sexuality, but rather the need to challenge discrimination and promote the respect and equality of all people, regardless of their sexuality. School ethos should not preclude a school from ensuring that all students and teachers feel safe and affirmed in their unique human identity.

It is important then, that all documentation including the staff handbook and student journals make it clear that the school does not tolerate discrimination or harassment of any kind including homophobia. This can also be made explicit in staff recruitment information and in student admissions policies as well as through the use of relevant posters. If the school ethos is rooted in the presumption that everyone is heterosexual, then school leaders will have to ensure that this ethos begins to change by making explicit reference to LGBT issues (see chapter 4) and providing resources and other materials for use in classrooms and around the school reminding everyone, including staff, that although often invisible, people who identify as LGBT are equally valued members of the school community. What is most important is that no member of staff, parent or student is left with any ambiguity in terms of where the school, including trustees, stands on the issue of bullying including homophobic bullying.

Student voice and bystanders

The most effective way to obtain the support and co-operation of students in addressing bullying is to involve them in developing ways of challenging discriminatory behaviour by their peers. Due to numbers, it is unlikely that it will be possible to engage all of the students with every aspect of a school's response to bullying at the same time. However, it will be possible to engage groups of students with different levels of the school's response in different ways and thus over time all students should feel that they have contributed to and therefore own their school's anti-bullying policies and procedures. Where they exist, student councils can provide a platform for discussion about how to involve students in tackling bullying and discriminatory behaviour.

The main focus of a school's work in this area must be to reduce bystander effect and to empower students to take action when they witness bullying. Initiatives to address bystander effect (Darley & Latane, 1970) are important for two reasons. Firstly, research by Salmivalli, Voeten, and Poskiparta (2011) sugggests that bystander responses influence the frequency of bullying, which makes them suitable targets for anti-bullying interventions. However, a further and often neglected reason for paying attention to bystanders is the long-term negative effects on those who witness bullying without intervening. Research suggests that children and young people who witness bullying as bystanders can experience negative psychological effects similar to those who are bullied. A key finding on bystander behaviour is that they are strongly influenced to act or not to act to help someone depending on how they perceive their position with the wider social group (Thornberg, 2007). This highlights the importance of addressing how to respond to bullying within a whole-school approach.

The role of peer mentors has also been shown to be quite successful and within the limits of their competency they can sometimes act as a first port of call for those students who need to seek advice or support by assisting young children to have the courage to report bullying and mediating when conflict arises among their peers (O'Higgins et al., 2010; Cowie, 2014). This is definitely an area that could be developed further in schools. Senior management teams will need to identify funding to allow for the training of teachers and students who will provide this type of activity at a school level.

Provision of student support services

While many of the elements of a whole-school approach are focussed on addressing bullying across the school, there is also a need to provide support directly to individual students (and sometimes staff) who experience bullying.

Research in Ireland and the UK confirms the importance of relationships of trust and mediation for young people who find they experience difficulties in second-level schools (Coldron, 2002; Murphy, 2004; Sweeney, 2014). Generally, year heads, class tutors and other members of staff play an important role in helping young people to overcome the effects of bullying. This can be achieved by respecting requests for confidentiality from students and ensuring that a supportive atmosphere is maintained in tutor groups and subject classes.

Furthermore, key support personnel such as the school chaplain, guidance counsellor, and the home-school-community liaison have particular roles in terms of animating the pastoral ethos of a school by offering specialised support such as emotional counselling to students who are experiencing difficulties, especially those who might engage in bullying behaviour (O'Higgins Norman, 2014). These key staff will also need to be aware of the emotional health issues that surround bullying. In order to provide this support they will need adequate space and time to ensure that they are available when the students need them. A simple thing like placing an anti-bullying poster in a prominent place such as on an office door can send out the message that support is available. It is important that other students and members of staff are aware of the contribution that these key staff can make and that clear referral procedures are in place.

The school chaplain or guidance counsellor uses counselling skills in her/his work with young people and normally has been professionally trained in the use of counselling skills. The counselling aspect of the chaplain's role in schools ranks among the highest of all their activities (O'Higgins Norman & King, 2009). Many of the issues presented by the student in a session with a chaplain will be similar to those presented to a psychotherapist. However, the chaplain brings an extra spiritual dimension to the encounter with the student. The nature of the chaplain's or guidance counsellors helping role in terms of counselling can be termed 'pastoral counselling'. This is a supportive role for adolescents experiencing problems in their life. Although always working within a professional code of conduct, the pastoral counsellor works in a more informal setting to that of a psychotherapist and refers clients who have deep-seated issues to others. The pastoral counsellor uses counselling skills and strategies that help meet the student's needs. It is also important to remember that all members of staff take responsibility for the well-being of their students and should not abdicate responsibility to key staff such as the chaplain or guidance counsellor or home-school-community liaison.

Partnership with parents and local communities

Parents, guardians and local communities play an important role in a whole-school approach to tackling bullying. Successful schools seek ways of consulting and involving parents/guardians and members of the local community when responding to bullying, while remaining clear about the school's approach to the issue. Such a partnership will need to be planned and carried out in a very sensitive manner. Societal changes have been dramatic in contemporary Ireland and increasingly the school is expected to mediate between the contrasting cultures of home, community, media, churches and other stakeholders (Martin, 2006, p. 3.1). Schools should not presume that all students are from a 'traditional' family background and encourage all parents and guardians to attend meetings and visit the school regularly.

Recent research on cyberbullying shows that parents and teachers often feel anxious about addressing this issue among their children and students (O'Higgins Norman & Ging, 2013; O'Higgins Norman & McGuire, 2016), relying on students to self-report if they have a negative experience online. With only 18% of parents reporting that they monitor their child's activity on social media (O'Higgins Norman & McGuire, 2016), there clearly is a need for parents and teachers to work together on this aspect of bullying. Research has shown that when parents and teachers work together, children and young people are more likely to feel safe, perform better at school work and take action when they encounter bullying (O'Moore, 2010).

Conclusion

Implementing a whole-school approach to addressing the problem of bullying will not be achieved over night. It will involve all of the elements outlined above and will evolve over time. However, our research has shown it is possible to make a start and to build on success no matter how small or insignificant it may appear. It is vital that school leaders provide opportunities to validate and celebrate successes while keeping the school focussed on what future challenges need to be met. Cultural change is slow and staff, parents and students will need constant support and training to assist them in achieving their goals of eliminating bullying from the school. Students will need to be continually rewarded for contributing to a school community where diversity is appreciated and respected and where bullying is not accepted. Finally, a whole-school approach to bullying is more than about protecting young people from being bullied. It is as much about developing a school ethos where staff, parents and students alike feel they are accepted and can be free from discrimination on any ground.

References

Bradshaw, C.P. (2015). Translating research to practice in bullying prevention. *American Psychologist, 70*(4), 322–332.

Brennan, J., & MacRuairc, G. (2011). Taking it personally: Examining patterns of emotional practice in leading primary schools in the Republic of Ireland. *International Journal of Leadership in Education, 14*, 129–150.

Chirot, D., & Seligman, M. E. P. (2001). *Ethnopolitical warfare: Causes, Consequences and possible solutions.* Washington, DC: American Psychological Association.

Coldron, J. (2002). *"We just talk things through and then she helps me . . ." Relationships of trust and mediation.* Paper Presented at the British Educational Research Association Annual Conference, University of Exeter, England.

Cowie, H. (2014). Understanding the role of bystanders and peer support in school bullying. *International Journal of Emotional Education, 6*(1), 26–32.

Darley, J. M., & Latane, B. (1970). *The unresponsive bystander: Why doesn't he help?* New York, NY: Appleton Century Crofts.

Day, C., Harris, A., & Hadfield, M. (2001). Grounding knowledge of schools in stakeholder realities: A multi-perspective study of effective school leaders. *School Leadership & Management, 21*, 19–42.

Devine, P. G., & Vasquez, K. A. (1998). The rocky road to positive intergroup relations. In J. L. Eberhardt and St. T. Fiske (Eds.), *Confronting racism: The problem and the response* (pp. 234–262). Thousand Oaks, CA: Sage.

Dewey, J. (1902). *The child and the curriculum.* Chicago: University of Chicago Press.

Dobson, A., & Ringrose, J. (2016). Sext education: Pedagogies of sex, gender and shame in the schoolyards of Tagged and Exposed. *Sex Education, 16*(1), 8–21.

Farrington, D. P., & Ttofi, M. M. (2009). *School-based programmes to reduce bullying and victimization* (Campbell Systematic Reviews No. 6). Oslo, Norway: Campbell Corporation.

Ferguson, C. J., Miguel, C. S., Kilburn, J. C., & Sanchez, P. (2007). The effectiveness of school-based anti-bullying programmes: A meta-analytic review. *Criminal Justice Review, 32*, 401–414.

Fullan, M. (2005). *Leadership and sustainability.* Thousand Oaks, CA: Corwin Press.

Ging, D., & O'Higgins Norman, J. (2016). Cyberbullying, conflict management or just messing? Teenage girls' understandings and experiences of gender, friendship, and conflict on Facebook in an Irish second-level school. *Feminist Media Studies, 59*(1), 1–17.

Hadley, M. (2003). Relational, indirect, adaptive, or just mean: Recent work on aggression in adolescent girls – Part I. *Studies in Gender & Sexuality, 4*, 367–394.

Kelly, A. V. (2009). *The curriculum: Theory and practice* (6th ed.). London: Sage.

KIVA Bullying Prevention Programme, University of Turku, Finland. Retrieved from www.kivaprogramme.net/ (accessed 26 September 2016).

Kochaneck, J. R. (2005). *Building trust for better schools: Research based practices.* Thousand Oaks, CA: Corwin Press.

Kumpulainen, K. (Apr-June 2008). Psychiatric conditions associated with bullying. *International Journal of Medicine and Health, 20*(2), 121–132.

Lodge, A., Gowran, S. & O'Shea, K. (2008). *Valuing visibility: An exploration of how sexual orientation issues arise and are addressed in post-primary schools*. Dublin: GLEN.

Looney, A. (2014). Curriculum politics and practice: From 'implementation' to 'agency'. *Irish Teachers Journal, 2*(1), 7–14.

Looney, A., & Klenowski, V. (2008). Curriculum and assessment for the knowledge society: Interrogating experiences in the Republic of Ireland and Queensland, Australia. *The Curriculum Journal, 19*(3), 177–192.

Martin, M. (2006). *School matters: The report of the task force on student behaviour in second-level schools*. Dublin: Department of Education & Science.

Merrell, K. W., Gueldner, B. A., Ross, S. W., & Isava, D. M. (2008). How effective are school bullying intervention programmes? A meta-analysis of intervention research. *School Psychology Quarterly, 23*, 26–42.

Meyer, E. (2008). Gendered harassment in secondary schools: Understanding teachers' (non) interventions. *Gender and Education, 20*, 555–570.

Minton, S., & O'Moore, A. (2004). The effectiveness of a nationwide intervention programme to prevent and counter school bullying in Ireland. *International Journal of Psychology and Psychological Therapy, 8*, 1–12.

Murphy, S. (2004). A study of pupils' perceptions and experiences of school chaplaincy. In J. Norman (Ed.), *At the heart of education: School chaplaincy and pastoral care*. Dublin: Veritas.

O'Higgins Norman, J. (2008). *Homophobic bullying in Irish secondary education*. Palo Alto, CA: Academica Press.

O'Higgins Norman, J. (2014). *Education matters, readings in pastoral care for school chaplains, guidance counsellors and teachers*. Dublin: Veritas.

O'Higgins Norman, J., & Ging, D. (2013). Cyberbullying among adolescent girls: Issues and responses: A case study from Ireland. In B. Flanagan & S. Thornton (Eds.), *The Bloomsbury Guide to Pastoral Care*. London: Continuum.

O'Higgins Norman, J., Goldrick, M., & Harrison, K. (2010). *Addressing homophobic bullying in Irish second level schools: Case studies*. Dublin: The Equality Authority.

O'Higgins Norman, J., & King, P. (2009). *School chaplaincy activity rating study: A research report for the School Chaplains Association*. Dublin: Dublin City University.

O'Higgins Norman, J., & McGuire, L. (2016). *Cyberbullying in Ireland: A survey of parents internet usage and knowledge*. Dublin: National Anti-Bullying Research and Resource Centre.

Olweus Bullying Prevention Programme, Hazeldene Foundation. (2007). Retrieved from www.violencepreventionworks.org/public/index.page (accessed 26 September 2016).

Olweus, D. (1993). *Bullying: What we know and what we can do*. Oxford: Basil Blackwell.

O'Moore, M. (2010). *Understanding bullying: A guide for parents and teachers*. Dublin: Veritas.

Pettigrew, T. F., & Tropp, L. R. (2006). A meta-analytic test of inter-group contact theory. *Journal of Personality and Social Psychology, 90*(5), 751–783.

Pollastri, A. R., Cardemil, E. V., & O'Donnell, E. H. (2009). Self-esteem in pure bullies and bully/victims: A longitudinal analysis. *Journal of Interpersonal Violence, 25*(8), 1489–1502.

Salmivalli, C. (1999). Participant role approach to school bullying: Implications for intervention. *Journal of Adolescence, 22*, 453–459.

Salmivalli, C., Voeten, M., & Poskiparta, E. (2011). Bystanders matter: Associations between reinforcing, defending, and the frequency of bullying behaviour in classrooms. *Journal of Clinical Child & Adolescent Psychology, 40*(5), 668–676.

Smith, J. D., Schneider, B. H., Smith, P. K., & Ananiadou, K. (2004). The effectiveness of whole school anti-bullying programmes: A synthesis of evaluation research. *School Psychology Review, 33*(4), 547–560.

Sullivan, K. (2010). *The anti-bullying handbook*. London: Sage.

Sweeney, N. (2014). An introduction to counselling in schools. In J. O'Higgins Norman (Ed.), *Education matters, readings in pastoral care for school chaplains, guidance counsellors and teachers* (pp. 71–87). Dublin: Veritas.

Thornberg, R. (2007). A classmate in distress: Schoolchildren as bystanders and their reasons for how they act. *Social Psychology of Education, 10*, 5–28.

Williams, K. (2000). Understanding ethos: A philosophical and literary exploration. In L. Monahan (Ed.), *School culture and ethos, cracking the code.* Dublin: Marino.

Chapter 17

Convivencia

A strategy that prevents school bullying and promotes emotional health and well-being

José María Avilés Martínez, translated from Spanish by Sarah Griffin-Mason

What is convivencia? What is education for convivencia?

The term *convivencia* is a Spanish word that expresses the dynamic and interactive concept of living harmoniously in human groups, the art of living together. As with any discipline, it demands various competencies (Grado, 2016) with optimal results only available where training and cultivation of these is provided. Hence, the act of convivencia in itself is not sufficient; the active sharing of space and time must be complemented with intentions, actions and forms of interpersonal interaction that produce and affect the collective climate of relationships and the affective and emotional well-being of individuals to produce satisfaction or unhappiness. Convivencia must therefore be fostered and worked upon as a preventive tool, in order to decrease opportunities for violence and abuse.

Satisfactory convivencia in the school environment demands the facilitation of appropriate structured channels of communication for organisational purposes. Ideal interaction techniques and management mechanisms will provide opportunities to the participants, allowing them to gain awareness of the difficulties implicit within this along with an understanding of the opportunities available for resolution in a collaborative and peaceful manner. To teach children about convivencia, we must facilitate the related learning, working on the content in order to make them competent (Fernández & de Vicente, 2014). This must be achieved in a positive manner with their participation, fostering their social competence and making them protagonists within management of the process. As the educational agents with whom they cohabit, the teaching staff must intervene in a manner that is planned, professional and integrated within the school curriculum. Departing from any other premise would simply leave the way open to coercion and bullying.

For students in particular, the convivencia content must be planned and taught with careful intention. We must help them to internalise the guidelines that will shape their action and to understand the educational scaffolding available in the management of emotions and expectations. Similarly, we must help them learn to face correction and sanction in order to help them change attitudes and behaviours where necessary. All these elements are involved in education for convivencia.

The convivencia plan

A convivencia plan analyses the current situation in each school establishing a baseline on which to build a response to the main deficits, including bullying and cyberbullying, in a constructive form. This is approached from the basis of the main content (Jares, 2006) starting with principles inherent to human nature (to include, the right to life, dignity, happiness, passion for life), those related to interpersonal relationships (to include respect, nonviolence, acceptance of diversity, rejection of discrimination, elimination of prejudice, solidarity, equality) and those of citizenship, using the concept of human rights as a regulatory framework for convivencia.

Convivencia plans have, to some extent, been requested within the regulatory demands placed upon Spanish education centres by the educational administration for some time under various laws (Law, 2/2006; Law, 8/2013), collecting and channelling work initiatives undertaken in the centres. However, there have been no specific plans to draw together and promote all the tools available in the fight against bullying or cyberbullying, although there have been some partial proposals, protocols and references that have been non-prescriptive in application (Ananiadou & Smith, 2002). In educational practice, the treatment of abuse has until now been subsumed within general approaches to convivencia, with no clear outlining of the issue. Just as not all problems of convivencia can be classed as abuse, bullying demands differentiated and specific treatment within Convivencia Plans. Working to improve convivencia helps prevent situations of abuse arising, but when these do occur, specific anti-bullying interventions must be enacted.

It is therefore necessary to outline a specific framework strategy against abuse, in order to have this legitimated with consensual documents established within the heart of the educational community on the basis of participation from all of the stakeholders involved (students, families and teachers). This is where the strength of this proposal lies. We believe that having the support of plans, projects or policies that discriminate positively for work against bullying and cyberbullying at the heart of the Convivencia Plans is indispensable in visualizing intentions, driving actions and providing references for consultation. This approach has been named the Anti-bullying Project (Ananiadou & Smith, 2002; Avilés, 2015).

When Convivencia Plans are evaluated, key descriptors are established that reflect indicators for positive convivencia practice in school institutions, some of which are intrinsically and directly linked to bullying prevention. Other vital elements include: the existence of recognised structures and working parties; the system of relationships and participation; the form of conflict management; the protagonism granted to the student body; the weighting given to the voices of families; openness to the surrounding environment; live collaboration networks; the dissemination and communication systems and the increased visualisation of convivencia; the diversity of responses to problems; the work undertaken on competencies for convivencia; the supporting documentation upon which this rests; the training and innovation this promotes; the analysis of underlying causes made; the management of the data obtained etc. Some of these will be considered below.

Convivencia as a preventive strategy against bullying

Work on convivencia in schools is thus proposed as a desirable educational strategy, both for the benefits it brings to both the academic and personal relationships between students and because of the improvement it produces in the social atmosphere within the classroom – which has a knock-on effect on classroom management (Marchena, 2016) – and in the improvement of the system of relationships between members of the educational community. It also has a positive impact on emotional health and personal well-being (Palomera, 2016). Work has been underway for some time to multiply the effects of this strategy on the basis of several strong concepts:

- *Structures*. Promote collective structures among the student body in response to proposals for individual or individualistic actions, promote support networks of Welcome Teams, Help Teams, Mediators or Cybermentors as opposed to similar strategies that promote individualism (Torrego, 2012; Fernández, Villaoslada, & Funes, 2002). Work with teaching staff on convivencia as teacher and parent associations and circles (De Vicente, 2016) to provide other opportunities for collective reflection and leadership on decision-making to prevent abusive behaviour.

  Teamwork in the educational terrain encourages coordinated action between families and teachers on the basis of 'educational loyalty' (Avilés, 2012), which is useful in establishing and coordinating actions in the same direction, especially when the problems affect convivencia both within and outside of the school, as is the case with cyberbullying. The educational loyalty of families and teachers legitimates both to act. This loyalty is shaped and rests upon documents such as the Anti-Bullying Declaration (Rigby, 2013) or the Re-education Accords (Alonso & Avilés, 2012), both of which provide reflection on a planned and shared educational intention between those who participate in the education of children.
- *Orientation*. Working on Positive Convivencia. Guiding the intervention toward prevention and the restoration of damaged relationships is essential (Cowie & Jennifer, 2007). This line of action promotes the construction of personal and collective abilities for conflict resolution that counteract

abuse and that also allows for action to be taken when difficult situations occur, establishing participatory routines with the convivencia process. This offers a proactive module as opposed to a merely reactive one (Boqué, 2006; Smith, 2011; de Vicente, 2016). Such a perspective approach can be classed as *Values-Based Education*, with the collaborative resolution of conflicts and the making of responsible decisions as backdrops, promoting actions that foster social competence, emotional education, service learning and cooperative work upon the basis of the teaching and learning environment (Minton, 2014). The process compels the school to become a more friendly, participatory and tolerant environment that is less hostile for the student body, for example, by offering positive protection mechanisms and opportunities for success, integrating mobile devices and the responsible use of these as opposed to demonization and, promoting passionate and creative curricular content against traditional content, interchanging the teacher-student role within the processes of teaching and learning to promote responsibility and competence in learning to learn amongst the students themselves.

- *Positive discrimination.* This involves drawing together all measures to improve convivencia specifically directed toward the prevention and combating of abuse through shared action around a specific project. The Anti-bullying Projects (Avilés, 2015) can be used to guide actors through the process, providing routes to participation with students, teachers and families in the campaign against abuse, that will prove their worth when the planned actions are eventually effective. As with the other convivencia instruments, we must make these sustainable over time (De Vicente, 2016) by ensuring longer-term commitments to these individuals and teams.
- *Visualisation.* Make the convivencia approach explicit within the daily life of the school as a way of breaking down communication barriers, tacit situations and the law of silence present in situations of bullying or cyberbullying. This is achieved by sharing spaces, occupying these, flooding school time with actions that encourage appropriate treatment, emotional well-being and interpersonal relationships. Commemorative events, competitions, school publications, radio transmissions, profiles in the social networks, tutorials, classroom behaviour and management, are all good spaces within which to make institutional messages against abuse visible and audible. This will help spread the institutional message of the fight against abuse and set democratic management habits for convivencia within the heart of groups, creating an anti-abuse climate.
- *Social discourse.* The predominant social discourse must be changed when bullying occurs in the midst of groups of peers. Work on convivencia seeks to change the focus from the negativity and silence that tends to be linked to bullying in group culture, the fear of speaking out or defending the bullied, toward a focus on positivity and communication that allows for work with students on aspects of a moral nature. Some of these include:

individual decision-making in the face of group pressure, the collective defence of those who are experiencing mistreatment or changes that must be produced within the figurative conception of the 'tell-tale' within the heart of the groups.

Working with convivencia as a form of bullying prevention

Bridges have been built and links made between work on convivencia and work on bullying (Avilés, 2016) that impact upon the well-being of individuals and their relationships.

- *Identifying the competences needed for convivencia and intentionally using these to work in a preventive manner.* The construction of social and citizen competency forms the basis of the prevention of behaviours that work against convivencia, including bullying. We must help to build emotional skeletons in the form of the social abilities and moral values that will help the student body to build the foundations of, and manage, their interpersonal relationships, to know how to cohabit in peace, to understand the society of which they form a part and to foster their desire and knowledge of how to participate in its development and improvement. We need to make them enthusiastic and to foster good feeling about participating in this as citizens.
- *Ensuring that the convivencia plan contemplates specific measures to prevent and approach bullying.* Research backs this hypothesis (Cowie & Myers, 2016; Farrington & Ttofi, 2009; Smith, Pepler, & Rigby, 2004; Smith, Salmivalli, & Cowie, 2012). Current and active mechanisms for collaborative and peaceful conflict resolution in school cohabitation alone are simply not sufficient. Abuse among peers does not operate in the same way as overt conflict (Rigby, 1996) as it can be hidden behind the 'rule of silence' and can occur as part of the dysfunctional group dynamics of those involved within a schema of latent and consensual domination-submission. It is therefore necessary to take organizational, curricular, group, educational etc. decisions to purposefully approach abuse in its very essence (disequilibrium), process (dynamic and structure) and maintenance (silence and inaction), dynamics that do not occur in the same way within conflict situations. If we do not do this, we will have no guarantees of success (Cantone et al., 2015; Ttofi & Farrington, 2011).
- *Set out the anti-bullying measures within a plan: the Anti-bullying Project.* Educational communities need to build upon and make more visible all those initiatives intentionally promoted to eradicate abuse (Avilés, 2015). This approach has been named the Anti-bullying Project (Avilés, 2015; Chalmers et al., 2016). This plan must be given a firm framework, made visible and legitimated in the educational community and must be connected

in a coordinated manner to other plans operating within the centres (for example, health, antiracism, emotional education, diversity, culture of peace, service learning). It must serve as guidance and reference material to be consulted when designing, leading, revising and reformulating intentions and proposals against bullying and cyberbullying; it must form part of the policy and day-to-day language of the centre, the educational practice among teachers and families, and the relationship and group culture of the student body.

- *Demonstrate in the day-to-day convivencia of the educational community a clear and frequently repeated anti-abuse policy.* The language predominant in the discourse of community sectors must not lend itself to misinterpretation. The Anti-bullying Declaration and the concept of Educational Loyalty (Avilés, 2015) must be references accepted consensually by all parties with mutual legitimation for action. They must have been worked through, so that when cases of assault do occur, correct and coherent responses may be given, even when the aggression occurs outside or from outside the education centre. The normal events, commemorative occasions and meetings of the educational community must be used to make these position statements visible.
- *Adopt a model of restorative practice as opposed to punitive practice, even with bullying.* The benefits of this practice must be extended (Cowie & Jennifer, 2007) beyond mere conflict resolution, providing a suggested form of relationship reparation in cases of bullying, once the abuse has ended (Avilés, 2012). It is important to ask exactly why we want to resolve cases of bullying and to shape the response that is given. Punishment is not sufficient to resolve the situations; indeed, it is sometimes not even necessary in the form in which it is proposed. Anti-abuse education is needed alongside the reconstruction of interpersonal relationships as an objective and, if we are to achieve this, we must draw in those who threaten the conflict resolution process in the quest for a way forward (Pikas, 1989). The relationship restoration circle must be closed with a request for forgiveness, recognition of the action and restitution of the damage from the aggressor, and the granting of forgiveness from the person who received the abuse. The witnesses provide a guarantee that the behaviour will not continue. And this is not easy, because this restorative practice must be coherently linked to the disciplinary policies practiced in the centre. In many cases of bullying the option chosen is to remove the victim, which does not resolve the problem (for them), conceding the aggressor the 'privilege' of punishment and allowing them to continue aggression within the same context.
- *Organize and maintain Working Groups in the centres.* The recognized structure in the centre must foster cohabitation and work against abuse (ABUSE). The benefits of having working teams within organizations are widely accepted (Baker, Day, & Salas, 2006; Orengo, Peiró, & Zornoza, 2011)

along with the idea that some individuals must be actively occupied in this pursuit, not only from among the teaching staff. These groups must also include representatives of the families and the student body. Furthermore, any anti-bullying working group must have access to training on self-management and be given time in which to act. Information alone is not enough (knowing what it is, how it happens etc.), the group must tackle socio-emotional and moral processes, practice techniques, design strategies, plan actions, develop actions, evaluate programmes etc.

- *Involve all sections of the educational community, especially the teaching body.* The model is decisive, the focus placed on bullying and the teaching style are important in transferring messages to the student body on how power relationships are understood and the degree of tolerance given to abuse (ABUSE). From this stance, support networks can be built within the student body, encouraging involvement, participation and guidelines for families. The active involvement of families is crucial for the development of anti-bullying actions (Cross et al., 2011; Smith, 2011; Smith et al., 2004).
- *Give the students a protagonistic role in seeking solutions.* The students must be part of the solution and not the problem; organizing the student body into support networks against bullying or cyberbullying (Fernández & de Vicente, 2014; Smith et al., 2012) facilitates an anti-abuse group culture. Playground Assistants, Welcoming Committees, Support Groups, Cybermentors (Cowie & Smith, 2013) are only a few examples of how witnesses can be involved in the support culture for those experiencing bullying.
- *The class-group as an intervention space. The weight of onlookers and their culture on aggression.* Work must be undertaken with the group to establish key ideas. The first of these refers to the system of relationships and the network of power (the organisational); every teacher must be aware of and able to manage this group power. The second refers to the shared group perception of bullying, the culture of the 'tell-tale' and the silence that protects them, the rights of the individual among the component members of a group (Salmivalli & Poskiparta, 2012) and how defence of these rights takes place (historical-cultural). The third refers to group rules against abuse and how these are respected (regulatory) and the final section concentrates on peer-to-peer social support structures built within these rules and how useful these can be (social operational).
- *Deal with the individuals involved within specific programmes.* Undoubtedly, either by action or omission, those involved in abuse are shaped by it. *The bullied* must receive the necessary support and treatment. The awareness and implementation of immediate specialist attention is indispensable, as is visualisation of reference points for safety in their surroundings. Training in how to respond to confrontation is central, alongside the provision of protective environments. Furthermore, work must be undertaken to improve the position of these individuals within the group, gaining respect for the

dignity of their person. With *the bullies*, therapeutic and educational process must be initiated, within the regulatory framework present in the school. Some of these individuals will need cognitive restructuring of their perception of relationships of power and the exercising of these. They will need to be taught to build alternative behaviours and to structure and manage the consequences of their actions. They will need to be offered methodologies that do not automatically attribute blame to them from the outset, but that will offer them ways out on the basis of a compromise solution (Pikas, 1989). Reflection spaces (Avilés, 2015) can provide a good option here. *Witnesses of abuse* must be trained to help in situations of abuse, with collective work against bullying and cyberbullying within the curriculum, emphasising the moral connections (Tognetta, Avilés, Rosario, & Alonso, 2015). They must be offered legitimate structures they can fit into, both within the school and outside of this, in order to stand up and be counted, teaching them that when they act together they have greater capability as there are more of them.

- *Prepared responses. Knowing how to run sessions to deal with the issue within the curriculum.* The socio-emotional and moral competencies of the student body form part of the curriculum (Bisquerra, Pérez, & García, 2015) and bullying must be covered in classroom content. Dealing with these situations allows students to be prepared and offers another opportunity for the teacher to demonstrate openness to communication, guiding the message, the implication and the anti-abuse commitment. The abused will appreciate the support, the abusers will receive a message on the moral nature of these situations, and the witnesses will feel the moral demand to act and become involved. Planning the development of these competencies on a curricular basis offers an opportunity to promote cohabitation and the need to prevent abuse and cyber abuse among individuals who will increasingly be facing professional and workplace demands to work effectively and efficiently as members of a team in the future.

In conclusion, work on convivencia is a collective task, in the educational community and society itself. Awareness of the abilities needed to develop competencies is an educational mandate that must be undertaken by teachers and families. Developing an Anti-bullying Project in an educational community demands, without doubt, the existence of certain preconditions that will lead to support, efficacy and success. While it is true that not all of these are present in all situations, we cannot wait for them to be provided before we begin. We must pull into this Anti-bullying Project (Avilés, 2015) all of the frameworks available for reflection, design, planning, implementation and evaluation of the effectiveness of actions, along with all the constituent initiatives. This should hopefully lead to the production of a consensual anti-abuse commitment translated and built into an Anti-bullying Project owned by and shared by the members within each educational community.

References

Alonso, F., & Avilés, J. M (2012). Los acuerdos reeducativos como instrumento preferente de resolución de las situaciones de indisciplina escolar. In J. L. Pais, I. Leal, A. Pereira, A. Torres, I. Direito, & P. Vagos (Eds.), *9º Congreso de Psicología da Saude* (pp. 400–406). Aveiro: Placebo.

Ananiadou, K., & Smith, P. K. (2002). Legal requirements and nationally circulated materials against school bullying in European countries. *Criminal Justice, 2*, 471–491.

Avilés, J. M. (2012). *Bullying. Guía para educadores*. Sao Paulo: Mercado de Letras.

Avilés, J. M. (2015). *Proyecto Antibullying. Prevención del bullying y el cyberbullying comunidad educativa*. Madrid: CEPE.

Baker, D., Day, R., & Salas, E. (2006). Teamwork as an essential component of high reliability organizations. *Health Research and Educational Trust, 41*(4p2), 1576–1598. doi:10.1111/j.1475-6773.2006.00566.x.

Bisquerra, R., Pérez, J. C., & García, E. (2015). *Inteligencia emocional en educación*. Madrid: Síntesis.

Boqué, C. (2006). *La convivencia en los centros. Programmeas y actuaciones*. Retrieved from www.deciencias.net/convivir/1.documentacion/D.convivir.conflicto/Actuaciones_convivencia Boque-20069p.pdf (accessed 28 January 2016).

Cantone, E., Piras, A., Vellante, M., Preti, A., Danielsdótttir, S., D'Aloja, E., Lesinskiene, S., Angermeyer, M., Carta, M., & Bhugra, D. (2015). Interventions on bullying and cyberbullying in schools: A systematic review. *Clinical Practice and Epidemiology in Mental Health, 11*(1), 58–76.

Chalmers, C., Campbell, M., Spears, B., Butler, D., Cross, D., Slee, P., & Kift, S. (2016). School policies on bullying and cyberbullying: Perspectives across three Australian states. *Educational Research, 58*(1), 91–109. doi:10.1080/00131881.2015.1129114.

Cowie, H., & Jennifer, D. (2007). *Managing violence in schools*. London: PCP.

Cowie, H., & Myers, C. (2016). *Bullying among university students: Cross-national perspectives*. London: Routledge.

Cowie, H., & Smith, P. K. (2013). La ayuda entre iguales como instrumento para la mejora de la seguridad en los centros educativos y para la reducción del bullying y la violencia. In A. Ovejero, P. K. Smith, & S. Yubero (Eds.), *El acoso escolar y su prevención* (pp. 263–285) Madrid: Biblioteca Nueva.

Cross, D., Epstein, M., Hearn, L., Slee, P., Shaw, T., & Monks, H. (2011). National safe schools framework: Policy and practice to reduce bullying in Australian schools. *International Journal of Behavioural Development, 35*(5), 398–404.

De Vicente, J. (2016). Modelo democrático de convivencia. In *IX Congreso de Educación*. Santander: Consejería de Educación.

Farrington, D. P., & Ttofi, M. M. (2009). Reducing school bullying: Evidence-based implications for policy. *Crime and Justice, 38*, 281–345.

Fernández, I., & De Vicente, J. (2014). Estructuras escolares al servicio de la participación del alumnado. *Convives*, 7(3), 22–31.

Fernández, I., Villaoslada, E., & Funes, S. (2002). *Conflicto en el centro escolar*. Madrid: La catarata.

Grado, A. (2016). La educación de las competencias para la convivencia. In *IX Congreso de Educación*. Santander: Consejería de Educación.

Jares, X. (2006). *Pedagogía de la convivencia*. Barcelona: Graó.

Ley Orgánica 2/2006. (2006). *Boletín Oficial del Estado*. Madrid. 4 de mayo de 2006.

Ley Orgánica 8/2013. (2013). *Boletín Oficial del Estado*. Madrid. 10 de diciembre de 2013.

Marchena, R. (2016). Convivencia y gestión de aula. In *IX Congreso de Educación*. Santander: Consejería de Educación.

Minton, S. J. (2014). Prejudice and effective anti-bullying intervention: Evidence from the bullying of 'minorities'. *Nordic Psychology, 66*(2), 108–120. doi:10.1080/19012276.2014.928485.

Orengo, V., Peiró, J. A., & Zornoza, A. (2011). Equipos de trabajo en las organizaciones. aportaciones recientes de la investigación y sus implicaciones para la práctica profesional. *Papeles del Psicólogo, 32*(1), 2–6.

Palomera, R. (2016). Educación emocional como pilar ineludible del clima escolar positivo. In *IX Congreso de Educación*. Santander: Consejería de Educación.

Pikas, A. (1989). The common concern method for the treatment of mobbing. In E. Roland & E. Munthe (Eds.), *Bullying: An international perspective* (pp. 91–105). London: David Fulton.

Rigby, K. (1996). *Bullying in schools: And what to do about it*. Londres: Jessica Kingsley.

Rigby, K. (2013). *Elements of a school anti-bullying policy*. Retrieved from www.kenrigby.net/05Elements-of-a-school-antibullying-policy (accessed 12 January 2015).

Salmivalli, C., & Poskiparta, E. M. (2012). Making bullying prevention a priority in Finnish schools: The KIVa antibullying programme. *New Directions for Youth Development, 133*, 41–53.

Smith, P. K. (2011). Why interventions to reduce bullying and violence in schools may (or may not) succeed: Comments on this Special Section. *International Journal of Behavioural Development, 35*, 419–423. doi:10.1177/0165025411407459.

Smith, P. K., Pepler, D., & Rigby, K. (2004). *Bullying in schools: How successful can interventions be?* Cambridge: Cambridge University Press.

Smith, P. K., Salmivalli, C., & Cowie, H. (2012). Effectiveness of school-based programmes to reduce bullying: A commentary. *Journal of Experimental Criminology, 8*(4), 433–441. doi:10.1007/s11292-012-9142-3.

Tognetta, L., Avilés, J. M., Rosario, P., & Alonso, N. (2015). Moral disengagement, self-efficacy and bullying. *Revista de Estudios e Investigación en Psicología y Educación, 2*(1) 30–34, doi:10.17979/reipe.2015.2.1p.34.

Torrego, J. C. (2012). *La ayuda entre iguales para mejorar la convivencia escolar*. Madrid: Narcea.

Ttofi, M., & Farrington, D. (2011). Effectiveness of school-based programmes to reduce bullying: A systematic and meta-analytic review. *Journal of Experimental Criminology*, 7, 27–56.

Chapter 18

The impact of Social and Emotional Training (SET) on school bullying in Palestine and Sweden

Birgitta Kimber

Introduction

Social and Emotional Training (SET) is a Swedish social and emotional learning programme, which was started in 1999 to promote mental health among the young. It was evaluated after two and five years. SET was not specifically an anti-bullying programme, but it can be said that all its elements have some bearing on bullying, and some measurements of bullying (quantitative in Sweden and qualitative in Palestine) were taken in the course of implementing the programme. Positive and significant effects were found on internalising problems, externalising problems, mastery, self-image and contentment in school. Students who needed the intervention benefitted the most, and the programme seemed to be especially effective among high-risk students.

In 2006, after the Palestinian SET project coordinator made a visit to Sweden, the Swedish SET programme was introduced into Palestine, through collaboration between the Palestinian Bible Society (PBS) and a Swedish Pentecostal church, with funds from the Swedish International Development Agency (SIDA). Palestinian children report feeling unsafe and vulnerable to attack, injury or arrest. In other words, there are strong parallels between the everyday experiences of Palestinian children and those who are bullied regularly at school.

Social and Emotional Training (SET) in Sweden

SET was implemented in Sweden between 2000 and 2005. The teachers taught SET to junior and intermediate students (grades 1–5) twice a week, each session with a duration of 45 minutes, and to senior students (grades 6–9) one 45-minute session a week over the school year. The programme is guided by detailed manuals for the teacher, three in total. One for ages 6–9, one for ages 10–12, and one for ages 13–15.

SET focusses on helping to develop the following five functions of the students: 1) *Self-awareness* – being aware of what one is feeling and thereby being able to use one's feelings when taking decisions, making realistic assessments of one's own capacities and having a sound self-confidence; 2) *Managing one's emotions* – knowing why one is feeling a certain way, and how to handle one's feelings so that – instead of being destructive – they may aid coping with tasks, and enable control of feelings and waiting for rewards in order to achieve a goal; 3) *Empathy* – understanding how others feel and seeing things from their perspective, recognising that others feel differently, and being able to cope with and understand the differences between oneself and them; 4) *Motivation* – using one's own internal "engine" for goal achievement, learning to take the initiative and strive for improvement, managing setbacks and frustrations on the path to goal achievement, and being able to put up with any reward having to come later; and 5) *Social competence* – being able to handle emotions in relation to others, to recognise social situations and to manage in different social environments. These aspects of personal and social development are frequently used in anti-bullying initiatives to help victims enhance their coping strategies, to empower bystanders to intervene when they witness a bullying episode and to encourage bullies to reflect on their actions and the impact on the emotions of their targets. They also feature in many peer support training programmes.

Accordingly, there were five separate, albeit overlapping, components to the programme, each one highly relevant in addressing the issue of school bullying. Typically, the components merge into one another, and therefore an exercise according to the manual may address several functions. The following themes recur in the tasks: responsible decision-making, problem-solving, coping with strong emotions, appreciating similarities and differences, clarification of values, conflict management, interpretation of pictures and narratives, doing more of what makes one feel good, resisting peer pressure and being able to say "No", knowing what one is feeling, recognising people and situations, cooperation, communications skills, setting goals and working to attain them, giving and receiving positive feedback, and stress management.

Two evaluations were carried out, one after two years and one after five years, in the Stockholm metropolitan area. There were a total of 110 classes in the two SET schools taken together; one had six classes per grade, the other five. A special re-test study was carried out on 119 students in grades 4, 8 and 9 in three schools (two intervention and one control) in Botkyrka.

The SET programme has been subject to extensive quantitative evaluation. All the instruments employed were well-established and had documented reliability and validity. I Think I Am (ITIA) is the Swedish self-rating instrument, "*Jag tycker jag är*" (Ouvinen-Birgerstam, 1985), which has roots in previous American research (Coopersmith, 1967), and is intended to map the young person's self-image and self-esteem. Youth Self-Report (YSR) (Achenbach & Edelbrock, 1987), used in an abbreviated Swedish (Lindberg, Larsson, & Bremberg, 1999), measures mental-health symptoms and problems. Besides the two subscales, internalising problems and externalising problems, suggested by Lindberg and colleagues, four new subscales were derived: anxiety, aggressiveness, assertiveness and attention-seeking. Mastery (Pearlin, Liebman, Menaghan, & Mullan, 1981), in one of its Swedish versions, which, broadly speaking, measures self-efficacy, or the extent to which people regard their life chances as under their personal control. The Social Skills Rating System (SSRS) (Gresham & Elliott, 1990) has four subscales, measuring cooperation, assertion, self-control and empathy. Contentment in school, or school satisfaction by analogy with job satisfaction, refers to a single item, "How do you like it in school?", taken from a Swedish health behaviour questionnaire administered annually by the Swedish Council for Information on Alcohol and Other Drugs (CAN) (Hibell et al., 1997). Bullying in three aspects (being insulted, physically assaulted or frozen-out) was assessed. Drug (substance) use refers to the use by students (only those in grades 7–9) of tobacco, alcohol, volatile substances and illegal narcotics.

Empirical evaluation of the SET intervention in Sweden has been presented in four papers in which comparisons were made between outcomes for SET and No-SET students, and also in a separate validation analysis (see Kimber, 2011). There is one main data set but five analyses, covering different time periods and using different statistical techniques. The first study (Kimber, Sandell, & Bremberg, 2008a) concerned all aspects of SET after two years among all students, except for substance use among grades 1–6; the second, emotional and social aspects after five years among senior students (Kimber, Sandell, & Bremberg, 2008b); the third, substance use among grades 7–9, again after five years (Kimber & Sandell, 2009); the fourth, heterogeneity of responses to the programme (Sandell & Kimber, 2013). We also performed a post-hoc validation analysis to check for non-linear relationships (see Kimber, 2011).

We found the impacts of SET to be generally favourable. After two years, there were positive impacts on 4 out of 5 of the scales covering social and emotional aspects for the juniors, aged 7 to 10 (the exception being body-image) and on 18 out of 20 of the scales for the seniors, aged 11 to 16 (the exceptions being mastery and cooperation). After five years, the impacts of SET, by contrast with our findings after two years, were found to be greater for internalising than for externalising problems, but in a validation analysis, a better fit-to-data for externalising was found in a quadratic (curvilinear) model than in a linear model. There was no evidence of any effect of gender or socioeconomic status.

There was virtually no recorded differential impact on the social skills scales (assertion, cooperation, empathy and self-control) after either two years or five years, but, in our validation analysis, we found a significant difference between the SET and No-SET students in relation to social skills after fitting a quadratic (curvilinear) model to the data.

In sum, there was considerable heterogeneity in the effects of SET. The intervention seems to be especially effective in inhibiting internalising problems and decreasing externalising problems, such as bullying, among high-risk students. Further, a qualitative analysis suggests that the practice of SET promotes the development of teachers, both professionally and personally, and also improvements in the classroom climate. Finally, an economic analysis has shown SET to be financially beneficial, with a benefit-to-cost ratio of 1:13.9 being reported (Belfield et al., 2015).

With regard to bullying, measures of reliability (over two years) of the scale used are presented in Table 18.1.

The main results are shown in Figure 18.1 and Table 18.2. Over the years, there was no statistically significant difference between the SET and No-SET groups in terms of the level of bullying, but there was considerably less fluctuation between years in the SET group (see Figure 18.1).

Although bullying had a small effect size, it showed a highly significant SET/No-SET-by-years interaction (df 4, 2255; F 3.86; p 0.004). This is explained by the fact that there was a stable mean level over the years in the SET group and a quite variable one in the No-SET group, which ends up only slightly higher than the SET group after five years of intervention. The regression coefficient and effect size (over five years) are shown in Table 18.2.

Table 18.1 Reliability (Cronbach's alpha) and re-test correlation for the bullying scale

Grades	*Instrument/ scale*	*t1 (May 2001) α*	*t2 (May 2002) α*	*r (t1 t2)*
4–9	Bullying	0.71	0.65	0.25

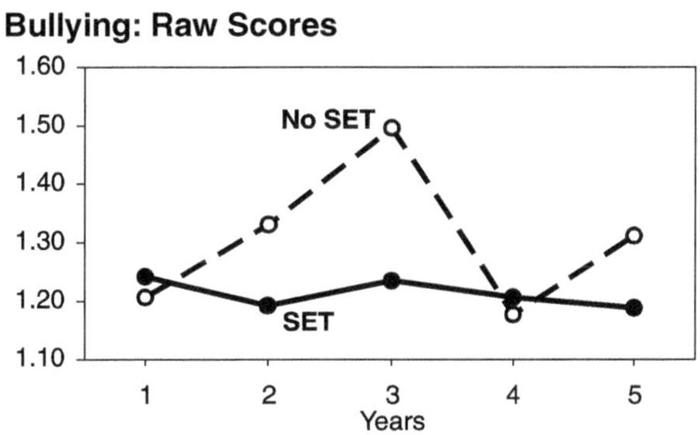

Figure 18.1 Bullying scores over five years of SET

Table 18.2 Regression coefficient and effect size for SET/No-SET by group

Outcome variable	*SET*		*No-SET*		*Δ*	*Zb*
	β	*d1–5*	*β*	*d1–5*		
Bullying	0.03	0.11	–0.02	–0.24	0.35	0.72

Social and Emotional Training in Palestine

The SET project in the Palestinian Territories was designed to address the psychosocial needs of children due to the ongoing violence and instability, and their side-effects on the situation on the family. This was to be accomplished by contributing to the improvement of their social and psychosocial well-being.

The Palestinians involved in the programme wished to address the following issues: children are traumatised, and many lack support to handle their difficult situation in a healthy way; teachers and parents often use physical punishment, which is culturally accepted in Palestine; and, all parts of society need to join together to provide better support for children (teachers, social workers, NGOs).

After getting acquainted with the main methods, headings and threads in the SET programme with the assistance of Swedish practitioners, SET was introduced on a small scale as a pilot project for the purposes of checking its adaptability to the Palestinian context and establishing the best methodology to be used for future activities. We wanted to see if a Swedish programme would work in a different society. Taking a process-oriented perspective, we experimented with how a programme could be contextualised and implemented in Palestine.

As well as training 10 teachers/social workers and 10 PBS staff members, activities included: implementation of the SET methodology in a Palestinian context; a survey of any other programmes implemented within the Palestinian territories related to the topics covered by SET programme; production of a manual (a small collection of SET exercises) in Arabic (by the project leader) targeting children and youth; and, finally evaluating the overall effect of the programme through the gathering of observations throughout the implementation period.

Five schools tested an abbreviated version of SET in 2007, and the project team reported on changes, in particular with regard to how the teachers treated the children.

The evaluation suggested that the Palestinian team had successfully implemented the programme, within its original proposal, of promoting less violent action and abusive behaviour and language, within its targeted schools (as defined by various indicators). Hence, based on the achieved indicators and on the change attained throughout the pilot phase, the project team realised the need for a second phase to work to maintain the emotional and psychological health of the traumatised children, and also grown-ups.

There was a need for a second phase whose main goal was to train teachers and social workers as trainers. A time period of 15 months was agreed upon. The full SET manual with all its exercises needed to be translated into Arabic and already-gained experiences incorporated (to replace the brief version used at Phase 1). Processing the manual to obtain cultural adaption was an important task. The Arabic manual applied to school years 1–10 (ages 6–15). Translation and adaption had to be achieved on the basis of observations and focus group discussions and through process evaluation by group leaders and the team. The project was to be implemented within private schools as well as by the United Nations Relief and Works Agency (UNRWA), where the PBS had received the consent of the school administration to implement the project.

There were two forms of training: training of the teachers and social workers from the first project phase for them to act as trainers of new target groups at the second phase; and the training given by these trainers to the six groups of new participants. The trainers of trainers visited Sweden for almost a week as part of the contextualisation process, showing how SET is being implemented in Swedish schools and how experiences might be transferable to Palestine. We evaluated the impact of SET on trainers, trainees and students with regard to the development of a vibrant and democratic civil society on the following indicators: increased trust, participation and reciprocity in communication and decision-making, increased networking, cooperation, and interchange, increased sharing of rights-based norms and values.

At the second phase, the PBS built on the achievements of the first phase and invested in the capabilities of the trained teachers/social workers, as well as its employees. More detailed and in-depth training was provided for five main beneficiaries (teachers/social workers), selected from the first phase, in order to integrate and mainstream all the knowledge into a larger programme with a special focus on children. The five teachers/social workers had been selected on the basis of their performance, enthusiasm, implementation and learning skills, as well as their capacity to pass their knowledge on to other teachers and social workers (who would benefit from the second phase).

Follow-up and evaluation, qualitative and process-oriented, took place throughout the implementation period. It was performed by the five group leaders and the eam, as well as the project leader. And there was a final evaluation session with the participation of all the beneficiaries of the project, based on open questions and questionnaires. Effects were measured by observations, evaluation sessions, interviews and the journals kept by the teachers during the educational sessions.

According to the observations and analyses of the Palestinians involved, the project has contributed to promoting the development of a vivid and democratic civil society in the targeted project areas. The programme content itself, specifically the SET exercises, seems to have worked towards building a democratic mind-set. An example is how individuals were enabled to express themselves and give space for others to express themselves. Throughout the project period, we have seen the democratic impact, on both the trainers and the trainees (and the children and youth they then trained), through the following indicators, all of which bear on bullying to a greater or lesser extent.

- Increased trust, participation and reciprocity (mutuality) in communication and decision-making. These are qualities that are usually absent in schools with high levels of bullying. "I have learned how to show my feelings and express what I think, it has allowed me to dream," said one 10-year-old girl from the West Bank. "I have learnt how to communicate, and I now have a very good relationship with my father," said a nine-year-old boy from the West Bank.

- Increased networking, co-operation and interchange. Again, constructive communication and collaboration across friendship groups are important components of a school with effective anti-bullying policies and practices.
- Increased sharing of rights-based norms and values (supporting the empowerment of people to take charge of their own life situation). "Differences are good, and we all complement each other," said one teacher. "I am not only a better teacher, but a better husband and father," said another. Concern for children's rights is a key component of all anti-bullying policies.

There were other impacts of SET on civil society:

- Growing awareness of children's rights and respect for their equal value among societal actors and educational institutions.
- Promotion of competent educational actors equipped with theoretical and practical knowledge of how to work with children's psychosocial development.
- More peaceful, constructive behaviours and respectful attitudes; and better communications between teachers and students, and among students/children: "We have had fewer cases of violence in the school," said one teacher.
- Development of a well-functioning network within the educational sector for supporting children's development.

Discussion and conclusion

In Palestine, there were, of course, obstacles to overcome and risks with which to deal. Externally, there was the instability of the political situation and the risk of closure of the targeted areas from time to time. Despite these obstacles, the principal finding was that, although the overall level of bullying was not significantly reduced among SET students in Sweden, there was greater constancy (fewer highs and lows) in its level over time. In Palestine, positive changes were reported, especially on how teachers and parents treated the children, i.e. less bullying of children by adults.

Looking back after completion of the second phase of the Social Emotional Training (SET) project in Palestine and previous experiences in Sweden, we are encouraged by the impacts it has had at different levels: on children and youth, on trainers of other potential trainers and within the family unit. We must remember, however, that no quantitative study of outcomes in Palestine has been performed. We have relied on process evaluation and the qualitative assessment of outcomes. Also, it should be noted that adaption of programme to context and implementation are of key importance (Humphrey, 2015), which certainly applies to SET in Palestine We are looking forward to the point where we will be able to show measured, scientific results for the effects of the SET programme in Palestine on the attitudes and behaviours, and also the life skills, of children and youth.

We have described the application of SET in two very different contexts in which children bring very different sets of issues with them to school. In Sweden, issues of self-esteem have become increasingly important, particularly among girls. In Palestine, there is the issue of harsh parent and teacher practices, and, of course, high levels of hardship, tangible threats and violence. There are difficulties in transferring an approach developed in the West to a different culture, but it might be fruitful to raise comparative issues. It might be that in Palestinian circumstances, bullying is perceived as a less serious issue than the violence that the children experience as a result of the conflict situation. Clearly in this context it is essential to take account of the particular social environment in which these children are growing up and the extremely negative impact on them of the frequent violence and aggression both within their communities and from outside their country. Nevertheless, the research findings indicated an overall improvement in the quality of interpersonal relationships among the students and this is the bedrock of any anti-bullying intervention.

Acknowledgement

I would like to thank Diana Samaan from the Palestinian Bible Society for her work on the Palestine project and her contribution to this chapter.

References

Achenbach, T., & Edelbrock, C. (1987). *Manual for the youth self-report and profile*. Burlington, VT: University of Vermont, Department of Psychiatry.

Belfield, C., Bowden, B., Klapp, A., Levin, H., Shand, R., & Zander, S. (2015). *The economic value of social and emotional learning*. Center for Benefit-Cost Studies in Education, Teachers College, Columbia University.

Coopersmith, S. (1967). *The antecedents of self-esteem*. San Francisco: WE Freedman and Co.

Gresham, S., & Elliott, S. (1990). *Social skills rating system manual*. Circle Pines: American Guidance Service.

Hibell, B., Anderson, B., Bjarnason, T., Kokkevi, A., Morgan, M., & Narusk, A. (1997). *The 1995 ESPAD Report. Alcohol and other drug use among students in 26 European countries*. Stockholm, Sweden: The Swedish Council for Information on Alcohol and Other Drugs.

Humphrey, N., personal communication. (2015). *Adapting for success: Implementation variability and student mental health outcomes in the PATHS curriculum* (presentation).

Kimber, B. (2011). *Primary prevention of mental health problems among children and adolescents through social and emotional training in school*. Stockholm, Sweden: Karolinska Institutet.

Kimber, B., & Sandell, R. (2009). Prevention of substance use among adolescents through social and emotional training in school: A latent-class analysis of a five-year intervention in Sweden. *Journal of Adolescence*, *32*, 1403–1413.

Kimber, B., Sandell, R., & Bremberg, S. (2008a). Social and emotional training in Swedish classrooms for the promotion of mental health: Results from an effectiveness study in Sweden. *Health Promotion International, 23*, 134–143.

Kimber, B., Sandell, R., & Bremberg, S. (2008b). Social and emotional training in Swedish schools for the promotion of mental health: An effectiveness study of 5 years of intervention. *Health Education Research, 23*, 931–940.

Lindberg, L., Larsson, N., & Bremberg, S. (1999). *Ungdomars psykiska hälsa. Utvärdering av ett mätinstrument Rapport från samhällsmedicin.* Stockholm, Sweden: Centrum för Barn – och Ungdomshälsa.

Ouvinen-Birgerstam, P. (1985). *Jag tycker jag är.* Stockholm, Sweden: Psykologiförlaget.

Pearlin, L., Liebman, M., Menaghan, E., & Mullan, J. (1981). The stress process. *Journal of Health and Social Behaviour, 22*, 337–356.

Sandell, R., & Kimber, B. (2013). Heterogeneity in responses to a universal prevention programme. *Journal of Primary Prevention, 34*(6), 405–412.

Theme 6

Commentaries and epilogue

In this final section three authors give their opinions on the book as a whole from a range of perspectives: In chapter 19, Bauman discusses continuities in the education system from school into university, noting continuities of bullying roles across developmental periods. She discusses ways in which insights from evolutionary psychology can give us deeper understanding of the phenomenon of bullying. In chapter 20, Coyne explores ways in which conceptualisations of workplace bullying relate to school bullying – two areas which have developed in parallel rather than as an integrated field. As he argues, workplace bullying has focussed less on the protagonists and more on aspects of the work environment such as poor leadership, work pressure, role ambiguity and organisational change. So the emphasis on workplace bullying is more on the social context and the quality of the environment than the individual characteristics of bullies and victims. In chapter 21, Barker critiques the whole book from the perspective of the practitioner. As a frontline teacher, specialising in children with emotional and behavioural difficulties and mental health needs, she demonstrates the value of the book with regard to restorative approaches, successful interventions and the need to demonstrate inclusive policies that help everyone within the school environment and the particular needs of marginalised groups.

Chapter 19

Continuities into the university

Sheri Bauman

The chapters in this volume provide thorough coverage of school bullying research from both theoretical and practical perspectives. As I read these informative chapters, I found myself wondering how the information might apply to the university setting. We now know that despite the considerable attention paid to bullying in children and adolescents, bullying does not disappear when students complete their high school careers. Bullying is present in workplaces, in national and international politics, and in institutions of higher education. In this commentary, I focus on bullying in university settings. I will note continuities of bullying roles across developmental periods, and then share insights from evolutionary psychology that shed light on the phenomenon. Finally, I discuss how prevention and intervention might occur in that context.

In chapter 2 of this volume, Pörhölä discusses several theoretical perspectives that explain the relative constancy of the bullying roles taken early on in the lifespan. She proposes that treatment by peers results in internalised attributions about the self, which then perpetuate the role in a variety of contexts. That is, because he is feared and/or admired by others, the bully sees him or herself as powerful and influential and deserving of deference, and behaves accordingly in multiple contexts. The victim may attribute their plight to their own shortcomings, and internalise a picture of themselves as weak and ineffectual, deserving of mistreatment. This explanation is persuasive and in line with many social-cognitive theories. It is consistent with findings that many participants in bullying and cyberbullying at universities had been similarly involved at elementary and secondary levels. Although this helps explain why some individuals continue to be mistreated in young adulthood, it begs the question of the presence of bullying in all societies in which it has been studied.

Evolutionary psychology and dominance theories have been applied to bullying (e.g. Ellis et al., 2011) and suggest that as a social species, human groups organise hierarchically, so that the group can be more efficient about meeting the needs of its members. Consider the case when there is an imminent danger from an external threat. If the group members were to take the time to discuss the situation from multiple viewpoints and reach consensus upon a plan of action, the group could easily be decimated before the discussion concluded. Similarly, if there were several members shouting conflicting instructions about how to reach safety, a similarly grim outcome is likely, with confused members uncertain about whom to follow. Thus, it is in the interest of species survival to have a hierarchical social organisation, with the person of highest status in a position of authority. The status rank of members is likely to remain in place until a change is necessary in such situations as the death or illness of the leader, a joining of several groups, or a successful challenge from a lower status individual who is supported by the group.

If we consider that as a species, this status-based ranking served to ensure survival, it is likely that the instinct to adopt hierarchical organisations for human groups is a nearly universal tendency. We see such organisation in societies around the world, in both informal and formal groups. Thus, bullying could have emerged as a strategy to both attain and maintain the status hierarchy necessary for survival.

If that is the case, then the purported increase in bullying behaviours at school transition points is consistent with that explanation. Whatever status had been constructed at previous levels would be disrupted when children move ahead to a larger and more complex social environment (e.g. middle school from elementary, high school from middle school, university from high school).

The change in organisation from elementary to middle school is the result of a combination of factors: change from a usually smaller school to a larger one with new people previously unknown to each other. In the US, promotion to middle school usually includes a change from a single teacher to multiple teachers for different subjects, so the group (class) configuration is constantly changing. In addition, the beginning students are youngest in the school, and bullying by older students may be an attempt to ensure the established hierarchy is not disrupted. During middle school, the onset of puberty results in higher awareness of potential romantic partners. In evolutionary terms, adolescence is a peak reproductive phase of the lifespan, and the time when individuals are competing for access to potential mates (Ellis et al., 2011).

Although this developmental period begins with puberty, in many developed countries adolescents typically postpone finding mates and procreating due to the competing demands of education and economics. Adolescence is in a sense protracted by this modern expectation/opportunity to advance one's status via educational attainment. When young people enter university, they are still adolescents and are in competition for resources, including sexual partners. Universities present some of the challenges experienced by middle school students in the beginning stages of puberty. Universities are typically much larger and more diverse than most high schools, and students who attend are likely to come from a variety of secondary settings, so that old hierarchies are no longer functional. There is pressure to find one's place and establish one's status position, and the task is likely to be more challenging than in the smaller more familiar environs of one's secondary school.

Ellis et al. (2011) observed that bullying and dominance behaviours are common in the animal kingdom, due to competition for resources necessary for survival, including sexual partners. The reported prevalence of bullying in universities is evidence that the evolutionary scenario is exhibited in that context as well. Bauman and Baldasare (2015) found that cyberbullying was significantly more prevalent among those students who are members of sororities and fraternities, organisations with selective membership that provide affiliation and identity with a high status group on campus. To preserve that status, members may perceive an attack on any member to be an attack on the group (Simmons, Bauman, & Ives, 2016) that threatens the status of the group. Such offences are considered particularly egregious.

Although the evolutionary need to reproduce and contribute to the survival of the species and of one's DNA is present throughout adolescence, among university-age adolescents, this need may be more pressing as they approach the normative age for forming committed relationships that hold promise to produce offspring. The social context of adolescents is often defined by their universities (in the US, loyalty to university athletics is common and celebrated) and so this is the venue in which the need for status and dominance is likely to be pronounced. A corollary of this context is that bullying, a way for dominance to be sought and ensured, is not a rare behaviour.

When we think about bullying prevention at the university level, we recall that whole-school approaches are recommended for primary and secondary schools. Many universities are organized by colleges, and within colleges there may be schools and departments. In terms of prevention and interventions to reduce bullying, it is challenging to determine how and to what audience a universal programme could be implemented.

At the elementary and secondary levels, universal programmes are the first line of defence, although success at those levels is less than resounding (Ttofi & Farrington, 2015). Research findings suggest that contemporary anti-bullying messages may not be as effective in later adolescence (Yeager, Fong, Lee, & Espelage, 2015). Furthermore, most new university students will have been exposed to prevention programming earlier in their educational career, and might be insulted and/or bored by messages they have heard before, possibly multiple times.

One approach that shows promise is to reach students using techniques of social media marketing (Spears et al., 2016). University students are highly engaged with social media, and are accustomed to receiving relevant information via that channel. Spears et al.'s project in which social media marketing techniques were used to disseminate anti-bullying messages shows promise. Another approach is to offer counselling services for students who are involved, if they can be identified. In addition, residence halls could be a venue for prevention messages, but students should be engaged in designing those messages to ensure they are relevant and appropriate for students at the university level. Future research should seek innovative ways to explore ways to reduce bullying and cyberbullying among university students.

References

Bauman, S., & Baldasare, A. (2015). Cyber aggression among college students: Demographic differences, predictors of distress, and the role of the university. *Journal of College Student Development, 56*, 317–320.

Ellis, B. J., DeGuidice, M., Dishion, T. J., Figueredo, A. J., Gray, P., Greskevicius, V., Hawley, P. H., . . . Wilson, D. S. (2011). The evolutionary basis for risky adolescent behaviour: Implications for science, policy, and practice. *Developmental Psychology, 48*, 598–623.

Simmons, J., Bauman, S., & Ives, J. (2016). Cyber aggression among members of college fraternities and sororities in the United States. In H. Cowie & C. Myers (Eds.), *Bullying amongst university students: Cross-national perspectives* (pp. 120–144). London: Routledge.

Spears, B. A., Taddeo, C., Barnes, A., Kavanagh, P., Webb-Williams, J., Stretton, A., & Karklins, L. (2016, July 20). Safe and well online: Findings from a five year multidisciplinary project. Presented in the Symposium: *Bullying, cyberbullying and online aggression: Multiple perspectives and approaches.* International Society for Research on Aggression, University of New South Wales, Australia.

Ttofi, M. M., & Farrington, D. P. (2015). Effectiveness of school based programmes to reduce bullying: A systematic and meta-analytic review. *Journal of Experimental Criminology*, 7, 27–56.

Yeager, D. S., Fong, C. J., Lee, H. Y., & Espelage, D. L. (2015). Declines in efficacy of anti-bullying programmes among older adolescents: Theory and a three-level meta-analysis. *Journal of Applied Developmental Psychology, 37*, 36–51.

Chapter 20

Continuities into the workplace

What can we learn from research into workplace bullying?

Iain Coyne

Before debating the workplace bullying research, I wish to extend my congratulations to the authors and editors for providing a comprehensive, stimulating and informative volume. The scope of the discussion into school bullying covering conceptualisation, through consequences and antecedents, to interventions is impressive. I am also particularly pleased to observe that the volume encompasses a wide range of aggressive behaviours within a school context including homophobic bullying (Rivers), sexual violence (Lee), religious bullying (Aznar, Tenenbaum, & Ruck) and hate crimes (Aziz). Advantageously, the volume promotes a multi-cultural perspective from leading experts in school bullying research.

Given the quality of this volume and the extensive research in school bullying, it is a little daunting to compose a commentary on how such research can learn from the workplace bullying literature. To focus the commentary; rather than trying to address all debates presented, this discussion will examine the workplace bullying literature as it pertains to conceptualising and researching bullying, fairness and attributions in bullying and the role of the bystander. Where appropriate within these areas the embryonic research on workplace cyberbullying will also be considered.

Conceptualising and researching bullying

In this section I wish to focus on two specific issues (see Coyne, 2016 for deliberation on how conceptualisations of workplace bullying relate to school bullying). Firstly, it is interesting to note that school bullying definitions continue to include the notion of intent (Cowie & Myers). By contrast, workplace bullying has shied away from adopting this criterion because of the difficulty in measuring intent (Einarsen, Hoel, Zapf, & Cooper, 2011) and the notions that perpetrators may disguise their true intentions to rationalise their behaviour to others (Samnani, Singh, & Ezzedeen, 2013) or deny it was negatively intended (Rayner & Cooper, 2006). The problem of including intent is perhaps more clearly evidenced in workplace cyberbullying. Technology-based negative acts may be ambiguous or often leave a trail. As a result, perpetrators may be more adept at disguising cyberbullying behaviours (Coyne et al., 2016). Perhaps whether or how intent is included in definitions needs to be reconsidered.

Secondly, the adoption of an inclusive stance on types of school bullying seen in this volume is something to be applauded. The workplace bullying literature is awash with different 'types' of interpersonal negative workplace behaviour, each professing defining characteristics highlighting their conceptual differentiation from each other. However, scholars are advocating a higher-level/superordinate conceptualisation of bullying (e.g. Lutgen-Sandvik, Tracy, & Alberts, 2007) where specific defining features (e.g. intention) are viewed as contextual factors or moderators in a causal path between aggression and outcomes (Coyne & Monks, 2011; Hershcovis, 2011). Similar to Myers (this volume) workplace bullying and other forms of harassment may be differentiated legally. There is currently no UK workplace bullying law, although certain aggressive acts could be dealt with under the Equality Act (2010), health and safety legislation and the other non-school specific acts detailed by Myers. Nonetheless, a legal/non-legal criterion should not be the defining criterion used to distinguish different forms of interpersonal negative behaviour. Overall, by adopting a superordinate conceptualisation, organisations can highlight clearly that all forms of aggression are unacceptable, rather than trying to shoehorn negative acts into academic-led definitional criteria.

Understanding workplace bullying

Contrary to the school-bullying literature, albeit adopting predominantly a victim perspective, workplace-bullying research has tended to focus less on the actual protagonists and more on promoting the work environment such as poor leadership (Hoel, Glasø, Hetland, Cooper, & Einarsen, 2010), job demands (Salin, 2015) role ambiguity (Notelaers, Witte, & Einarsen, 2010) and organisational change (Harvey, Treadway, & Heames, 2006) as the dominant explanation for bullying behaviour. Perhaps the extensive literature here can help school-bullying researchers better understand the environmental factors which promote bullying behaviours.

The role of victim disposition in bullying is controversial with some authors (Aquino, Grover, Bradfield, & Allen, 1999; Coyne, Seigne, & Randall, 2000) suggesting personality may explain the submissive or provocative nature of bullying victims (this links closely to resilience outlined by Cefai and Sims-Schouten & Edwards this volume); while others have posited personality as an outcome rather than an antecedent of bullying (Leymann, 1996). Similar to Cowie and Colliety (this volume) scholars have suggested workplace bullies possess an inflated self-esteem and ego-defence mechanism (Zapf & Einarsen, 2011), although there are a dearth of empirical studies of narcissism and bullying.

Pörhölä highlights the need to pay more attention to the social relationships between perpetrators and victims. Extending the dispositional hypothesis of both victims and perpetrators, Aquino and Lamertz (2004) may offer some insights here. They propose a dyadic model of victim and perpetrator interaction outlining the types of bullying which result from an interaction between submissive and provocative victims and domineering and reactive perpetrators:

- Dominating perpetrator – submissive victim = predatory bullying where the perpetrator controls an 'easy target' victim.
- Dominating perpetrator – provocative victim = dispute-related bullying resulting from the need to dominate being met by resistance.
- Reactive perpetrator – provocative victim = dispute-related bullying emerging from perceived provocation from a victim (e.g. ego defence).
- Reactive perpetrator – submissive victim = no/little bullying.

Fairness and attributions in workplace bullying

Discussions around fairness and attributions are prominent throughout in this volume. Theoretically, justice (Parzefall & Salin, 2010) and attribution models (Bowling & Beehr, 2006; Hershcovis, 2011) have been applied to help explain the process and/or outcomes of workplace bullying. While models do not agree fully on the order of each construct in predictive pathways, fairness and attributions are predicted to impact employee work behaviour and well-being. Interestingly, within workplace cyberbullying (Farley, Coyne, Sprigg, Axtell, & Subramanian, 2015) findings have indicated different predictions depending on attributions of blame: self-blame related to mental strain indirectly through negative affect; perpetrator blame related to job dissatisfaction indirectly through justice perceptions. These ideas and findings may be helpful in understanding the processes underlying school bullying.

Bystanders

Hanif and Zaheer and Pörhölä suggest the need further to consider participant roles within school bullying. In comparison, understanding participant roles or bystander behaviour in the context of workplace bullying is relatively unexplored to date (Paull, Omari, & Standen, 2012) – even though bystanders are the largest group negatively affected by workplace bullying. Conversely, examining cyberbullying at work, Coyne et al. (2016) reported non-significant relationships between witnessing workplace cyberbullying and witness mental strain. These authors suggest: "the online nature to cyberbullying may reduce the likelihood of a witness experiencing social bonds with the victim, potentially reducing their empathic responding" (p. 27).

Leading from the discussion of attributions, Bloch (2012) posits witnesses of workplace bullying create blame attributions based on a moral schema of the behaviour. As a result, three participant roles (not unlike school-based bullying) emerge:

- Defender – a bystander perceives the victim's actions as within and the perpetrator actions as outside workplace norms.

- Prosecutor – the victim is characterised as to blame for the bullying because his/her behaviour is outside of workplace norms.
- Commuter – the bystander fluctuates between sympathising with the victim and viewing the victim as deviant.

Empirical evidence on these roles within work bullying contexts is very sparse. Some recent research that I have been involved in, adopting a quasi-experimental vignette design, has illustrated that bystanders were least likely to adopt a defender role and more likely to agree with perpetrator actions when bullying was online and work-related. One hypothesis for this result is the potential for online/work-related acts to be ambiguous in nature and hence potentially not viewed as bullying by a bystander (Coyne et al., in review). This links back to the question of intent within bullying definitions.

Perhaps an area workplace bullying research may be fruitful for school bullying researchers to consider derives from theoretical explanations of bystander behaviour. Robinson, Wang, and Kiewitz (2014) detail three theories which may help explain bystander behaviour:

- Justice theory suggests witnesses who perceive a sense of moral outrage/injustice to the behaviour are compelled to act to restore the justice (e.g. defender role).
- Stress theory implies that witnesses experience secondary trauma potentially resulting in cognitive and emotional empathy with the victim's circumstances (e.g. defender role).
- Social learning theory intimates that witnesses may view negative behaviour as socially acceptable, model it or perceive the behaviour does not warrant intervention (e.g. prosecutor or commuter role)

In conclusion, workplace bullying research on the impact of fairness, attributions and emotions in the bullying process could offer insights for school-bullying researchers. These ideas are not only applicable to the victim perspective, but can also be applied to the perpetrator and bystander roles. Potentially, these models could help with "understanding of interaction processes in which the different participant roles are produced" (Pörhölä, this volume, page ??) and lead to evidence-based prevention and intervention strategies to reduce bullying.

References

Aquino, K., Grover, S. L., Bradfield, M., & Allen, D. G. (1999). The effects of negative affectivity, hierarchical status, and self-determination on workplace victimisation. *Academy of Management Journal*, *42*, 260–272.

Aquino, K., & Lamertz, K. (2004). A relational model of workplace victimization: Social roles and patterns of victimization in dyadic relationships. *Journal of Applied Psychology*, *89*, 1023–1034.

Bloch, C. (2012). How witnesses contribute to bullying in the workplace. In N. Tehrani (Ed.), *Workplace Bullying* (pp. 81–96). East Sussex: Routledge.

Bowling, N. A., & Beehr, T. A. (2006). Workplace harassment from the victim's perspective: A theoretical model and meta-analysis. *Journal of Applied Psychology, 91*(5), 998–1012.

Coyne, I. (2016). Commentary: What universities can learn from workplace bullying research. In H. Cowie & C. A. Myers (Eds.), *Bullying among university students: Cross national perspectives* (pp. 203–206). Abingdon, Oxon: Routledge.

Coyne, I., Farley, S., Axtell, C., Sprigg, C. A., Best, L., & Kwok, O. (2016). Understanding the relationship between experiencing workplace cyberbullying, employee mental strain and job satisfaction: A dysempowerment approach. *International Journal of Human Resource Management, 28*(7), 945–972.

Coyne, I., Gopaul, A.-M., Campbell, M., Pankász, A., Garland, R., & Cousans, F. (in review). Bystander intervention intention to negative acts at work: The role of mode, type, organisational action and relationship to target. *Journal of Business Ethics.*

Coyne, I., & Monks, C. P. (2011). An overview of bullying and abuse across settings. In C. P. Monks & I. Coyne (Eds.), *Bullying in different contexts* (pp. 231–256). Cambridge: Cambridge University Press.

Coyne, I., Seigne, E., & Randall, P. (2000). Predicting workplace victim status from personality. *European Journal of Work and Organizational Psychology, 9*(3), 335–349.

Einarsen, S., Hoel, H., Zapf, D., & Cooper, C. L. (2011). The concept of bullying and harassment at work: The European tradition. In S. Einarsen, H. Hoel, D. Zapf, & C. L. Cooper (Eds.), *Bullying and harassment in the workplace: Developments in theory, research and practice* (pp. 3–39). Boca Raton, FL: CRC Press.

Farley, S., Coyne, I., Sprigg, C., Axtell, C., & Subramanian, G. (2015). Cyberbullying: The experience of trainee doctors. *Medical Education, 49*, 436–443.

Harvey, M. G., Treadway, D., & Heames, J. T. (2006). Bullying in global organizations: A reference point perspective. *Journal of World Business, 41*, 190–202.

Hershcovis, M. S. (2011). 'Incivility, social undermining, bullying . . . oh my!': A call to reconcile constructs within workplace aggression research. *Journal of Organizational Behaviour, 32*(3), 499–519.

Hoel, H., Glasø, L., Hetland, J., Cooper, C. L., & Einarsen, S. (2010). Leadership styles as predictors of self-reported and observed workplace bullying. *British Journal of Management, 21*(2), 453–468.

Leymann, H. (1996). The content and development of mobbing at work. *European Journal of Work and Organizational Psychology, 5*, 165–184.

Lutgen-Sandvik, P., Tracy, S. J., & Alberts, J. K. (2007). Burned by bullying in the American workplace: Prevalence, perception, degree and impact. *Journal of Management Studies, 44*, 837–862.

Notelaers, G., De Witte, H., & Einarsen, S. (2010). A job characteristics approach to explain workplace bullying. *European Journal of Work and Organizational Psychology, 19*(4), 487–504.

Parzefall, M.-R., & Salin, D. M. (2010). Perceptions of and reactions to workplace bullying: A social exchange perspective. *Human Relations, 63*(6), 761–780.

Paull, M., Omari, M., & Standen, P. (2012). When is a bystander not a bystander? A typology of the roles of bystanders in workplace bullying. *Asia Pacific Journal of Human Resources, 50*, 351–366.

Rayner, C., & Cooper, C. (2006). Workplace bullying. In K. Kelloway, J. Barling, & J. Hurrell (Eds.), *Handbook of workplace violence* (pp. 121–146). California: Sage Publications.

Robinson, S. L., Wang, W., & Kiewitz, C. (2014). Coworkers behaving badly: The impact of coworker deviant behaviour upon individual employees. *Annual Review of Organizational Psychology and Organizational Behaviour, 1*, 123–143.

Salin, D. (2015). Risk factors of workplace bullying for men and women: The role of the psychosocial and physical work environment. *Scandinavian Journal of Psychology, 56*, 69–77.

Samnani, A. K., Singh, P., & Ezzedeen, S. (2013). Workplace bullying and employee performance: An attributional model. *Organizational Psychology Review, 3*(4), 337–359.

Zapf, D. & Einarsen, S. (2011). Individual antecedents of bullying: Victims and perpetrators. In S. Einarsen, H. Hoel, D. Zapf, & C. L. Cooper (Eds.), *Bullying and harassment in the workplace: Developments in theory, research and practice* (pp. 177–200). Boca Raton, FL: CRC Press.

Chapter 21

The perspective of the Special Educational Needs Co-ordinator (SENCO)

Anna Barker

Introduction

I work as an Assistant Head for Inclusion in a small, inner city school where mental health issues are common among our diverse intake of pupils. My role encompasses the breadth of inclusion and I coordinate the needs of children with behaviour issues, English as an additional language, special educational needs and medical diagnoses. I am responsible for ensuring that all children have access to the whole-school curriculum and make equivalent progress and attainment as their peers, irrespective of the needs they have. I work closely with parents, other professionals (such as Educational Psychologists and Speech and Language Therapists) and the school staff. At my school, we have a whole-school restorative justice approach in which the core themes of listening to what has happened, talking through the impact of events and finding ways forward are the approach we use when dealing with conflict between students. This book is important for Special Educational Needs Coordinators (SENCOs) or those working within inclusion because the chapters focussed on schools offer practical advice which is underpinned by research and evidence-based practice.

Why this book is important for a SENCO

The overall theme of this book (the first in a series on the mental health and emotional well-being of children and young people) concerns the mental health risks to school pupils from being involved in bullying, whether as perpetrators, targets or bystanders. Bullying is a particular risk for children who are different in some way from their peers; children with educational, behavioural and emotional difficulties can so easily feel rejected and excluded by others. This is highlighted in chapter 4 by Ian Rivers who discusses the cruel treatment experienced by LGBT pupils, many of whom become depressed or even suicidal as a result of bullying, cyberbullying and social exclusion. It is also highlighted in chapter 7 by Ana Aznar et al. who describe the impact of xenophobia on asylum seekers. These chapters document the issues but also offer some hope in action that schools, families and communities can take.

What can schools do in practice?

For me, one of the most illuminating approaches is described in chapter 12 by Carmel Cefai who, with colleagues from other European countries, has developed a curriculum relating to children with disabilities or special needs that targets negative attitudes and actively promotes inclusion through child-centred methods, such as puppet play, stories and role play; his team also identify practical ways in which teachers and parents can build up the resilience of vulnerable children. I also found chapter 15 by Marilyn Campbell useful as she outlines the crucial role of policies that actively promote inclusion and challenge bullying. Her work in Australia has important messages for SENCOs in the UK. It is well established that to move forward with any new initiative takes a whole-school approach; however, this can be challenging to implement. James O'Higgins Norman and Keith Sullivan, in chapter 16, give valuable insights into practical, evidence-based ways of embedding good practice into every day school life as well as on developing a whole-school ethos which actively embraces an anti-bullying message. In addition, in chapter 18, Birgitta Kimber explains how Social and Emotional Training (SET) can give all young people the skills and confidence to express themselves authentically which in turn enables them to challenge negative social and emotional experiences within the peer group. All primary schools in the UK will have some form of Personal Social and Health Education (PSHE) on their timetable in which a whole range of topics are taught. SET, with its range of well-developed activities, would complement these greatly when dealing with other areas of the PSHE Curriculum, such as Sex and Relationships Education.

Conclusion

The important message I take away from this book is that we, as educators, cannot underestimate the value of children being taught how to talk and express their feelings in an authentic and genuinely communicative way. By giving children the necessary skills and tools to respond appropriately, particularly when dealing with conflict and the difficult emotions that disputes, social exclusion and intimidation always generate, we as educators give them resources that will make them more resilient in their everyday lives, not only in school with the peer group but also at home with their parents and siblings and in the community. The process of enabling these children to become more self-aware and more confident in their peer relationships has the potential to lessen the devastating impact that bullying can have on individuals' self-esteem and in turn reduce the possibility of mental health difficulties in the future. The ethos of a school is critical when embedding these restorative approaches in everyday school life. Children need to believe that, when faced with a difficulty, no matter how small to the outside person, they will be listened to and a solution sought. This can start in nursery school when children are taught the basic social skills of sharing and their upsets over seemingly small things are taken seriously by the adults looking after them.

I recommend this book to schools for the following reasons:

1 When implementing positive change in any area of the curriculum the value of evidence based practice cannot be underestimated;
2 This book highlights the strengths of research as well as giving positive approaches that could be adapted in any school setting;
3 This book also affirms restorative, child-centred approaches in tackling the problem of bullying.

Chapter 22

Epilogue

Implications and considerations for future research in the field of young people's mental health

Helen Cowie and Carrie-Anne Myers

Bullying is a serious problem for children and young people and one that greatly affects their emotional health and well-being. Bullies abuse their power over others in a whole variety of ways that make the target or targets feel uncomfortable, unwelcome, worthless, excluded and endangered. Institutions that ignore the damage done by condoning such behaviour create contexts that are not conducive to mental health. Research in the field of bullying – whether at school, university or the workplace – provides many signposts for researchers in the wider field of mental health. Large-scale surveys such those by Sourander et al. (2010) and Lereya, Copeland, Costello, and Wolke (2015) consistently indicate that those children and young people who are involved in bullying, whether as targets or perpetrators, are at heightened risk of mental health difficulties and that the consequences can be severe and long-lasting. More in-depth studies of the individuals who are affected by bullying reveal a range of risk factors and personal characteristics that interact to increase the emergence of emotional and social distress. Luca, in chapter 8, demonstrates vividly the long-term impact of bullying on a child's mental health that can persist well into adult life, and the role of counselling in alleviating that person's suffering over the years. Cowie and Colliety, in chapter 9, overview a number of therapeutic approaches for dealing with the mental health issues experienced by those who bully, each of which illuminates the factors that underlie the bully's tendency to engage in negative behaviour towards vulnerable peers.

At the same time, research into bullying has also revealed the complexity of the social contexts where it happens and highlights the significant role played by others in the peer group who adopt a range of participant roles, whether as reinforcers or assistants to the bully, defenders of the target, or passive bystanders who witness the event but take no action. The understanding generated by participant role theory (Salmivalli, 2010) (see chapter 2 by Pörhölä and chapter 14 by Hanif and Zaheer) is of immense relevance to researchers in the wider field of youth mental health since it gives insights into the impact of others on the emotional health and well-being of the individual. As Pörhölä points out in chapter 2, there is considerable continuity in abusive peer relationships from school to further and higher education. In this context, she proposes several theories including positioning theory (Harré & Moghaddam, 2003) and attribution theory (Heider, 1958) for giving insight into the processes through which individuals integrate (or fail to integrate) with the networks in their youth culture. To this end, of course, mental health researchers are right to focus directly on the perpetrators and victims of bullying since they, in different ways, are especially vulnerable to mental health problems in their lives. The suffering of victims points to the need for counselling and other forms of social support, at an *individual* level. However, mental health researchers also need to be mindful of the *social* contexts within which mental health difficulties evolve.

Much research into the mental health of children and young people has focussed on the quality of relationships within the family. This valuable research examines the nature of the family and community contexts in which children grow and develop so that we can be aware of the risk and protective factors that influence the emotional health and well-being of children and young people. However, there is less emphasis in the mental health literature on the peer group with its potential for thoughtless indifference and cruelty on the one hand and active concern through befriending, peer support and mediation on the other. The authors in the present book have shown us from a range of perspectives how crucial it is to address the issue of bullying in different contexts. The knowledge that has been built up over the years about school bullying has been harnessed in this book to demonstrate not only how to counteract negative behaviour on the part of individuals but also how to be active in promoting a school community which embodies such values as respect for the person and the celebration of diversity. These values create a social environment that is supportive of children's mental health.

As the authors here argue, therapeutic work can also be done in everyday situations by fellow students. Peer supporters can be trained and empowered to defend the victims of bullying and to befriend those among their classmates who feel rejected or excluded from the life of the school. Avilés, in chapter 17, argues compellingly that, in schools where *convivencia* underpins the core values of the institution, there exists a context that advocates the equal rights of all members of the school community to live and work together, and that positively creates a social environment that promotes the mental health and well-being of students and educators alike. Again, there is enormous scope for mental health researchers to unravel the complex factors that interact to create environments that are conducive to emotional health and well-being.

At a wider level, there are serious issues to confront in today's society, not least the rise of xenophobia and racism (Aziz in chapter 6) as well as callous indifference to the suffering of such groups as asylum-seekers (Aznar et al. in chapter 7) or those who are viewed negatively on the grounds of their sexual orientation (Rivers in chapter 4). Such forms of bullying transcend into the arena of criminal activity, and more specifically 'Hate Crime'. In this volume, authors have begun to open up the debate with regard to crime and criminal behaviour masquerading as "simply bullying". Lee (in chapter 5) demonstrates the blurred boundaries with regard to sexual violence on school premises while Myers (in chapter 3) discusses the complexities of the policies that institutions, such as schools, must adopt while balancing their duty of care for each student with the requirements of the law. There are often clear solutions that can be used but the changing nature of bullying and its long-term effects are often not being considered in educational contexts. Although claims to criminalise bullying are not being made in this book, the editors are acknowledging that, as bullying takes on increasingly severe forms, the impact, consequences and lasting mental health needs of those involved have to be addressed. There is definitely a requirement for more research looking at the extreme end of the bullying scale which crosses into the criminal context.

Bullying and cyberbullying emerge when there is an imbalance in power between individuals or groups or where certain people are perceived to be vulnerable. Children and young people need guidance in their schools to debate and discuss the great issues of the day and to develop a frame of mind that is open to considering a range of perspectives on any issue. They need opportunities to challenge prejudice when they encounter it and to step out of the role of passive bystander when they see a xenophobic, homophobic, disablist or sexist incident. They need the experience of restorative practices to address conflicts and the opportunity to participate in systems of peer support and conflict resolution in everyday settings. Crucially, they need to comprehend the lasting consequences of such actions from beyond the school grounds, often continuing throughout the lifespan. The mental health impact of, for example, sexual bullying, will stay with the victim forever. These aspects of child experience are in urgent need of research if we are to prevent further unnecessary suffering among youth.

As we have seen throughout this book, researchers who address the issue of bullying are, at the same time, providing evidence for the value of creating safer spaces in which children can learn to help others, to develop qualities of empathy for peers in distress and to take responsibility for their own actions. This form of citizenship has far-reaching consequences for improving the social climate of classrooms, the school as a whole and even the community. Again, mental health researchers can learn from this wealth of knowledge that has been built up in the literature on bullying over a period of nearly thirty years.

This book is the first in a series on the mental health of youth. We as editors hope that we are setting the scene for deeper understanding of interpersonal relationships and the social settings that foster empathy for others and a respect for the right of all children to fulfil their potential as active, creative and productive citizens in the future.

References

Harré, R., & Moghaddam, F. (Eds.). (2003). *The self and others: Positioning individuals and groups in personal, political, and cultural contexts.* Westport, CT: Praeger.

Heider, F. (1958). *The psychology of interpersonal relations.* New York: Wiley.

Lereya, S. T., Copeland, W. E., Costello, E. G., & Wolke, D. (2015). Adult mental health, consequences of peer bullying and maltreatment in childhood: Two cohorts in two countries. *Lancet Psychiatry*, *2*(6), 524–531.
Salmivalli, C. (2010). Bullying and the peer group: A review. *Aggression and Violent Behaviour*, *15*, 112–120.
Sourander, A., Brunstein, K. A. B., Ikomen, M., Lindroos, J., Luntamo, T., Koskelainen, M., Ristkari, T., & Helenius, H. (2010). Psychosocial risk factors associated with cyberbullying among adolescents. *Archives of General Psychiatry*, *67*, 720–728.

Index

abuse 18, 36–7, 46, 60, 67–8, 83, 97, 119, 120–4, 131, 170, 192–9; sexual 44–7, 48–50, 53–5, 81, 84–5, 226–8
anger 8–9, 85, 97, 98, 103, 108
anti-bullying legislation *see* legislation
anti-bullying policies *see* policy
anti-cyberbullying legislation *see* legislation
anti-cyberbullying policies *see* policy
anxiety 3, 6, 7, 39, 79, 82–3, 85–8, 91, 101, 103, 106, 108, 119, 123–4, 182, 203
Asperger's Syndrome 63
assistants to the bully *see* participant role approach
Association of Chief Police Officers 59, 62
asylum seekers 25, 61, 67–75, 223, 227
attachment 85, 88, 94
attribution theory 16–21

Brexit 61
bullying: interventions 169–210; perceptions of 145, 149–50; policies 169–77, 183, 223–5; prevention 192–9; social context of 92–3, 154–65, 226–8; university 213–15; workplace 217–20
bystander apathy 7, 9, 25
bystanders 1, 3, 6–9, 12, 14, 19, 25, 27, 43, 92–5, 113, 156, 164, 169, 186–7, 203, 217, 219–20

change management 181–2
child centred approaches 224–5
Children and Young People's Safety Survey 51–2
children who bully 3, 4, 8, 33, 90–8
community 1, 3–5, 8, 9, 16, 18–19, 30, 93–8, 115, 131–4, 138, 170, 173–5, 177, 182–8, 192–9, 224, 227–8
continuities and discontinuities 1, 12–21, 91–3, 213–15, 217–20
convivencia 10, 167, 192–9, 227
coping strategies 82–3, 85–6, 88, 131, 135–9, 144, 146, 148–9, 203
counselling 6, 79, 83, 95, 97, 119, 159–60, 187–8, 215, 226–7
crime 4–5, 25, 27, 30–3, 37, 46, 49–52, 58–65, 115, 217, 227
Crime Survey for England and Wales (CSEW) 51–2, 62
criminal law 31–3, 58, 122–3
culture 10, 25, 35, 39, 58, 60–1, 64, 70, 84, 102, 113, 132, 145, 154–64, 177, 188, 195–8, 209, 227
cyberbullying 3–9, 27, 29, 31–3, 36, 43, 46, 90, 101, 115, 117–24, 172, 174, 188, 193–5, 197–9, 213, 215, 217, 219, 223, 228

dating violence 18, 91, 117
defenders *see* participant role approach
depression 3, 6, 38–9, 79, 82–3, 87–8, 91, 101–5, 108, 119
disability 4, 30, 58–9, 62–4, 93, 121, 130, 132, 136, 149, 170, 224

eating disorders 79, 82
emotional wellbeing 3–4, 75, 79, 102, 113, 192–9, 223, 226–7
empathy 1, 4, 6–10, 43, 71–5, 91, 133–4, 136, 156, 203–4, 220, 228

Equality Act 2010 27, 30–3, 218
ethnicity 58, 60, 67–8, 74, 121, 155
exclusion 4, 13, 30, 35, 46, 49–50, 62, 67–9, 73–4, 132, 136, 171, 174, 223–4

fathers *see* parents
friends 4, 16, 18–21, 70–4, 83–5, 104, 121, 134, 136, 159, 183, 208

guidelines *see* policy

harassment 5, 18, 25, 27, 30–2, 36–8, 43, 46–7, 49, 51–5, 62, 67, 91, 123, 170, 183, 186, 218
hate crime 25, 27, 30, 32, 58–65, 217, 227–8; action against 63–4; disablist 62–3, 65; LGBT 59–62; racist 59–61; religious 60–1
homophobic, biphobic and transphobic bullying (HBT) 35–44, 130–1, 180, 185–6

inclusion 223–5
interpersonal relationships *see* peer relationships

leadership 173, 180–3, 185, 194, 211, 218
legislation 27–34, 39, 122, 169–77, 175, 218
lesbian, gay, bisexual, transgender (LGBT) bullying 35–44, 59, 61–2, 64, 130–1, 173, 185–6, 223

Media Heroes 9
mental health 1, 3–4, 33, 38–9, 62–4, 79, 81–2, 87–8, 90–4, 98, 108, 119, 144, 148, 150–1, 157, 170, 202–3, 211, 223–4, 226–8
moral disengagement 1, 6, 8–10, 25, 91, 120–2, 124, 134, 195–9
mothers *see* parents

national guidelines *see* policy
neoliberal framework 133, 144–51
nurture groups 94–6

obesity 144–5, 147–9; childhood 144–5, 147–9
Office for National Statistics (ONS) 61–2
outsiders *see* participant role approach

Parent Acceptance Rejection Questionnaire (PARQ) 105–9
parent-child relationship 103–4
parents 9, 20–1, 28–9, 32, 63, 69–74, 83–8, 92, 94, 97–8, 102–6, 115–19, 121–4, 132, 135, 138–40, 144–51, 154, 159, 169–70, 173, 180, 182, 188–9, 206, 208, 223–4
participant role approach 4, 7, 8–10, 12–13, 19–20, 93–4, 97, 113, 154–64, 187–8, 219–20, 226
peer community integration theory 13, 19
peer relationships 4, 13, 15, 17–20, 90–2, 97, 159–64, 224, 226–8
peer support 7, 88, 145–6, 151, 159, 164, 195–6, 198, 203, 227–8
perpetrators 3–4, 6, 9, 40–43, 48–54, 58, 59, 61–2, 64–5, 67, 79, 88, 90–8, 113, 117, 119, 121, 156, 169, 175, 183, 217–19, 223, 226, 227; persistent 91–3
police 27, 30–3, 37, 46, 50, 59, 62–4, 115, 123, 173–4
policy 4, 28–30, 33, 47–8, 54–5, 60, 117, 144, 154, 167, 169–77, 183–4, 224, 228
positioning theory 13–14, 18, 227
power: abuse of 67–75, 81–7; relationships 6, 92–3
Prevent strategy 61, 63–4
Promoting Issues in Common (PIC) Method 95–7
psychotherapy *see* counselling

race/racism 32, 59–63, 94, 227
refugees *see* asylum seekers
reinforcers *see* participant role approach
religion 4, 30, 58, 60, 64, 71–2, 185
RESCUR 132–9
resilience 1, 10, 25, 87–8, 104, 113, 130–41, 144–51, 218, 224
restorative practice 34, 64–5, 197, 228
rights 14–15, 20, 68–75, 122

Savile, Jimmy 54
School Culture Scale 154–64
school ethos 7, 138, 155, 181, 185–7, 189, 224
Second Step 43
self-esteem 7, 17, 42, 82, 84, 87, 92, 94, 108, 134, 151, 203, 224
sexism 53, 93
sexual bullying and violence 25, 30, 46–55, 84–5, 217, 228
shame 1, 3, 8, 35, 85
Social and Emotional Training (SET) 10, 167, 202–9, 224
social context of bullying 92–3, 115–24
social media 113, 115–24, 150, 188, 215

social networking 116–25
Special Educational Needs Coordinators (SENCOs) 223–5
student support services 187–8
student voice 82–4, 181, 186–7
suicide 6, 32, 36, 38–9, 62, 79, 82, 91, 119, 131, 170, 173; suicidal ideation 79, 88, 91
Support Group Method 94–5
symbolic convergence theory 13–21

Teacher Voice Survey 46
theoretical perspectives 4, 12–21
therapy *see* counselling
transphobic bullying 35–55

university bullying 1, 12, 37, 39, 53, 84, 86, 97, 102, 104, 106, 211, 213–15

victimisation 3, 16–18, 21, 30, 32–4, 36, 48–9, 51–3, 58, 67–8, 74, 79, 82, 101–9, 119, 130, 157–8, 171–2
vulnerability 6, 25, 86, 88, 92

whole-school approach 10, 30, 55, 138, 151, 180–9, 215, 224
witnesses *see* bystanders
workplace bullying 1, 13, 211, 217–20

xenophobia 93, 223, 227

For Product Safety Concerns and Information please contact our EU representative GPSR@taylorandfrancis.com
Taylor & Francis Verlag GmbH, Kaufingerstraße 24, 80331 München, Germany

www.ingramcontent.com/pod-product-compliance
Ingram Content Group UK Ltd.
Pitfield, Milton Keynes, MK11 3LW, UK
UKHW020011200926
475702UK00014B/1813

* 9 7 8 0 3 6 7 1 9 0 1 8 7 *